Fire on the Beach

Recovering the Lost Story of
Richard Etheridge and the Pea Island Lifesavers

DAVID WRIGHT
AND
DAVID ZOBY

A LISA DREW BOOK

Scribner

NEW YORK LONDON TORONTO SYDNEY SINGAPORE

SCRIBNER
1230 Avenue of the Americas
New York, NY 10020

SCRIBNER and design are trademarks of Macmillan Library Reference USA, Inc.,
used under license by Simon & Schuster, the publisher of this work.

Designed by Kyoko Watanabe

Set in Plantin

Manufactured in the United States of America

1 3 5 7 9 10 8 6 4 2

Library of Congress Cataloging-in-Publication Data
Wright, David.
Fire on the beach : recovering the lost story of Richard Etheridge
and the Pea Island lifesavers / David Wright and David Zoby.
p.   cm.
Includes bibliographical references and index.
1. Etheridge, Richard, 1842–1900. 2. African American lifeboat crew
members—North Carolina—Pea Island—Biography. 3. United States.
Life-Saving Service—History. 4. Lifesaving stations—North Carolina—
Pea Island—History. 5. Pea Island (N.C.)—History. I. Zoby, David. II. Title.

VK1430.A1 W75 2001
363.12'381'09756175—dc21
00-068728

ISBN 0-684-87304-4

To William C. Bowser III,
Pea Island surfman, 1935–38,
and the people of Roanoke Island,
whose memories and heart
made this book possible.

CONTENTS

PART THREE: *The Life of a Surfman*

No subject at the present moment is more replete with vital and romantic interest at home and abroad than that of the American Life-Saving Service. Its brief history teems with incident and instruction. Its wonderful achievements have given it wide celebrity the world over . . .

—*"The American Life-Saving Service,"*
Harper's Weekly, *February 1882*

It is fair to say here that there was not a life-saving station within twenty miles in either direction, but the men did not know this fact and in consequence they made dark and opprobrious remarks concerning the eyesight of the nation's life-savers . . .

"Funny they don't see us."

—*Stephen Crane,*
The Open Boat

Gulls wheel like from a gun again,
And foam gone amber that was white,
Lighthouse and stars start making friends,
Down every beach the long day ends,
And there, on the last stretch of sand,
On a beach bare of all but light,
Dark hands start pulling in the seine
Of the dark sea, deep, deep inland.

—*Derek Walcott,*
"The Schooner Flight"

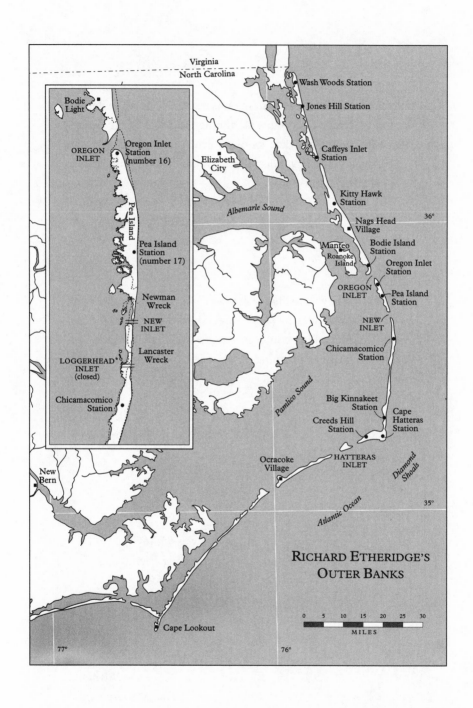

Virginia
North Carolina

Wash Woods Station

Jones Hill Station

Caffeys Inlet Station

Elizabeth City

Kitty Hawk Station

Albemarle Sound

Nags Head Village

36°

Manteo
Roanoke Island

Bodie Island Station

Oregon Inlet Station

OREGON INLET

Pea Island Station

NEW INLET

Chicamacomico Station

Pamlico Sound

Big Kinnakeet Station

Creeds Hill Station

Cape Hatteras Station

New Bern

Ocracoke Village

HATTERAS INLET

Diamond Shoals

35°

Atlantic Ocean

RICHARD ETHERIDGE'S OUTER BANKS

0   5   10   15   20   25   30

MILES

Cape Lookout

77°

76°

Bodie Light

OREGON INLET

Oregon Inlet Station (number 16)

Pea Island

Pea Island Station (number 17)

Newman Wreck

NEW INLET

Lancaster Wreck

LOGGERHEAD INLET (closed)

Chicamacomico Station

Fire on the Beach

PROLOGUE

In the early-morning hours of October 5, 1881, William B. Daniel, the number three surfman from Life-Saving Station 17, on Pea Island, North Carolina, passed the cragged shapes of several old shipwrecks as he walked the south patrol. Just over the dunes from the station, broken seas ripped across the odd, cylindrical boilers of the sunken federal transport *Oriental,* a bearing Daniel took each night before setting off into darkness.

This stretch of coast was a graveyard for many ships and their crews. One-half mile away, the brig *Star.* Two hundred yards farther, an unknown wreck that had been ashore here as long as anyone could remember. Another one hundred fifty yards, the brig *Parry.* And a little farther still, where the rough surf washed over the beach, the schooner *M&E Henderson.* Surfman Daniel knew these and many more. Since his boyhood, he had heard the stories about this coast and its ghost fleet.

While most of the nation mourned President Garfield's death, surfmen along the Sand Banks of North Carolina were monitoring a rainy front with severe surf and fresh northeast winds. William Daniel had been assigned the 3 A.M. to sunrise beat, the final patrol of the night. Patrolling the beach was exhausting, a cryptic combination of darkness and sound, an often frightening trek, though no surfman worth his salt would admit it. A year before, directives had come down from headquarters in Washington that surfmen could not carry lighted lanterns on patrol, as ships at sea might mistake the beam for one of a ship in deep water and be drawn into the breakers. Using only their knowledge of beaches and storms and their sense of duty to illuminate the way, surfmen went each night into the darkness.

When a surfman returned from his six-mile march, he got whatever sleep he could, then a day of exhaustive drilling and hard work waited. Such was the life of a surfman. Daniel, with two years' experience, knew what to expect. But on this night in early October, the weather was out of the ordinary. Even from within the station's walls, the men could hear the terrific breakers detonating offshore, roaring up the slope of the beach, then hissing as they retreated back into the sea. Winds blazed across the sands, lifting bits of shell and grit into the air and giving the entire beach-front a fuzzy appearance. Through the wind and waves the crews of the ghost ships seemed to be crying their tales of doom to the living.

Not one month before, Surfman Daniel had drawn the same patrol in a storm. In the station's log, Keeper Etheridge had called the weather "smoky" and observed the dramatic shift as a strong low-pressure system had descended on the Banks. A rainy front with southeast winds had persisted for several days, then changed over to rough surf and fresh northeast winds. Surfman Daniel had trekked southward to New Inlet, where he found great breakers burying under a torrent of seawater the old wrecks he used for reference. The waves rushing over the beach had nearly knocked him off his feet. This storm was turning out to be equally frightening.

With winds blasting at his back, almost shepherding him down the coast, Daniel reached New Inlet, just over two miles away, by 4:30 A.M. He looked south, but could only see the tide racing up the beach and the wind-whipped spindrift rolling into the dunes like tumbleweed. The inlet had been shoaling up for years, and he wondered if this storm would close it for good or open a deeper passage like the one at Hatteras. Through the sheets of rain and banks of fog, he did not see anyone on the opposite shore.

Normally, a patrolman would meet his neighbor from the adjacent station and exchange a stamped badge to prove to the keeper that the entire beat had been covered. Because the Outer Banks were broken by several inlets, many stations were cut off from their neighbors. To the north of Station 17, surfmen from Station 16 were cut off from their northern counterparts by swift, deep currents of Oregon Inlet. The two stations, Pea Island and Oregon Inlet, were stranded together on a tiny strip of barrier island. Men from each met halfway on patrols, worked in unison during shipwrecks, and shared rides back and forth to Roanoke Island. On the other end of the patrol, a time clock stood at the tip of the sandy bight separating them from the opposite shore. Men would turn a key in the clock, the keeper checking it daily to guarantee fastidiousness.

The southern patrol from Pea Island wasn't always a solitary march. Some nights, the man from Chicamacomico, Station 18, would arrive at New Inlet at about the same time. Though the sound of the breakers made it too noisy to communicate, Daniel might raise an arm to let the other man know all was well. Then each man would turn his key in the clock and head back, eyes fixed on the sea. Yet much more than the waters of New Inlet separated the men from those on the opposite bank. On this night, nobody appeared on the far bank of New Inlet. It was worth noting, but probably nothing out of the ordinary.

Over a hundred years later, it's difficult for present-day readers to visualize the patrolmen of the Life-Saving Service (LSS), the forerunner of the modern Coast Guard, setting off to cover the beaches under a wash of stars. Their methods of launching light boats into hurricane-driven seas or using stout cannons to fire rescue lines out to stranded schooners seem, today, a manifestation of Victorian romanticism. Yet in the late nineteenth century, keepers and surfmen were the guardians of thousands of miles of shoreline and hundreds of coastwise ships. Like clockwork, surfmen walked our coasts each night and in the foulest weather, trekking north or south to meet the patrolman from the neighboring station. These men were the only hope a stranded crew had when their ship struck the shoals.

The Life-Saving Service was set up in the maritime tradition of nightly watches, rotating duty, and adherence to strict codes. The men who worked in the stations that dotted the coasts experienced a fellowship with their seagoing counterparts that has all but vanished today. A system of coded flags allowed surfmen to communicate with passing ships. In this manner, each station could relay important information from shore— such as latitude and longitude coordinates and storm warnings—to the bridge of a cruising vessel. Each station was under the supervision of a station keeper, usually referred to as "Cap'n" by his crew of six surfmen. The keeper, recommended and reviewed by a government inspector, hired and trained crews, which, without exception, were local men, men who could keep stroke with an oar, knew the local currents, and had the sort of disposition that allowed for high risks at low pay. The stations were organized into regional districts, with North Carolina and three outposts in Virginia composing the Sixth District.

As in duty aboard a schooner or whaling vessel, each crewman was assigned a nightly watch, but instead of walking the decks and peering over the railings into the dark sea, coastal surfmen trudged over the dark beaches and looked seaward for ships in distress. While most of the nation slept, the service boasted in its annual reports, these men faced "all natural vicissitudes, all hardships, all exposure known between the autumnal and vernal equinoxes, bitter cold, rain in torrents, cutting sleet, blinding flights of sand and spray . . ." Over the LSS's history, coastal lifesavers often went beyond duty and performed rescues that, today, are hardly fathomable. However, in its early years, incompetence, particularly in its North Carolina stations, marred the efficacy and reputation of the Life-Saving Service—to the degree that its future was imperiled.

In January of 1880, African-American Richard Etheridge was appointed to replace the ousted keeper of Station 17, who, like many Outer Banks keepers, had failed to respond to a ship in distress. Etheridge recruited and trained a crew of black surfmen, forming the only all-black station in the entire LSS. But vestiges of the Civil War still very much influenced daily life. Already, veterans from the North were traveling to battlegrounds in North Carolina where they could reflect on the war and pay tribute to their fallen friends. For Southerners, memories of the war brought pain—lost comrades, fallen heroes, a vanquished way of life. The postbellum South was a place where previous animosities died slowly. To some Outer Bankers, the Pea Island crew echoed all of those losses.

Depending on who was asked along the Banks, Richard Etheridge and his "colored crew" were a curiosity, a lark, or an outrage. Before Etheridge had hired them on at Pea Island, the best a black surfman could hope for, whatever his experience with the sea, was the lowest-ranking position at a station, as the number six man or as a substitute. Isolated from the rest of the crew, he'd be expected to cook, to do menial tasks such as cleaning the galley or tending the station's ponies, if they had any—that is, except when a ship came ashore. Then, the black surfmen would be right there in the surfboat with the others, stroking out to a wreck in mast-high seas. They wanted to be there, despite the daily humiliations. It was the reason that they, like all good lifesavers, joined the service. Now, at Pea Island, African-American surfmen could aspire to more.

On the same night in October 1881, Benjamin O'Neal watched the storm take shape from the window of the Chicamacomico Life-Saving Station, seven miles south of Pea Island. He saw the stars vanish one by one from the heavens and a thick bank of clouds sweep up from Hatteras. As a substitute, filling in for number one surfman Israel B. Midgett, who was at home sick, O'Neal had drawn the last watch of the night, from 3 A.M. to sunrise. O'Neal had grown up on this stretch of North Carolina coast, fishing when the immense schools of mullet, blues, and shad blackened the waters, and "wrecking" when heaps of lumber and cargo tumbled ashore after storms. In small spritsail skiffs, he trapped terrapin and gathered shellfish with his uncles, always keeping a watchful eye on the long horizon. He was all too familiar with the sea's sudden changes, and he could tell by the way the clouds assembled in the south that the storm would soon be over the beaches of Chicamacomico. Just his luck.

In heavy oilskins and weatherproof boots, O'Neal stepped out into the storm. On the winding footpath that led to the sea, O'Neal met an approaching figure: Surfman James Meekins, returning from the northern beat. Meekins slipped his leather satchel from his shoulder and handed it to O'Neal, then continued slack-shouldered toward the station.

With a rising wind in his face, O'Neal crossed a few hummocks and paused to survey the Atlantic. Great walls of white surge were rolling onto shore, backlashing and kicking up spray as they struck the beachfront. The thick and misty weather made it impossible for the patrolman to see the breakers, but he could hear them rumbling, building out in the darkness. A scent accompanies a coming gale, and O'Neal had known it since childhood: the briny odor of fresh seas mingling with the hint of seaweed, wet wood, and sweet sea grass.

He walked along the high-water mark, slogging over driftwood, windrows of seaweed, and nests of spindrift that had blown in from the raging ocean. Occasionally, the seas would catch him off guard, racing up past the wrackline, dousing his pants and sluicing into his boots. He soon found himself walking up near the cliffed dunes, the storm surge intensifying with each oncoming wave. From the north, the winds continued to whip the surf into a frenzy. Salt water and blowing sand stung his eyes and forced him to walk with his head down, chin tucked into his jacket. As it passed over the hummocks and dunes, the wind began an eerie chorus of moans or whistled through old shipwrecks abandoned on the beach.

He counted the minutes remaining in his patrol, anxious to be back in his bunk at the station. Just then, a wave rushed up his leg and he felt something collide sharply against his shin. Expecting to find a length of driftwood, he reached down and, to his astonishment, found a piece of ice the size of a dinner plate. The Banks, owing to its proximity to the warm Gulf Stream, rarely experience a freeze, and the fall of 1881 had yet to see temperatures even approaching the freezing mark. In fact, the water temperature usually stood above fifty degrees at that time of the year.

His mind raced. He looked out into the breakers, but saw nothing. Stumbling north, he continued to come across more and more fragments of ice, then fresh planking, a bucket, and several broken barrels. Soon, out on the outer bar, approximately three hundred yards from where he stood, O'Neal made out the faint outline of a schooner grounded head-on toward the beach. Beneath the roar of the sea, he could hear her bell ringing and ringing. She was still together, but swaying and pounding in the gale.

Before dashing back to his station for help, the shaken patrolman rummaged through his satchel for a Coston flare. The first refused to burn. He hurried to find another. Once lit, its red bloom illuminated the surf. From the deck of the schooner, a faint light flickered in response. He turned and fled headlong toward the station. Ship ashore! There was a ship ashore!

During the Age of Sail, the ocean off the Outer Banks was known throughout the world as both beautiful and unforgiving. Still today, the dark, looming shapes below the surface are testimony to the hundreds of vessels that have wrecked off North Carolina, many taking entire crews with them. Some 650 ships are known to have been lost off the Outer Banks, and mariners rightly came to call the area "the Graveyard of the Atlantic."

Modern maps that depict the location of shipwrecks are busy with information. The entire 180-mile stretch of windswept barrier islands as it arches away from the mainland like an arm bent at the elbow is littered with sunkers. While it is hard to find a single location where shipwrecks did not occur on the Tar Heel coast, it's clear that the forty-five-mile span from Oregon Inlet to the horn at Cape Hatteras claimed the most vessels. Here, the frigid, southward-flowing Labrador currents collide with the tepid, north-flowing Gulf Stream, forming hidden shoals where depths can go from 125 fathoms to 2 in just a few yards.

Since Colonial times, mariners have taken advantage of the prevailing currents to dramatically reduce their travel time, and the shipping lanes off the Outer Banks became the supply lines for the United States. In the heyday of American shipping, a spectator could watch from the beaches as many as one hundred vessels tacking about, maintaining a holding pattern until conditions permitted them to clear Cape Hatteras. The area became the most dreaded on the Atlantic coast.

Weather forecasting in the 1800s was a vague and mysterious science, and most shellbacks thought of storms as unavoidable hazards that, like salted beef and sea biscuits, came with the profession. Hurricanes and nor'easters could rise up from the Atlantic with no warning, stunning and destroying whole fleets at once. To the north, mariners could anchor and ride out the gales in the relative safety of Chesapeake Bay. Likewise, to the south, sea-battered ships could limp into the deepwater ports of Charleston and Savannah for a certain degree of safety.

Ships caught off the Outer Banks had few alternatives. Captains would just reef their sails and hunker down or drop both anchors and hope they wouldn't drag or part lines—the idea being simply to outlast the storm. Many failed to do so. Adrift in these enormous seas, ships would be driven ashore and dashed to bits on the shoals. Like iron shavings to a magnet, vessels seemed to stack up on this coast in each storm. In October 1806, surveyor and scientist William Tatham reported the macabre effects of a single hurricane. "Such was the scene of distress," he wrote, "that we lay on the oars and counted." The wrecked hulls and twisted masts of no less than thirty-one ships lay foundered off Hatteras and Ocracoke Inlets.

The federal government constructed four lighthouses to beacon this coast and aid navigation—inadequate protection for the volume of maritime traffic. With so much destruction, the government was relatively slow to create a system of coastal lifesaving. The outbreak of the Civil War delayed efforts, but as lives and valuable cargoes continued to be lost in staggering numbers, Congress finally understood that the nation couldn't prosper with its fleet grounded on shoals and pitched on beaches. A slow trickle of funds became available, and from them emerged the United

States Life-Saving Service. By drawing keepers and crews from local communities, the LSS had the appearance and luster of communal pride, not just another gaffe and abuse of the Reconstruction Era.

On October 5, 1881, at the time of Daniel's and O'Neal's patrols, 189 Life-Saving Stations dotted the American coastline. These lonely outposts were situated on the most wretched stretches of shore from Maine to Florida, as well as along the Great Lakes. Even as far away as the Pacific coast, life-saving stations kept watch over the busy sea. Organized in 1871, the LSS began as a tiny, underfunded branch of the already existing Revenue Marine Service, in the Treasury Department.

During these first years, a scent of doom tainted the service, with its keepers and surfmen known more for their foibles and follies than their rescues. The *Huron* and *Metropolis* disasters, two of the worst in maritime history, occurred off the Outer Banks in the 1870s, making headlines that horrified Americans from coast to coast. There were tales of stations being padlocked and off-limits to fishermen just yards from a ship in distress, of surfmen capsizing their lifeboat and drowning along with the mariners they had come to rescue, of lifesavers rifling through the pockets of victims washed ashore.

Popular magazines such as *Harper's* and *Frank Leslie's Illustrated Newspaper* blasted the Life-Saving Service, using the North Carolina incompetence to lobby that the entire operation be turned over to the navy. "[T]he lifesaving stations there [in North Carolina] are scarcely able to rescue the crew of a fishing smack. Let this service be divorced from politics, let it be placed under the Navy . . . ," cried one editorialist.

For the captains who sailed along America's storm-battered coasts, the stories from the Outer Banks were unnerving. If their vessel struck the shoals at Hatteras or grounded off Kitty Hawk, would the lifesavers respond?

Built in Seaford, Delaware, in 1874, crafted of oak and held together with thousands of galvanized rivets, the three-masted schooner *Thomas J. Lancaster* of Philadelphia was a solid 653 tons. Her captain, George L. Hunter, was also her owner. The *Lancaster* departed from Boston on September 22, 1881, bound for Savannah with a cargo of one thousand tons of ice. Thirteen people were on board. Captain Hunter had employed a crew of eight men, and as was often the case in the 1800s, his family—his wife and their three young daughters—had joined him.

On the night of October 4, 1881, the *Lancaster* pushed south past Bodie Island Light off the coast of North Carolina. The beacon, with its distinctive black and white bands, marked the beginning of a hundred-mile stretch of nearly uninhabited beach. The schooner would keep a southeastern course following the arch of barrier islands to Cape Hatteras. Then, after clearing Diamond Shoals, she would continue south and fold in toward the South Carolina coast. Hunter observed moderate conditions: "the wind was light from the north-west, and the sea smooth." The first mate took over at midnight, and the captain joined his wife and family in their cabin.

During the early hours of the morning, something went terribly wrong. A heavy squall came up and broadsided the schooner from the northeast. While the crew was busy taking in the sails, the first mate sighted breakers, long-cresting lines of them, directly starboard—they were over shallow water. The *Lancaster* jolted, pitching violently, and her masts whined and shook. Hunter immediately appeared topside and began barking orders.

The ship had been eight miles off the coast as it passed Bodie Light, but a mistake in navigation had brought her in toward shore sometime between three and four o'clock that morning. The sea built and crashed over the railing. Then, the ship's hull rose massively in the air and fell upon the sandbar. Surrounded by total darkness, the captain had no choice but to assume they were stuck on the treacherous Diamond Shoals, where, as the seafaring world well knew, few ships ever survived once grounded. Even with her heavy oak construction, the *Lancaster* would soon break apart under the murderous pounding waves.

On board the *Lancaster* was a booklet published by the United States Department of the Treasury. Mass-produced and copiously distributed through the nation's customhouses so that every ship's captain would own one, it contained instructions in both English and French that could mean the difference between life and death for a shipwrecked crew. Aside from basic navigational information, the booklet directed mariners on the proper actions to take in an emergency. "Often when comparatively smooth at sea a dangerous surf is running which is not perceptible four hundred yards off shore, and the surf when viewed from a vessel never appears as dangerous as it is," the book read. "Many lives have unnecessarily been lost by the crews of stranded vessels being thus deceived and attempting to land in the ship's boats."

Outer Banks history is full of accounts of mariners, inexperienced in handling small boats in heavy surf, who lost their lives when they tried to reach the shore by their own devices. Lifesavers on the beach would use flags, flares, whistles, and pantomime to warn the shipwrecked not to launch their boats. Mariners who ignored them usually drowned or had to be wrenched out "by desperate and dangerous grapples in the surf and undertow." Lifesaving crews were much more experienced at getting their narrow surfboats through the steep breakers. They called it "the art of surfing."

If the station keeper judged the surf too heavy, instead of risking capsizing his boat, he would order that a line be fired out to the wreck. The booklet instructed: "Get hold of the line as soon as possible and haul on board until you get the tail-block with a whip or endless line rove through it." Setting up the rescue lines and lifesaving apparatus required the assistance of able-bodied sailors on board the vessel as well as competent lifesavers onshore.

Hunter knew the book. He also knew the reputation of the Life-Saving Service.

In North Carolina, the first lifesavers were fishermen and inlet pilots, chosen for their lifelong association with the sea. Hurricanes were mysterious forces with supernatural strength, and predicting their arrival was, to some degree, an exercise in clairvoyance. Outer Bankers watched the sea while they worked, especially at the end of summer when bands of dense, gray clouds might appear in the south. "June, too soon. November, all over" was a common saying along the coast. They watched the way shorebirds gathered on the beach and livestock became nervous and began wandering haphazardly over the dunes. Some looked to the heavens, claiming a "blazing planet" was a portent of things to come.

Hurricanes packing winds of up to 140 miles an hour and inundating the beaches with a dome of storm surge raked the Carolina coast in unpredictable patterns. In 1842, 1846, 1856, 1861,1876, and 1879, hurricanes swept up the Banks, leveling dwellings, drowning livestock, and uprooting trees. Between storms, Outer Bankers lived in a state of suspended anticipation.

The Outer Banks was a frontier, and only industrious, hardworking men and women lived there. In the heat of the summer, the white sands danced with mirages of ponds, though there was usually no freshwater to be had. All along the sounds, swarms of mosquitoes and deerflies rose from the stagnant pools of brackish water. Winter brought flocks of migrating geese and ducks so immense that it was said they could completely darken the sky as they passed between the earth and the low, white winter sun. Freezes, though rare, might drop temperatures to the basement of the thermometer, raising squalls of blowing snow over the slate-gray Atlantic, and leaving a rime of new ice across the sound.

Boats designed on the Outer Banks, with its shallow channels and tight spaces, had a distinct character. Not only could Bankers recognize local boats at a glance, but in many cases, they could tell the maker and when it was made.

Although industrious and self-sustaining, Bankers were also reputedly unruly and ungovernable. Folklore casts an infamous picture of these coastal inhabitants using various means to trick captains into beaching their ships. Many claim that the name Nags Head originated in an era when malicious wreckers would tie a lantern around an old horse's neck and lead it up and down the dunes. From the sea, the rising and falling light would give the impression of a ship safely moored in a harbor, taunting unsuspecting ship captains to sail to their destruction.

In these coastal communities, the cry "Ship ashore!" was followed by a frenzy of salvaging activities. Wrecking was a tradition woven into the culture from its earliest days. "Your loss, our gain" might best describe the local attitude. In the villages along the Sand Banks and on Roanoke Island, "progging"—walking about after a storm in search of valuables—was viewed as a viable occupation. At one time, the beaches were strewn with a wreck every mile, each with its own story of disaster and doom. From the deck of a wrecked schooner, the Outer Banks must have seemed a barbarous no-man's-land.

*   *   *

Over the centuries, the Outer Banks has been a racial hodgepodge, largely white, but speckled with blacks, both free and slave. Little arable land, a treacherous coast, undependable inlets, and a lack of deepwater harbors made the region ill-suited for the proliferation of the "peculiar institution," and only in certain areas were enough slaves kept to constitute small communities of blacks: in the southern reaches of the Banks, on Portsmouth Island, where they served as "lighters," loading and unloading the cargo of ships as they passed through Ocracoke Inlet; and on Roanoke Island, where small farms were maintained and a few families accumulated relative wealth by wrecking, fishing, and piloting ships. Here, about a quarter of the population were bondsmen.

Slavery accounted for the majority of African-Americans on the Banks, but free blacks had also long populated the coast. Mostly the descendants of slaves who had drifted down from the settlements in Virginia, they presented little economic threat and, so, shared the limited resources on more or less equal footing with their white counterparts. Naturally, when push came to shove, they were usually left out.

While whites may have tolerated blacks in some roles, they were, when threatened, likely to use power and influence to bar them from economic endeavors. During the Colonial era, pilots at Ocracoke, the main point of entry to the settlements along the Neuse and Pamlico Rivers, protested to Governor Josiah Martin in 1773 against the competition "sundry Negroes as well as free men as slaves" were creating for their businesses, "to the great prejudice and injury of your petitioners contrary to law and again the policy of this country and to trade in general." Apparently, Governor Martin did not act on the pilots' complaint.

Richard Etheridge was born a slave on the beaches north of Pea Island on January 16, 1842. He grew up knowing the tides and currents, the channels and shoals, and early on, he learned the savage power of storms. The hurricane of September 7, 1846, blew so strongly that winds and flood waters from the Pamlico Sound burst through Bodie Island and opened an inlet near Richard's childhood home. The storm caused the tide to rise nine feet higher than normal. Farther north, it carried away the market house and destroyed the warehouse of the Nags Head Hotel, littering its stores for a half mile along the beach. Beach dwellers had to climb to safety in the attics of their homes, hoping the houses would stay moored to their foundations. Household property, cooking utensils, and clothes were all destroyed. According to lore, Jonathan Williams's ship, the *Oregon*, on a return trip from Bermuda to its home dock of Edenton, on the Albemarle Sound, was caught in the storm surge—thousands of metric tons of rushing water—that cut the inlet open through Bodie Island, leaving the ship stranded but intact on a sandbar in the newly opened channel. Area residents began calling it Oregon Inlet.* The same hurricane opened Hatteras Inlet the next day.

From the prow of the *Lancaster*, no land could be seen. The ship's heavy oak moaned and shuddered. She was in the grasp of other forces now and would soon be just another victim of the sea. Hunter had mistakenly put his location on Diamond Shoals off Cape Hatteras. Given his knowledge of the dangers of these shoals, he thought their best chance to save themselves was in the lifeboat, instructions from the Treasury Department be damned.

Hunter decided that at daylight, he, his family, and crew would board the boat and make a run for shore. Though daunting, it seemed to be their only course. At around four o'clock in the morning, Hunter ordered the men to lower the lifeboat on the leeward side of the wreck. Dawn was still hours away, but the captain wanted to be ready should the pounding sea snap the hull in two and the *Lancaster* come apart.

The lifeboat seemed wholly insignificant against the backdrop of crosshatched breakers. As if impatient, the sea began to buck the small boat against the hull of the schooner. To prevent it from being dashed to pieces, the second mate and three seamen boarded her and attempted to hold it away from the ship. They used their arms, legs, and a couple of oars—anything to keep the boat from striking the thick oak hull.

O'Neal's Coston flare was a sudden surprise against the dark night, a brilliant red glow surrounded by a halo of bright light. The sight of the flare relieved all on board, for it meant land was close by.

In fact, the *Lancaster* was much closer to shore than Hunter had pre-

---

*Other sources claim that the steamboat *Oregon* was the first vessel to pass through, announcing the inauguration of the new passageway and giving it her name.

viously thought—just three hundred yards. And the lifesavers on shore knew they were there. Perhaps this revelation, had it come sooner, might have changed the captain's decision to launch the boat. Perhaps he might have been able to call his shipmates back on board. But already the crew of the *Lancaster* had sealed their fate.

As Surfman Daniel worked back toward Pea Island, the storm reached its greatest intensity. The Signal Service stations at Hatteras and Kitty Hawk recorded wind gusts up to sixty-seven miles an hour, with sustained winds around forty. At times, the downpour made it impossible for Daniel to see even ten feet in front of him. When he arrived at the station, he was soaked to the bone, runnels of water streaming from his jacket. He stopped at the window and looked back to the south.

A heavy bank of fog lifted. The sun must have risen just above the horizon, for a faint, pearlescent glow inhabited the fog, giving it body and form. This first suggestion of sunrise revealed tremendous surf, miles and miles of broken, white seas. To the south Daniel saw an interruption in the fury of the white breakers, a black spot that, from a distance, resembled a lump of coal. Far to the south, more than five miles away, he could make out the masts and spars of a ship; the black shape in the surf was a grounded schooner. He notified the keeper.

Keeper Etheridge wasted no time rousing the crew, his voice booming through the wooden station as the first strokes of daylight painted the eastern skies. "Ship ashore! Ship ashore to the south! Put on your oilskins!" The floorboards thumped and creaked as the surfmen dashed for their jackets and boots.

While they hustled into their foul-weather gear, Etheridge surveyed the wreck from the crow's nest atop the station. Through the viewing glass he could see the masts, three in all, still standing—a good sign that the ship was holding together. He estimated the distance to be no less than five miles, probably no more than three north of Chicamacomico. That put the vessel directly on the sandbars at Loggerhead Inlet, a passageway that had recently shoaled up and closed. Keeper L. B. Midgett's Chicamacomico crewmen would probably be at the scene by then.

Crossing New Inlet with the beach cart would be impossible. The cart, which housed the half-ton beach apparatus containing the heavy mortar and shot, sand anchor and hawsers, would get swamped and lost. Instead, the Pea Islanders traveled light that morning, hauling only what they would be able to ford across the coarse waters of the inlet. Etheridge ordered his men to load the boat wagon with the medicine chest, cork life-saving jackets, a Merriman suit (an 1881 version of a wet suit), and the heaving lines and sticks. The Chicamacomico crew would bring their beach cart or boat, whichever Keeper Midgett judged most expedient.

The Pea Island surfmen wasted no time. In their excitement, they did not pause to eat anything. Two men slid the boatroom door open and the crew burst forward with the boat wagon. They were six crewmen: Lewis Wescott, Robert Tolar, William Daniel, William Davis, William Bowser, and Benjamin Golden. Wescott, the number one man, was young and promising, a leader who could fill in for Etheridge in a pinch. Tolar, known to take a drink now and again, had entered lifesaving with Etheridge at the Bodie Island station in the LSS's first years. William Bowser was a talented boatbuilder; William Davis, a decorated soldier of the U.S. Colored Troops during the war. William Daniel and his brother Henry, who was absent from the station delivering the mail to Manteo, were skilled watermen from Roanoke Island. Benjamin Golden, a reliable substitute, filled in for Henry. Bowser, Henry Daniel, and Davis had been surfmen under the white keeper at Pea Island when the *M&E Henderson* had come ashore and had witnessed the shakedown and the firing of the white crewmen that had ensued from it.

With a steady gale at their backs, the Pea Island crew started south, passing by the charred foundation of their old station, then over a series of hummocks and through pools of tidal wash. This would be the first major test for Etheridge and the all-black crew—the previous spring's troubles aside. Each of the men understood that the tenuous balance of circumstances that had gotten a black keeper and crew put in charge at Pea Island could just as quickly split them up, return them to their positions as cooks—or, worse still, drum them out of the service altogether.

They also recognized this as a test for the Life-Saving Service as a whole. Scores of lives had already been lost along this coast because of shady hiring practices, neglect, and a lack of leadership. Another failure might mean disbandment and annexation into the navy.

★　　★　　★

Down the coast, Keeper Little Bannister Midgett, a tall, intimidating man with a temper like the riptides of a winter storm, drove his crew from Chicamacomico with equal determination. Keeper Midgett—"L.B." to most—cut a curious figure along the Outer Banks, his biography the stuff of tall tales. Midgett, on a dare, was said to have once eaten a duck raw, just to prove it could be done. His quirky reputation aside, L.B. was a surfman through and through. He was appointed about the same time as Richard Etheridge, another of the men hired with the idea that the best leaders would shape the Tar Heel LSS into a first-rate organization.

Upon first seeing the foundered schooner, lying head-on to the beach, her masts swaying amid acres and acres of cross seas and cresting breakers, Midgett judged her close enough to shore to use the mortar and shot, and he ordered his men to prepare the beach cart. With the three horses they'd commandeered from local citizens hitched to the wagon, they started off.

The work of hauling the beach cart was tremendous. The crew bogged down in the gale and surf-swept beach, the cart's spoked wheels sinking into a beachfront that Midgett deemed "very Bad and overflown." Pieces of wreck-stuff—fresh planking, tackle, slabs of ice—crashed against the wheels of the wagon. Stanley Midgett, a nearby resident who was hauling wood to the station, pitched in, but progress was slow, even with the three ponies.

The Pea Island crew's march was equally arduous, and they had New Inlet to cross.

Surfmen Davis and Daniel had both been on patrol when the *Lancaster* had struck the strand and had had almost no sleep since the night before. Like most crews up and down the coast that fall, many of the Pea Islanders, Keeper Etheridge included, were fighting off bouts of what they called the ague—that is, malaria. The storm of the previous month had flattened yaupon bushes and left acres of standing water, breeding grounds for illness. Etheridge and Tolar had each spent the better part of September first stricken with, then recovering from, sickness. Just the week before, in fact, Etheridge had been so severely ill that Surfman Bowser had had to carry him home to Manteo for treatment. The keeper could still feel behind his eyes the throbbing heat of his most recent spell of fevers, not yet quite gone. But he, like the rest, knew himself to be up to the task at hand. When a ship came ashore, there was no other choice.

The men trudged on. Forty-five minutes. An hour. New Inlet still before them. Occasionally, Etheridge would break from the ranks and dash up a dune to peer at the wreck through his viewing glass. She was still holding together.

It is possible that no one aboard the *Lancaster* knew how to swim. Sailors of the era, who often harbored deep superstitions, typically thought it bad luck to learn. Swimming, they believed, would only prolong the agony of drowning. If they went down thirty miles offshore, this logic made a twisted sort of sense. As the sun began to draw the outline of dunes and bushy hummocks in plain view of the crewmen—not three hundred yards distance—those who didn't swim now rued their ignorance.

Even had they had the knowledge, long odds favored death over any of the mariners' ever reaching shore. Rip currents and undertows would hold swimmers in the "horse markets" while the steep, heavy faces of breakers fell upon them again and again. Floating debris, full of sharp rivets and jagged edges, churned in the surf, cracking bones and ripping the flesh of those caught in its path. And there was the risk of hypothermia. No, the more prudent plan was to run the surf in the boat when it was light enough to see. With the coming dawn, they were ready to go, with or without aid from shore. They would not wait on the lifesavers.

Before first light, however, breaking waves began to dump water into the lifeboat. The four men aboard bailed like mad. Suddenly, the painter snapped and the small craft was sucked under an enormous sea. Two of the men immediately drowned, while the second mate and another struggled frantically to hold on to a line tied to the schooner. The second mate's leg snapped when, tangled in the rope, his body was dashed against the hull. Those on board the *Lancaster* hauled the two exhausted and injured men in.

There was no time to tend to them, though. A huge sea broke over the vessel, shattering the windows of the cabin. As water poured into the hold, thousands of tons of ice came alive and began to bang and crash about below. The combination of water and ice caused the vessel's decks to rend, breaking up the hull at an alarming rate. The sound was incredible.

With the lifeboat gone, the survivors clung to the wreckage and peered toward shore. Far down the beach they could see a knot of men pulling a cart, coming slowly but coming nonetheless. The lifesavers were now their only chance.

New Inlet, located just eight miles south of Oregon Inlet, where Etheridge had grown up, was unpredictable: open one season, shoaled up the next. Keeper Etheridge maneuvered his crew to where he supposed they could wade across: on the sound side, where the water should be at its most shallow.

The Pea Islanders hauled the boat cart past fish houses on the backside of the island and into the inlet. Often chest-deep in water, the men formed a tight group and pushed forward. Once across, they headed southeast. As they pulled their wagon over the hummocks, they could see the masts of the wreck rising up above the beach.

With the ice battering the hull from within and powerful seas breaking on her sides, the *Lancaster* didn't stand a chance. In the early hours of October 5, her solid-oak decks began to split and tear away aft, so Hunter, his wife, the three young girls, and his crew scrambled toward the front of the ship. They lashed themselves to the fore-rigging, an adult helping each of the girls to hold on. Mrs. Hunter, lashed to the bitts, held her youngest child, only eighteen months old, in her arms. The survivors huddled on what was left of the bowsprit and jib, but even then they were not safe from the breaking seas.

Rising out of the darkness, a huge swell swept the forecastle, wrenching one of the girls from the steward's arms. She fell to leeward and vanished under the jib. Hunter immediately dove after and was able to grab her. But crashing waves never travel alone, and the next broke upon the captain, snatching his daughter from his grasp. He reached for her, but this time could not find her.

The same sea struck the wreck with enough violence to rip the baby from its mother's arms. Two children were now lost.

Frantically searching for his girls, the captain was dashed against the capstan by passing swells. Hunter, with a terrible head wound, was then swept overboard. He caught hold of the bobstay hanging from the bowsprit and was able to pull himself back onto the *Lancaster*. Dazed and injured, he just rested there awhile. Eventually, he dragged himself over the bow to his wife in the fore-rigging and huddled with her on what was left of his ship. Their last daughter was passed down to her, and to try to keep this child from slipping away with the next crashing sea, she tied her fast in the lines of the rigging.

This was the situation that greeted the crew of Chicamacomico as they came abreast of the disaster. Keeper Midgett surmised that the ship could come apart at any moment. He ordered his men to set up the beach apparatus and prepare the mortar to fire a rescue line to the wreck. Each man knew his task. Like a team of well-trained firefighters, they leapt into motion, but instead of ladders, buckets, and hoses, the lifesavers used a network of ropes, pulleys, and cross-beams.

To the untrained eye, the drill would look more like a circus act, though countless mariners had been rescued this way. The keeper chose a spot for the numbers five and six surfmen to bury the sand anchor. With long-handled shovels, these men sprinted to the position and buried the wooden cross-beam deep down in the beach. Numbers one and two unloaded the heavy cannon from the cart, placed the shot in the muzzle, and sighted the gun to Midgett's call, while numbers three and four unloaded the faking box, which held the lines, and prepared the traveling block that would carry the breeches buoy (a circular float with a pair of canvas trousers sewn in) out to the wreck. All of this took less than two minutes. Somebody on board would need to secure the line to an elevated place on the mast, but within minutes, the lifesavers would be hauling people to shore, one at a time.

With the schooner facing the beach, she made a difficult target. Crosswinds swept over beach and sea, and Keeper Midgett had to adjust his shot to account for their velocity. "Left! Left! Well!" he called as surfmen one and two aimed the cannon. Once set, the men hurriedly cleared away from the muzzle and covered their ears. Midgett called, "Ready!" then pulled the lanyard to ignite the powder, and the barrel blazed forth a white flash of fire. The twenty-pound shot rocketed toward the vessel, peeling line from the faking box, and fell directly into the mizzen rigging.

From shore, they saw one of the survivors attempt to reach the line. He looked feeble. He struggled from handhold to handhold, waves washing over the schooner. The lifesavers could only watch in misery as the current swept the line leeward, away from the broken ship, before he reached it.

The Pea Island crew arrived as Midgett was preparing another shot. It was eight-thirty; it had taken them two and a half hours to travel the five miles to the site. Their ponies jolted in their hobbles at the enormous blast from the gun. Rocketing out and over the wreck, the mortar looked like a hyphen on a blank, gray page. But the line fell just a few yards out into the surf and lay lifeless.

Etheridge knew right away that the muzzle blast had burned the line. Midgett cursed and ordered the men to prepare another shot. Without pause, the Pea Islanders jumped in with the Chicamacomico crew, black and white surfmen working side by side. Two began faking line into its box, winding new rope through the wooden pegs. Others went after another shot and secured it to the line. Keepers Midgett and Etheridge stood off a few paces and discussed the situation.

Midgett, the first on the scene, had final authority. Both men agreed that the seas were running too high to launch a surfboat. In addition to which, neither crew had brought theirs. The rescue would have to be performed with the mortar and line. Owing to the strong winds, the keepers decided that the cannon must be moved windward of the wreck.

Through his viewing glass, Etheridge counted the survivors. He could see a small group of men huddle around the jibboom. A woman was aboard—Etheridge saw her clearly. She was holding a child in her arms. A continuous assault of surge washed over the wreck, upsetting the sailors and causing them to jockey for better holds. Through the lens, the ocean seemed less imposing, a small sphere of restless water. Without the glass, the raging Atlantic was endless.

The fourth shot landed across the jibboom, where it was seized by one of the men. With a line finally secured to the schooner, the two crews prepared to deploy the breeches buoy. As they were sending the necessary tackle out to the wreck, though, the mariners suddenly stopped pulling the line. Tired or wounded or both, they had given up. Without their help, the lifesavers were powerless.

Seeds of panic began to roil in the bellies of the men on the beach. Midgett and Etheridge, away from the rest, discussed what to do next.

They decided to send three men with the horses to retrieve the surfboat from Chicamacomico. If the winds changed and the seas dropped off, perhaps they could launch and stroke out to the ship.

Aboard the *Lancaster,* despair had set in. None of those who remained had the strength to attach the line, and now it appeared that the lifesavers were abandoning them. Seaman John Lilley decided to take his chances. He abandoned ship. Diving away from the wreck, he stroked frantically with his last strength through the blocks of ice, razor-sharp debris, and loose lines. Somehow, Lilley made his way into the breakers.

Seeing him, Midgett donned the Merriman "life-saving dress" a cumbersome, rubberized bodysuit, and lumbered as quickly as he could into the surf. So strong were the waves that they swept him off his feet when he was only waist-deep in water. By a miracle, he was able to reach Lilley and drag him to shore. Etheridge took the sailor from Midgett, wrapped him in blankets, and gave him a dose of brandy to help revive him.

As this was happening, black and white lifesavers frantically signaled for the survivors to remain aboard the wreck. Yet another seaman, seeing Lilley's success, plunged into the drink. Caught in the swift currents of the "cut," he was carried down the beach, flailing but unable to make progress toward shore. After a struggle, he disappeared in the raging undertow.

Midgett once again entered the surf after the sailor. He dove under the waves, the suit pulling him back up; he thrashed about, searching, but could find no one. Richard and others, plunging after him, lifted the exhausted and distraught Midgett to his feet and towed him to shore, where he collapsed with fatigue. They had to carry him back to his station in the cart.

Thomas Midgett, the keeper from the Gull Shoal station, the next one south of Chicamacomico, arrived on horseback, drawn by the bright red halos of flares and the booming of the cannon. By now, it was nearly three o'clock in the afternoon. With six months seniority over Etheridge, Midgett considered himself the ranking officer and began directing men to prepare another shot. Etheridge had already witnessed the futility of this—no one aboard the wreck had strength enough to secure the line. But Keeper Midgett was determined to show the others it could be done.

Richard Etheridge did not challenge him. Instead, he directed three men to accompany him to Chicamacomico and assist the men already sent after the weighty surfboat.

The schooner had been grounded for nearly twelve hours now. The lifesavers had been toiling on the beach without much success for almost as long. Some of the men Thomas Midgett commanded had been up for nearly twenty-four hours, and none had had a thing to eat.

Midgett succeeded in landing an excellent shot across the jibboom, right in reach of the remaining sailors. At worst, he expected to be able to send cork life jackets out along the line for the survivors to don, but, to Midgett's chagrin, the sailors "tuck it [the line] up and hove it over bord." This surprised none of the surfmen. The sailors had long since lost faith in being taken off by the breeches buoy.

Back at Chicamacomico, Keeper Etheridge and surfmen from both crews strained against the weight of the boat. With its high gunwales and a heavy hull, the surfboat acted as a sail against the gale, which still blasted from the north. The strength of seven men and three ponies hardly moved the boat forward. Progress was agonizingly slow. They spent more than five hours trying to get the boat to the wreck site. Finally, dejected and exhausted, Etheridge and his men left it where it stood and returned without the boat.

As evening set in, the mate of the *Lancaster* tied a piece of cork fender to his waist and plunged into the ocean in an effort to reach shore. Currents whisked him off. He disappeared below the water, never to be seen again.

At sundown, Captain Hunter, wounded and heartbroken, fell from the bowsprit and drifted away from the wreck. He had one arm through a life preserver, but lost his grip and drowned in plain view of his wife and daughter. Later, this child, exhausted and in shock, slipped from her hold. Tethered to the rigging, she hung head down by one foot beside the bowsprit, semiconscious and unable to cry for help, until one of the remaining seamen, Harry Brien, saw her there. Mrs. Hunter never saw her—or if she did, she could not move to free her. Brien slid down from his place on the jibboom, wrapped the girl in canvas, and lay her still body on the bowsprit.

★   ★   ★

The first corpse to come ashore was one of Hunter's young daughters. The men on the beach had all seen drowned bodies before. But this one was different. So young. So disfigured. Some must have thought of their own daughters. Etheridge probably remembered young Oneida, only eleven years old, playing at home, his wife, Frances, looking on.

Was this death somehow his responsibility?

L. B. Midgett, partly recovered, returned to the beach at sundown. With the wind falling off and the help of a fresh horse, he and his men were at last able to get the surfboat to the scene of the wreck. Pitching over the sandbar, the breakers hollowed out and had become steep and smooth. Some rushed up the beach with blocks of ice the size of woodstoves hidden in their surge. Despite this, Midgett and Etheridge, after a short discussion, concluded that a launch might be possible.

Etheridge ordered some of the men to collect driftwood and wreckage from which to build a fire. The blaze would light the surf and facilitate the attempt. Those who thought they might have to take up an oar in these conditions felt their stomachs rise to their throats. The lifesavers, each one sapped to the core, had been on the beach some fourteen hours.

The moon broke through the clouds, and Etheridge stood away from the fire and looked out through his viewing piece at the *Lancaster* one final time. He tried to count the survivors. He could see the woman, still huddled near the jibboom. She cradled the child in her arms. The man beside her was now gone. Etheridge's line of sight blurred, perhaps salt water on the lens, but when he wiped it clean and went to look again, his vision was even fuzzier. The horizon tilted, and Etheridge collapsed.

L. B. Midgett launched the surfboat into breakers so steep that men on the beach could see the oarsmen's knees as the boat rode up the crests. The small craft shipped water constantly. Although they were able to reach the wreck, Midgett decided that the surf was too rough to attempt to take the survivors off. The lifesavers waited beside the disintegrating carcass of the ship for a lull in the seas—a risky proposition—but strong currents wrenched them away. Unable to regain their position, Midgett directed them back to shore without the survivors.

Night passed. The seas calmed. At eight the next morning, over twenty-four hours since the schooner had grounded, Midgett and his crew were finally able to row out, board the wreck, and take off the remaining six passengers. The survivors, their clothes beaten off their backs, were in such poor condition that the lifesavers had to carry them. Mrs. Hunter clung to consciousness. The child was battered and pale blue, but still breathing.

"I give them a little Brandy and Wine to recsute them," Midgett reported. "I then wrapped the Capt's wife and child in Blankets tuck them all to the station And did all in my Power to save them." Midgett's wife and the wives of other lifesavers, already there, pitched in. They offered brandy, sugar, tea, and beef extract. Despite their efforts, the infant died that night, bringing the death count to seven.

They had still been mourning President Garfield in Norfolk when the storm had first struck, tearing the black drapes from their facets, flooding houses, and sending six vessels ashore along the Chesapeake Bay. At Hatteras, two others ran aground. But only at the *Lancaster* did people die.

The schooner itself was a total loss. In the days following the wreck, salvaging crews were only able to save a few sails and some of the standing rigging. Remorse fell heavy on the men of Chicamacomico as they recovered the bodies of the dead, made coffins, and laid them to rest in unmarked graves among the dunes and sea oats.

Rumors began to emerge. It was said that the captain's corpse was robbed of seventy-five dollars.

Assistant Inspector Frank Newcomb arrived from regional headquarters in Elizabeth City to piece together the story, to find fault, and if necessary, cast blame. Mrs. Hunter, after the physical toll of those hours on the wreck and the anguish from the loss of her family, was unable to give any information as to the cause of the disaster. Newcomb did not ask her. A gentleman in that era knew when not to further encumber a woman. Instead, he arranged for her passage, and she traveled North as soon as she was able. The inspector would have to rely on the testimony of the other survivors, as well as that of the lifesavers.

★   ★   ★

The weather stayed foul in the days that followed, the Atlantic, rough and gray. On October 10, the men from Pea Island observed seven schooners and one steamer pass in a brisk wind and cloudy weather. On the thirteenth, they recovered an oar, a whiskey barrel, a small can of oil, planking, and a small jug—remains from the *Lancaster*.

With the physical stress of the long day at the site of the disaster and his recent bouts with malaria, Etheridge had finally succumbed. Three Pea Island surfmen had pulled the empty boat wagon to where their keeper lay and lifted him into it. They dragged the cart back over hummocks and sand hills, through large standing pools of rainwater, across the inlet and past the fish houses, all silent as pallbearers. They carried him to his quarters and helped him into bed. Someone among them stoked the woodstove to warm the station house, then, as their code demanded, they went back to work, one man setting off north, another south, both patrolling the beaches. The third man hurried back to Chicamacomico with the box of clothes donated by the Women's National Relief Association to succor the survivors of the wreck.

Later that day, when he'd recovered enough strength to get up from bed, Etheridge must have silently grilled himself, wondering what the outcome would have been had he and his crew acted differently. Could they have done more? Pea Island had been there, right beside Chicamacomico, and neither had seemed able to do anything to save the sailors, the captain, his family.

Soon, the inspecting officer, Newcomb, would arrive at the station, interview each man, question each decision, each action. In recent years, keepers and surfmen were fired for failing. Would it happen again? Would they be disbanded, dispersed along the coast to serve as cooks and lackeys, as before? Was this already the end of Etheridge's career as keeper?

He could not know. He could only report the conclusion he'd drawn from the torturous self-scrutiny that had followed that terrible night. "Had the [*Lancaster*'s] crew all Remained by the wreck," he wrote in his log, "No life need to have been lost."

Inspector Newcomb, too, had thoughts to carry. The *Metropolis* and the *Huron*, the *Nuova Ottavia* and the *M&E Henderson*. Here was yet another disaster off the Outer Banks, accompanied by the needless loss of life, this one again within plain view of the government lifesavers. Newcomb could only pray he would not find the surfmen at fault. The Life-Saving Service might not survive another hailstorm of criticism.

After sending the *Lancaster*'s second mate to the Marine Hospital in New Bern where his broken leg would receive attention, Newcomb transported the remaining survivors aboard the sloop *Saville* and sailed north toward Elizabeth City over the now calm waters of the Pamlico Sound. This was a trip Newcomb had made too many times these past two years, working tirelessly to root out the persisting incompetence and inattention to duty that was ruining lifesaving along this shore.

As he traveled past Pea Island, the light from the oil lamps burning in the station were clearly visible. Newcomb had been instrumental in hiring Etheridge the year before. Something about Etheridge had inspired the young officer to stand up and fight for the idea of an all-black crew. Many had opposed the appointment, and with the wreck of the *Lancaster,* those voices might yet rise again.

Newcomb, with a breeze cupping the sails of the *Saville,* navigated toward Elizabeth City. A feeling burned inside, a clarity that hiring Richard Etheridge had been right, that Etheridge could be a key piece in solving the puzzle of the problems in North Carolina. The future—could the black crew but survive as a single unit to see it—would bear out Newcomb's wisdom.

PART ONE

Richard Etheridge

"A Man Among the Men"

To TELL THE PEA ISLAND STORY IS TO TELL THE story of Richard Etheridge, the station's first keeper. When Assistant Inspector Frank Newcomb made the surprising and unlikely choice of Etheridge to run the station, he justified the decision by describing Etheridge as "a man among the men" along the coast. He was that and more. The ability and daring in the surf, the resourcefulness and single-minded vision that drew Newcomb to him, despite warnings to the contrary, are at the heart of the inception of the all-black crew.

The source of Etheridge's appeal has its roots farther back than merely his beginnings in the Life-Saving Service. It starts with his childhood in slavery, encompasses his experience as a soldier fighting for freedom during the Civil War, when his leadership skills were forged, and continues after his return from the battlefield. During an era when African-Americans were invisible, mostly despised but always misunderstood by a larger society raging about the "place" of blacks within it, Etheridge was a beacon. He resisted this dehumanization, thrived when forces conspired to limit him.

1

Youth

The Outer Banks

> Nature has done almost nothing to prepare men and women
> to be either slaves or slaveholders. Nothing but rigid training,
> long persisted in, can perfect the character of the one or the
> other. . . . We were both victims to the same overshadowing
> evil. Nature had made us friends; slavery made us enemies.
>
> —*Frederick Douglass*, My Bondage, My Freedom

Richard was the son of the slave Rachel Dough, whose gravestone lies beside his own on Roanoke Island. Although Rachel Dough belonged to Warren Dough, Richard was the property of John B. Etheridge, a relatively wealthy entrepreneur from a family of local prominence.

The Etheridge family origins in the region dated back to the first half of the eighteenth century. Etheridges were one of a dozen families or so who became substantial landowners in eastern North Carolina before the American Revolution. By the turn of the nineteenth century, Etheridges owned sizable tracts of the northern "Sand Banks" and had solidified their status in the community by frequently intermarrying with other local landed families, most notably the Baums and the Midyetts (also spelled Midgett). The Etheridges, Midyetts, and Baums were by no means members of the Southern planter elite. They were fishermen and inlet pilots; some captained sailing vessels; most raised what crops they could and kept a few livestock on small plots of land. But, for the Outer Banks, they were all families of relative means and of good standing.

Born in 1806, John B. became a commercial fisherman in his adult life. By the time of his death in 1881, he owned property on the beaches at Nags Head and at Oregon Inlet, at Poke Pointe on the mainland side of the Pamlico Sound, and on Roanoke Island, as well as a thousand acres of marshland. In 1850, he owned nine slaves—including Richard—a goodly number for an Outer Banker. John's siblings, together, owned as many as ten more. Unlike in plantation slavery, where the only contact blacks had with whites was through an overseer, Banker slaves worked side by side with their masters. John B., his wife, Fanny (who was also his cousin), their four children, their ward Warren Burgess, and the nine slaves all divided their time between the home on Roanoke Island and the house built in the thicket and live oak on the sound side of Pea Island, south of Oregon Inlet.

John B. Etheridge was well liked in the community. He could spin a yarn with the best of them and was known as a repository of local lore. Like all Outer Bankers, he did not sustain himself and his family by just one occupation. He owned a schooner, *Syntax,* and several boats and provided fresh fish and other seafood to the Nags Head Hotel. His reputation as a fisherman was a selling point for the hotel, which boasted his catches in their newspaper ads. John B. also caught other game and maintained small plots of land on which he grew potatoes, melons, and other crops. It goes without saying that his slaves were instrumental in his financial successes.

The violent opening of Oregon Inlet in 1846, though a travail to live through, facilitated business ventures for the entrepreneurial John B. and created more labor and chores for his slaves. In 1849, Etheridge and his slaves netted 2,150 diamondback terrapin, a small, pesky turtle that, by its abundance, fouled fishing nets—much to many anglers' chagrin—but proved to taste excellent in soups and stews. The new inlet was the primary navigable link from sea to sound between Cape Hatteras and the Chesapeake Bay, and Etheridge used it to carry his huge bounty north and flood the markets in Norfolk. He sold the entire lot for four hundred dollars. There were no game laws at that time, and John B., showing savvy and daring, set his slaves after more. They trapped another 1,900, which he took farther north, up the Chesapeake to Baltimore, where he made another three hundred fifty dollars.

In 1850, John B. was appointed keeper of the Bodie Island Light, built in 1848 to indicate the entrance to Oregon Inlet. This was but one of several federal appointments he and others of his family would receive over their lifetimes.

Richard was treated different from most slaves, on the Outer Banks or elsewhere. Richard was born on the premises of John B.'s home at Oregon Inlet and, according to John B.'s children, was "raised as a member and one of the family." Sarah, John's daughter, who was ten years Richard's senior, claims to have helped raise him. Throughout the South, slave codes dictated slave behavior and how masters should keep them. These codes became more rigid after Nat Turner's 1831 revolt took the lives of fifty-nine white men, women, and children, just to the north of the Outer Banks, in Southampton, Virginia. According to the North Carolina codes, masters were prohibited by law from teaching slaves to read and write. But the Etheridges did just that for Richard. Other Outer Banks slaveholders rarely did.

The question of Richard's paternity is a puzzle that, though it will never definitively be solved, creates interesting scenarios. One is that Richard was John B.'s son. In the Banks, as throughout the South, interracial relationships were common. Some few even existed out in the open. More often than not, though, these liaisons and the biracial children they produced endured as commonly known, but publicly unacknowledged, realities of life.

Until well into the twentieth century, "mulatto" was a third possible racial category on the census, and over the decades, mulatto dependents crop up in the records of the extended Etheridge family (as well as in others). In 1850, fourteen-year-old William Bowser (who would later serve in the LSS with Richard) and his sixteen-year-old sister, Vicy, both of whom marked *M* for "mulatto," appear as members of the Adam (John B.'s father) Etheridge family, the only free people of color in the household.* As

---

*Bowser's grandson and namesake, William Bowser III, in an interview with the authors, stated that it was common knowledge within his family growing up early in the twentieth century that they had white forebears from a prominent Outer Banks family.

late as the 1880s, an illegitimate biracial boy was born to John B.'s nephew
Patrick, despite the strong social taboo of that era against the intermixing
of races.

Local lore remembers Richard as having been a mulatto, and an article that appeared in *The Coast Guard Magazine* in the 1930s supports this
claim, although its author reported that Richard was half Native American. By the time of his birth, no identifiable Native American groups were
left in coastal North Carolina, and the chances that a slave woman had
borne a child by a man who identified himself as Native American were
pretty slim. There may be another explanation for the claim to Indian heritage. During the conflicted times of Jim Crow segregation, summoning
Native ancestry was often a way to avoid acknowledging white ancestry,
and although in the census reports and other records Richard never identified himself as a mulatto, this may have been a way to avoid the sensitive
issue of miscegenation.

If this is so—that is, if Richard was, in fact, biracial—it is not incon-
ceivable that he was John B.'s illegitimate son, particularly given the special favor John Etheridge and his family bestowed upon Richard, which
persisted throughout his lifetime. Though Rachel Dough was never John
B.'s property, the Etheridges attest that Richard was born in the household, raised as one of the family, taught literacy. Later, after the end of the
Civil War, Richard chose to live with the Etheridge family and not with
Rachel Dough nor in any of the other black households on the island. In
fact, until his marriage in 1867, he lived with his former masters. John B.,
with his standing in the community and his influence in local politics,
helped Richard get his first position in the federal service—again, an act of
favoritism that John did not bestow upon other former slaves. John's children Jesse and Sarah remained close to Richard until his death. Sarah was
reported to have visited Richard's home many times over his life. These
facts all make for a compelling case. Still, his true paternity will likely
remain a mystery.

At seven in 1849, Richard was quite likely among the slaves who helped
John B. fatten his coffers in the terrapin trade, doing peripheral chores:
culling the catch, setting nets. As a favored slave, he may even have
accompanied John B. on his trips to market.

Youth was not an obstacle to participation in the ways of daily life on the barrier islands, it was an opportunity for instruction in those ways. All Outer Bankers, both well-to-do and not, learned the skills of their parents at early ages and worked right alongside them. They built boats from the sturdy lumber they chopped and planed and piloted them through the inlets and over the shoal waters of sea and sounds. They mended yards of nets and learned how and where to set them. They dredged for oysters, hauled tons of mullet from the churning surf, caught loggerhead turtles, cut blubber from beached whales and boiled it to make oil. These skills and the ones that he learned as an outgrowth of them—understanding the tides and weather systems; acquiring a deftness in the surf—would later serve Richard well when he would apply for one of the much-sought-after positions in the Life-Saving Service.

2

War

Let the colored men accept the offer of the President, take up arms, join the army, and then we will whip the rebels.

—African-American man in response to
Lincoln's authorization to recruit black troops

No matter how peculiar the "peculiar institution" may have been in the Outer Banks, no matter how much less harsh it might have seemed compared to bondage elsewhere in the South, it was still slavery. In 1859, John B. Etheridge passed Richard along to his son, Jesse, as though he were a reliable boat from which to cast his nets of future fortune and reap the wealth of the sounds and sea. Jesse, who was just two years Richard's senior, had been raised with Richard as "children together," and they shared a relatively close relationship. Yet, from early adulthood, their fates were sealed, the one the servant, forced to do the other's bidding, whatever that bidding might be. This fact, not lost on Richard, influenced his thinking for the rest of his life, and he would act on it at the first opportunity to present itself. That opportunity came with the outbreak of war.

The fall of Fort Sumter in April 1861 announced the coming of change for all Outer Bankers—indeed, for all Americans. North Carolina quit the Union fairly soon after the opening of hostilities, as did Virginia, Tennessee, and Arkansas, but Bankers, generally, were not so quick to take

sides and enter the fray. Outer Bankers had traditionally had as much contact with seamen from Northern ports or with ships from abroad as with
mainland North Carolinians; and while some owned slaves, slavery significantly benefited none among them. Few were willing to risk life and
limb for the benefit of people with whom they held a bond in name only.

While Bankers were struggling to maintain neutrality amid the growing hostilities, the rest of the state had other plans for the barrier islands.
Most North Carolina rivers empty into the sounds that lie between the
Banks and the mainland, the Banks being a natural shield against seaborne
invasion. Understanding the strategic importance of this, rebel North
Carolina governor John Ellis ordered that defensive positions along the
coast be established. Forts were built at each of the important inlets,
troops mustered to occupy them, and a makeshift naval squadron, the
"Mosquito Fleet," organized to patrol the sounds. Much of the preparations were being made farther down the coast from the Etheridge property, but the hustle and bustle soon touched their lives.

The Mosquito Fleet, five small steamers commandeered by the rebel
forces and armed with guns, began harassing shipping along the coast. For
the Etheridges and other Banker inlet pilots and fishers, war was proving to
be bad for business. Then, in early June, a Confederate steamer unloaded
engineers and laborers, along with crates of guns, ammunition, and tools,
on Roanoke Island and at Oregon and New Inlets. Fortifications were built
in all three locations, and soldiers began to amass. The commanding officer made an appeal to the citizens of Currituck County to send slaves and
tools to assist in the labor. Neutrality was increasingly difficult to maintain.

Before long, the federal forces also recognized the significance of the
Outer Banks. In early August, the Yankees sent a small expeditionary force
under veteran sailor Silas H. Stringham, accompanied by 860 troops
under Major General Benjamin F. Butler, to seal the "pirate" Mosquito
Fleet in by stoppering Hatteras Inlet with sunken schooners loaded with
stones. Stringham and Butler understood the importance of this site, the
main point of entry to the sounds north of Beaufort. With vastly superior
ordnance, Stringham bombarded Forts Hatteras and Clark, which
guarded the inlet, into submission, and Butler occupied them. Instead of
choking up the waterway and abandoning the position, though, they left a
contingent of soldiers to control the unobstructed passageway. Neither
had any intention of surrendering the position.

Butler, in his zeal to promote his actions at Hatteras, rushed back to Washington, arriving at the White House in the middle of the night. He awoke the sleeping president and boldly pronounced that the North had won its first important victory on Confederate soil. Coming so soon after the federal defeat at the First Battle of Bull Run, where the Union suffered 2,645 casualties, Lincoln, pleasantly surprised by the news, supported the occupation.

The fighting at Hatteras was too far down the coast for the Etheridges to witness, but they soon realized that the war had definitely come to the Outer Banks when, shortly after the fall of Forts Hatteras and Clark, the Confederate command of the fort at Oregon Inlet, near the Etheridge home, hurriedly abandoned the works, spiking the guns so they could not be of use to the Union, and retreated across the Pamlico Sound to Roanoke Island. Before fleeing, the Confederate commander ordered powder ignited in the tower of the Bodie Island Light. The explosion thundered across the quiet waters, leaving little of the federally constructed beacon that John B. Etheridge had overseen for the past decade.

With Hatteras in Union hands, Roanoke Island was the next key piece in securing control of northeastern North Carolina and southern Virginia. Both federal and Confederate leaders recognized this, as did the Bankers, some of whom began fleeing the imminent fighting for the safety of the mainland. The Etheridges stayed. When he could, John B., like the majority of the locals, hid any stock he deemed too valuable to lose, and the family tried to stay the course of noninvolvement. It is unclear whether Richard, who was now nineteen, was ever impressed into service for the rebels, as so many blacks were, both slave and free. If he was, he was never forced to leave the Etheridge household to serve the Confederates anywhere other than along the Banks.

While white Outer Bankers may have been largely indifferent to the issues that had started the war and, more than anything, wanted to stay out of it, the slaves from the barrier islands and the surrounding regions were far from neutral and implicated themselves in the Northern cause as soon as the chance presented itself. Blacks understood that, while the rhetoric about the war cited preserving union as its aim, the roots of disunion resided in the issue of slavery, its protection and propagation. Blacks had a stake in the Northern cause.

In late January 1862, the Yankees under Brigadier General Ambrose Burnside, a Mexican War veteran who had just fought during the defeat at the First Battle of Bull Run, began grouping at the Union forts at Hatteras to attack Roanoke Island. As Burnside amassed his army, small boats and rafts, mostly of escaped slaves, began arriving in the Union camp. Many arrived from the mainland, but others came from Roanoke Island and elsewhere along the barrier islands. Even if white Bankers, wherever their loyalties lay, cursed the coming conflict on principle, slave Bankers welcomed its arrival and the possibility of freedom that was heralded by the growing number of federal gunboats at Hatteras.

The morning of February 7, 1862, Burnside moved on Roanoke Island. The operation began with Union gunboats shelling the Mosquito Fleet and gun batteries on the island to provide cover for the landing. When the rebel guns were sufficiently silenced, a group of small shallow-draft steamers hauling a number of boats—each bearing as its standard the Stars and Stripes, and each filled with soldiers—set course for the shore. They landed ten thousand men on Roanoke Island.

Before nightfall, it had become a Union stronghold behind enemy lines, a site from which to control the waterways of the sounds, to strengthen Lincoln's naval blockade, and to open a second front into Virginia. More important, Burnside's success gave Lincoln and the Union forces a symbolic victory to rally around, to boost morale and garner support, after continued struggle along the more northern fronts.

Word of the Union victory spread quickly throughout the region. Just a few days after the battle, under the cover of night and in a heavy rain, a dinghy filled with escaped slaves landed on the northern shores of Roanoke Island. The group, composed of some twenty men, women, and children, had fled down the Chowan River to the northwest under fire from their former masters onshore, then paddled and sailed the thirty-five miles across the Albemarle Sound to the island. Once arrived, the escaped slaves rejoiced. They were led to General Burnside's tent, where they stood in a group and sang the hymn "The Precious Lamb, Jesus Christ,

Was Crucified for Me" as more and more Yankee officers began to collect around them.

That first dinghy was merely one in a series of dinghies, rafts, and other waterborne craft that runaways piloted to freedom at Burnside's camp. Some even swam the three miles across the sound to get to the Union lines. When Burnside took the island, its population included only 170 slaves. Within a few months, several hundred "contrabands" had collected there, many of them with their entire families. Along with the slaves came a number of poor whites, refugees from the fighting, but most were African-Americans. By the summer, Burnside's army controlled the North Carolina coast, including the Outer Banks, the sounds, and the port towns that bordered the Pamlico. Slaves poured into these Union-held areas.

Burnside decided to employ the escaped slaves in his army. They performed all sorts of skilled and manual labor, including building three earthwork forts—one on Roanoke Island—which freed the troops from these onerous tasks. Some among the contrabands took on more daring roles, serving as scouts, guides, and spies. Many of the women, who generally did not serve as manual laborers, helped in the Union hospital.

On Roanoke Island, the ex-slaves, both native and nonnative, began to establish a community. Mixing with the native black population, they built a school and two churches for themselves, along with the work they did for the army. One church, put together under a broad bower of trees, was no more than several lengths of cut pine, laid down parallel beside one another to serve as pews, and a pulpit made of discarded quartermaster's boxes. From this pulpit, a Yankee officer reported, "Many of their colored preachers exhort with great earnestness and power, and usually present the Gospel with simplicity and truth." The island's freedpeople rejoiced in the Union arrival. At least one "Burnside" was born to black parents during those years.

White natives, by and large, were hardly pleased with the developments in the war. Life in the Banks had undergone radical change. The federal occupation and naval blockade put a stranglehold on commerce. Plus, the island swarmed with jubilant blacks, former slaves, who not only squatted land with the approval of the Northern troops, but who were uniting, building a community. Excluding Northern soldiers, blacks now outnumbered whites on the island more than two to one.

The Yankees themselves were, for the white residents of the Outer

Banks, a plague worse than locusts. The day after Roanoke Island fell, a large group of Northern troops had raided island farms; they returned to their camp shouting "Hurrah" and laden with the carcasses of plundered cattle, carrying squawking fowl bound by the talons, and with tubers and other vegetables spilling out of pockets and haversacks. As the occupation continued, it was not uncommon for "foraging" parties to venture out to replenish the army's stock at the expense of those of the locals. Nor was the commanding general satisfied with Outer Banks neutrality. Burnside, who was officially appointed commander of the Department of North Carolina, sent officers out to administer oaths of allegiance, and the island's inhabitants quickly understood that it was in their best interests to vow their loyalty to the Union.

John B. Etheridge and his brother Adam took the oath of allegiance. The Union army was well entrenched in the Banks, and pragmatism, as much as anything, probably guided their decision. The larger family was split on the issue, though. Little John, John B.'s oldest son, declared himself a secessionist while Tart, John B.'s cousin, served in the Union navy. Division such as this was common among Outer Banks families, with many of the young men who harbored secessionist feelings slipping away to enlist in the Confederate army.

How much of the battle of Roanoke Island Richard Etheridge actually witnessed is impossible to know. It's clear, however, where he stood on the issue of secession: as would be expected, he, like most blacks, both free and slave, welcomed the federal invasion. Though he still resided with Jesse Etheridge, Richard was taking part in the growing black community.

Meanwhile, in the North, activists renewed their call for manumission. Free blacks and abolitionists used General Butler's "contraband acts," whereby Butler refused to return escaped slaves to their Confederate masters, as a means to build momentum toward the cause of emancipation. President Lincoln, to this point, had been resistant, convinced that manumission would be a dangerous political move. For the majority of Northern popular opinion, the war was being fought to restore union, not to end slavery. But with the rebels' impressive victories on the battlefield—at the Second Battle of Bull Run, Fredericksburg, then Vicksburg, Mississippi—the president realized that it would take overwhelming manpower to defeat them. As Union casualties rose and enlistment fell, Lincoln and his military commanders had finally to acknowledge that emancipation, though politically risky, made military sense. The use of black labor would free up more troops to fight.

Lincoln issued his Emancipation Proclamation on January 1, 1863. The edict was cautious, though: it did not abolish slavery, but rather, freed the slaves *only* in states that had seceded and in regions still held by the rebels. And it provided for their enlistment in the armed services. With this, the abolitionists had established a firm foothold from which to move forward in the fight for emancipation.

Military service was an important front upon which to combat slavery. The abolitionists believed that in taking up arms against the rebellion, the former slaves would be making a bold, public claim to their rights to freedom and citizenship. With the aid of other prominent abolitionists, Massachusetts governor John A. Andrew, who had been lobbying to raise regiments of African-American troops from among the free black population of his state, raised the Fifty-fourth Massachusetts Colored Volunteer Infantry Regiment—made famous by the 1989 film *Glory*. So great was the turnout that he continued the call to arms among his black citizens and raised a second regiment, the Fifty-fifth.

Massachusetts men who had fought in the Burnside Expedition reported back to Governor Andrew about the enthusiastic assistance that the freedmen had given the army. In early April, encouraged by the recent success in raising black troops in his home state, Andrew proposed to Secretary of War Edwin Stanton that he send "some able, brave, tried, and believing man" to North Carolina to organize black regiments there. He recommended Colonel Edward A. Wild, a close friend who had helped the governor raise the Fifty-fourth and Fifty-fifth.

In the late spring of 1863, as the appropriately named Wild was convalescing from devastating war wounds, Lincoln, upon the secretary of war's recommendation, promoted him to the rank of brigadier general and ordered him to North Carolina to raise four brigades from among the freed slaves there. Though incapacitated, Wild jumped at the opportunity.

Wild arrived in coastal North Carolina in June 1863 with the express purpose of forming an "African Brigade." Of slight build but enormous presence, he was an ardent abolitionist. While on duty in southern Virginia, Wild had William Clopton, a local planter with a reputation for cruelty toward his slaves, brought into regimental headquarters and publicly flogged by those very slaves, whom Wild ordered freed.

Wild cut a striking figure, with flowing hair, a full, reddish beard, and piercing eyes—reminiscent of John Brown's ascetic's glare. His empty left sleeve was folded and pinned just above where the elbow should be. The new recruits, awed by the man, speculated on the rumors that the general himself had overseen the amputation of the arm. And Wild found recruits aplenty. He sent white officers into the burgeoning freedmen's camps at New Bern, Beaufort, and Little Washington, and on Roanoke Island, to induce the able-bodied men to join the army. Wild himself traveled around the Union-occupied territories along the coast. He was such a dynamic stump speaker that, after he'd visited Hatteras in mid-June, all the freedmen there except those too old or infirm followed him back to his base at New Bern to join the African Brigade.

Secretary of War Stanton reported to Congress that "[t]he hardy young negroes of Roanoke [Island] were among the first to answer the country's call," and they answered in relatively large numbers. Of a total native black population of 197, nearly 100 signed on with recruiting officer Second Lieutenant Jerry McClair, who had been sent by Wild to the island.

Richard Etheridge, along with his boyhood friend Fields Midgett, joined at the end of the summer, on August 28. Richard was twenty-one. He asked no one's permission. He merely left the Etheridge household, where he still resided with his former masters, choosing to follow one-armed Wild and fight for his right to true freedom.

Whatever the Etheridges' feelings about Richard's enlistment, they, like the other island families, could merely watch in silence as their former slaves joined the flock of freedmen responding to the call to serve. Not John B. nor any of the other Banks slaveholders publicly contested the loss of their chattel.

Richard and a group of recruits left the island by boat bound for training camp at New Bern. Most left behind family, wife, and children. Richard left behind his mother and a burgeoning community that was coming to depend upon him and the other young men of his ilk. The enlistees entrusted the welfare of their loved ones to the troops occupying the island.

Richard was clear on the risk he was taking in joining the fight. Three months before he enlisted, as news spread of Wild's activities in the state, newspapers throughout North Carolina reported that a new law had been passed by the Confederate Congress, stating that any black soldier captured would not be treated as a prisoner of war but instead as a slave engaged in insurrectionary activities and would suffer the penalty for this offense: death. Captured white officers of black troops would also be executed.

Fully aware of this added risk, the black recruits, before signing on, demanded guarantees that their families would be taken care of should anything happen to them in the field. General Wild responded favorably and quickly. He authorized the creation of a freedman's colony on the unoccupied and confiscated lands of Roanoke Island, where each soldier's family would get a small plot of land. They would be provided rations, and the government would build and supply schools, a hospital, and other facilities in exchange for the military service of the men. By enlisting, the men had gone from slave to family provider in one bold step.

In all, more than five thousand black North Carolinians would join the Union ranks by the war's end, most from the coastal counties. In the summer and fall of 1863, Wild found a sufficient number of volunteers, about 2,150, to organize two full regiments and another partial one. In late July, just a few weeks before Richard Etheridge left his home for training camp in New Bern, Wild was ordered to Charleston with the First North Carolina (Colored) Volunteer Infantry regiment and a company from the Second NCCV for duty at Folly Island, outside Charleston. Wild hadn't properly organized the units nor completed his recruiting mission, but he welcomed the opportunity to send his troops into combat.

At Folly Island, the African Brigade was first employed to police the campgrounds of white troops, then, after vigorous protests from General Wild, in less demeaning but equally menial tasks—primarily, as laborers, digging trenches.

At New Bern, Etheridge, for the first time in his life, was examined by a doctor. No practicing physician lived on Roanoke Island, the nearest being at Elizabeth City, across the Albemarle Sound, or in Shawboro, near the Virginia border, each more than forty miles away—a distance too great to undertake for the examination of a slave. Etheridge queued up with the others outside the medical tent, the line moving fairly quickly, and when his turn came, he was called in by an orderly.

Etheridge removed his shirt, as ordered by the army surgeon. Standing five feet ten, he was wiry and lithe, his face made darker by the sun. He had chiseled features: angular cheekbones and honest eyes; he had a striking bearing. Without much prodding or probing, the surgeon declared Etheridge fit for service; he gave him a dose of quinine, told him to put his shirt back on, and instructed the orderly to call in the next man.

Etheridge and the other recruits of the Second NCCV were like fish in a barrel in the military camp. They were the object of scrutiny, all attention on them, and while some Northern troops were supportive of raising black regiments and many were indifferent, there was no lack of hostility toward the black soldiers among the Yankees. With the principal body of the brigade gone to South Carolina, the regiment was at less than half strength, with only three officers left. On these grounds, the quartermaster refused the black troops supplies and equipment until the unit was up to strength, compounding the problem. Training and drill were all but impossible. The regiment was in disarray.

Commanding Gerneral John G. Foster ordered Colonel Alonzo G. Draper, who was in charge of the remaining African Brigade, to move the Second NCCV north to Fortress Monroe, at the mouth of the James, where they would be used to labor on the trenches and batteries. Just a week after Richard Etheridge's and Fields Midgett's enlistment, they, along with the rest of the men of the Second, boarded naval transports bound for Tidewater, Virginia. Major General John J. Peck, the commander in North Carolina, was happy to see them go. Upon learning that the Second would be transferred, he expedited their departure, in spite of the fact that it left portions of his post unguarded. He would rather risk attack with an undermanned command than have the armed freedmen in his ranks.

For all that the men of the Second suffered from the racism of the top brass, they drew an ace in their commanding officer, Alonzo Draper. Draper *was* an advocate of the black fighting soldier. Very much so. He had been an instructor stationed in upstate New York when Governor

Andrew began raising black units. He immediately volunteered his ser-vices. "I am but twenty-seven years old," he wrote Andrew, "and am anx-ious after nearly two years of garrison duty, to distinguish myself in the field, by a fruitful devotion to duty, and, aside from my selfish motives, I have a sincere desire to assist in ameliorating the condition of the colored race, and in their enfranchisement from that social depression to which an ignorant popular prejudice has consigned them. This sentiment is not a novel one to me, but is consistent with the whole course of my life."

Draper was more activist than intellectual and was a proven leader. The eldest son of a family of modest means from Lynn, Massachusetts, he studied law while supporting himself, a new wife, and a child until a labor crisis set him on a crusade to help improve the condition of the ordinary laborer. In 1859, Draper became the editor of the *New England Mechanic,* a paper that advocated for the interests of journeymen shoemakers, and organized a large-scale strike after neither manufacturers nor retailers supported the workers when a glutted market led to their unemployment. He gave speeches as far afield as New York, raising money and awareness, and led mass, but orderly, demonstrations. Newspapers and magazines covered the strike, which grew to encompass fifteen thousand workers, male and female, from all over New England.

War put an end to the strike. Draper raised a company of volunteers and drilled them until they were mustered into the army. He was made their captain. When he learned of his governor's search for officers to command black regiments, his destiny appeared to have unrolled itself before him like holy writ.

A regiment at full strength contained one thousand men—ten companies of one hundred each. Draper found himself with only 371 officers and troops, the rest gone with Wild to Folly Island. Draper set up camp near Portsmouth, five miles south of Norfolk and across the James from Fortress Monroe. As best they could, Draper and his handful of officers organized the men into a regiment. Etheridge and Midgett, along with a number of other native Roanoke Islanders, were put into Company F. When the company's captain, George Ives, assembled his staff of non-commissioned officers, he appointed Etheridge as one of four sergeants.

Etheridge was a natural choice. He carried himself well and was respected by others. His ability to read and write also pushed him toward this. From an early age, other slaves, old and young alike, counted on literate ones to read for them and to provide information. In addition to which, Richard, following the example of the Etheridges, probably believed that leadership among his race was his calling, that he carried some obligation to rise to the head of his community. He stood out among them, as did Fields Midgett, who was made a corporal.

Fortress Monroe, opposite Norfolk—out on the tip of the peninsula between the James River and Chesapeake Bay—was built up and bustling with activity. People were everywhere: armed sentinels; companies in drill formation; hospital tents; sutlers' wagons. White tent towns laid out in orderly rows sprang up all across the open fields. The earth was scarred with trenchworks, marking the places beyond which it was not safe to venture. Warships, schooners, and steamers cluttered the waters surrounding the fort, their empty spars a blighted forest rising above the calm waters of the Chesapeake Bay. The black troopers were quick to get acclimated, though. They had to be. Within days of their arrival, detachments began being ordered out on labor details to fortify the camps around Portsmouth and Norfolk.

No sooner had Draper and his unit arrived at Fortress Monroe than the colonel began scheming for ways to get his men into the field. Daily, Draper sent out only the minimum number of men needed for labor duties. He drilled the rest—moving as a unit; wheeling and countermarching; shifting from column to line of battle and back to column formation again. Draper rotated his men so that all would receive equal measures of training and labor. When he could spare them, he sent out officers, commissioned and noncoms, to enlist black recruits. Dressed smartly in his uniform, Sergeant Etheridge made trips into the Virginia countryside to drum up prospective soldiers from among the slaves.

At Portsmouth, Etheridge and the rest of the unit suffered indignities daily, and they, like their colonel, grew increasingly frustrated with their lack of field experience. It was becoming clear to these men that the lesson they had learned from slavery—that, as an African-American, one had to constantly prove his humanity and worth to whites—applied as much, maybe more, to Northerners, who'd had so little contact with blacks, as it did to Southerners.

Colonel Draper seemed different. He inspired the confidence of his men. Like other abolitionists of his day, he held some paternalistic views about blacks, seeing them as children in the bodies of adults. In his command, however, Draper didn't make any distinctions in the authority with which he commanded his troops, white or black, and the freedmen respected him for this. The colonel wore a heavy, full beard to signal his gravity and was a strict disciplinarian.

Draper actually drove his officers harder than he did the troops. He felt the officers had to set a good example for the blacks in their charge, to help raise them up from their conditioning as slaves. At Fortress Monroe, though, these officers were under unique pressures. They were ostracized by their fellow white soldiers, regularly berated and ridiculed for serving in a black unit. Matters were made worse as the men they were leading were so green and often performed poorly on parade. Draper insisted upon sobriety among his officers, forbidding the use of alcohol altogether, but many were taking to drink as a way to relieve the stress.

Etheridge's company commander, Captain Ives, either because of the stress or because he was addicted to drink (or perhaps a measure of both), ignored Draper's prohibition. One day in the fall, Ives reported drunk for duty. Etheridge, the other sergeants, and all the men of the company knew it. Soon, the colonel knew it, too. Draper upbraided the man and booted him from the African Brigade. If the colonel would do this to an officer, one of the few in an understaffed regiment, the troopers did not doubt he would do it to them. Incidents such as this, though painful to witness, cultivated a respect for Draper among the men.

Normally, before seeing duty, regiments received two to three months of drill and preparation. The men of the Second learned as they performed the tasks assigned to them while also doing labor duty in the trenches. By November, morale was dangerously low. Despite Wild's respect for them as men, despite Draper's drive to make them soldiers, disillusionment set in among the Second.

To begin with, the black troops were paid less than their white counterparts, and all resented this. White privates received thirteen dollars per month including their uniforms, while blacks only got ten, minus a three-dollar allowance for clothing—seven dollars in all, a laborer's wage. This added insult to injury, and the men begrudged the army this overt racism.

Noncommissioned officers, such as Etheridge, earned a private's wage, not the supplement noncoms normally received. And to make matters worse, many of the men had yet to receive their pay at all.

The Second, as a unit, lacked proper supplies. The men had, in fact, been undersupplied since New Bern, when they were refused equipment for not being at full strength. As a result, Draper's command failed an inspection in early November, reportedly for not being "properly stockaded." The reviewing officer cited a "want and care of discipline" as the cause, indifferent to the real one: that they were caught in a ludicrous cycle, incapable of behaving as a proper regiment because of their insufficient number and the ancillary duties assigned them, and unable to remedy the situation for the same reasons. The men knew they were being singled out, but felt powerless to defend themselves from this attack.

Though frustrated, Draper and his men came to understand that only by proving their worth in the field would they get the respect and equal treatment they deserved. As difficult as the army was making service for these men, joining had been a key to feeling empowered in their newly won freedom. Continuing to serve held the best promise to assure freedom for all slaves. Maybe more than any other lesson, Richard Etheridge retained this one: that he had to do better, despite facing more trying circumstances. He would apply it in his dealings throughout his life, including later in the Life-Saving Service. What he could not yet know was that even doing better did not guarantee fair treatment.

General Wild returned from South Carolina that November. He could not have arrived at a better time; his return gave Draper and the Second the support they had been denied since their arrival at Fortress Monroe. To counter previous reports, Wild made an immediate, personal inspection of the Second and defended Draper before their superiors. He charged the brass itself with contributing to the poor performance of his regiment. Any unit, he argued, would be second-rate with worthless equipment. His endorsement eased the pressure placed on the men, but Wild, like Draper, knew that the African Brigade needed success in the field to be legitimated within the ranks.

As important to the future of the African Brigade as Wild's return was the appointment in November of Benjamin Butler to succeed Foster as commander of the Department of Virginia and North Carolina. Butler had witnessed firsthand the capabilities of black troops operating under black officers in the Louisiana Native Guards while he served as military governor of New Orleans in 1862. He knew them to be good soldiers and came to believe that the black trooper had the greatest stake in the fighting, to gain "freedom for himself and his race forever!" A savvy politician, he also had other ambitions that the use of black troops would facilitate.

Butler had been an active and influential anti-Lincoln Democrat from Massachusetts before the war. When Butler turned to soldiering after the fall of Fort Sumter, the president recognized him as an important political tool in sustaining the fragile bond between hawk-Republican and dove-Democratic factions, and Butler turned this to his advantage. He used his influence to maneuver his way up the ranks, hoping that his military service might lead to a high-ranking position in government, perhaps even to the presidency. Wanting to make his mark during the war but with few white recruits coming to his department, Butler realized that he would have to raise black regiments.

Among white soldiers, Butler was said to have "nigger on the brain." But the general understood something that those men did not: although many in the North still resisted the notion of fighting a war to free the slaves, Butler recognized that the Union could not be preserved without crushing slavery.

While his actions had political motivations, Butler made no pretenses at sympathizing in the least with slaveholders. He was a vehement enemy of the rebellion. While military governor of New Orleans, he had issued his infamous "Woman Order," which decreed that any woman showing disrespect for federal soldiers would be treated as a "woman of the street." He also ordered hanged a civilian who had belligerently lowered the Stars and Stripes from the U.S. mint in defiance of the Union occupation—an act for which the general was decreed an outlaw in the South. The rebels began calling him "Beast Butler." In his new command, he wanted to send a clear message to the slaveholders throughout the Department of the James: although they were not legally bound by the Emancipation Proclamation to free their slaves, emancipation would be the standard practice while he was in command.

As one might expect, Butler was drawn to General Wild. He approved the plan that Foster had resisted during his tenure, authorizing a military foray out in the field by the African Brigade. Draper was to lead the small expedition from Portsmouth into Princess Anne County, Virginia. The expressed purpose of the raid was to bring in recruits, but they were also to break up supply depots and confront any guerrilla activity the unit might encounter. The men all clamored to go. Etheridge's Company F was not among the party sent out, but they envied these men their good fortune and, understanding the importance of the foray, prayed for their success.

With 6 officers and 112 men from Companies A and B of the Second NCCV, Draper departed on November 17. He knew that the expedition was a test that would have major repercussions if anything went amiss. Draper had instructed the men to pack three days' rations—the expected length of the foray—overcoats, and blankets, and each trooper carried an Enfield rifled musket with forty rounds of ammunition. Draper reminded the troopers, "Preserve strict discipline throughout. March in perfect order, so as to make a good impression and attract recruits." He also cautioned them to keep "good order at night, to guard against surprise."

Butler, Wild, and Draper knew that rebel forces, particularly Confederate irregulars in the region, would soon become aware of their movements and might take a special interest in ambushing the black troops. General Wild advised Draper that, should his column encounter any irregulars, they were not to be taken alive. Any captured were to be hanged, a placard inscribed with the word *Assassin* or *Guerrilla* placed across the body. If the unit was fired upon from a house and the shooter not captured, they were instructed to burn the house. Wild allowed that his men might be especially tempting targets, but he would not let them be sitting ducks. With these directives, the expedition set off.

Nine days after leaving, Draper and his men marched back into camp to the cheers of those left behind. And what a sight it must have been for Etheridge, Fields Midgett, and the rest. More than 450 black refugees had joined the military train, including numerous prospective recruits for the brigade. Many of the freed slaves brought along farming implements, carts filled with furniture, whatever they could from the plantations. The returning soldiers had not encountered any irregulars, but they did capture a man suspected of being a guerrilla chief. Draper had brought him back to stand trial. The detachment also had in their column, and under heavy guard, a number of Confederate prisoners, who had been caught at home on furlough. Included among them were Major Edgar Burroughs and one of his sergeants from the Fifteenth Virginia Cavalry Regiment.

It was a glorious day for Draper and the regiment, one of celebration. Etheridge, Midgett, each man of the Second could not wait for the day he would get to prove his mettle in the field. And they didn't have long to wait. The Princess Anne County raid was but a prelude of things to come.

3

Wild's December Raid

At the commencement of the war General Wild was practicing
medicine in Brookline, Massachusetts. That he understands the
guerrilla pathology, and can give a prescription that will cure
every time, I think the Pasquotank bushwhackers will acknowledge.

—New York Times *correspondent,*
detached with the African Brigade

In late summer 1863, seventy captured Confederate officers aboard the
U.S. transport *Maple Leaf* escaped off the coast of northeastern North
Carolina and, with the help of local rebel sympathizers, regained their own
lines before the federal authorities could recapture them. The news
enraged the Union command at Fortress Monroe. It confirmed for them
that, in the counties around Elizabeth City, significant portions of the
population supported the rebellion. This needed little confirmation, however, as Confederate irregulars operated freely out of the swampy region
with little objection or obstruction from locals.

At the same time, the North Carolina Home Guard, known locally as
the Partisan Rangers, established camps in the marshland and thick
forests of the region. These irregulars sabotaged federal military operations and hampered use of the strategic Dismal Swamp Canal, which

linked the Union stronghold in southern Virginia to the ones in and around the North Carolina sounds.

Wild and Butler came up with a plan to address this two-pronged issue of guerrilla activity and local indifference to it. Wild would lead an expedition into northeastern North Carolina with the aim of raising recruits for his brigade—that is, he would liberate the slaves along his route. He was also authorized to clear the region of irregulars and confiscate any rebel property that might be of use to supply his command. It was understood between the two generals that the raid would be a proving ground for the African Brigade, giving them an opportunity to demonstrate for a doubting nation the value of arming the freedmen. With this, Wild readied his men to set out.

In the early-morning hours of December 5, 1863, the men of the Second NCCV along with those of the First United States Colored Troops (USCT—recently raised in the District of Columbia) arose to the sound of reveille trumpeting across the camp at Portsmouth. Most had probably slept little, in anticipation of the coming day. It was still dark out, the air ringing with cold, as Etheridge and his tent mate readied themselves for the long march south.

Etheridge put on his woolen, leather-brimmed forage cap first, the faster to bottle in his body's warmth. He pulled on sky-blue trousers over his long underwear, wore an extra shirt, and drew his blue frock coat over it. Lighter blue stripes sliced the navy field over his arm, a sign of his rank. He laced up his leather brogans—ankle-high boots the men called gun boats—then prepared his equipment.

He double-checked the leather cartridge "box"— not really a box at all but a pouch. His forty rounds were at the ready. Then his waist belt: attached were both his scabbarded bayonet and the pouch holding his percussion caps. The cartridge box draped over his shoulder on a wide-strapped leather belt. He carried his parade sword, although he couldn't imagine using it for fighting. It served him well, though, in commanding his platoon. He placed his canteen and haversack in his knapsack, beside his mess kit and jackknife. He and his tent mate disassembled their two-piece "pup tent," each one taking a section, rolling it with his blanket, and fastening the whole to his knapsack.

All around Etheridge, the other troopers were ready, too—knapsacks on their backs, wearing identical blue greatcoats. Across the face of every cartridge box and oval metal belt buckle were inscribed the letters *U.S.* Literate or not, everyone understood their significance. Each trooper took up his Enfield .577-caliber muzzle-loader and fell into formation behind his company's standard-bearer.

The long column, some eleven hundred strong, followed the Dismal Swamp Canal into North Carolina. For many, they were heading home, to the land where they had been slaves. They felt like men. They were soldiers.

Raids are usually thought of as rapid. Units small enough to strike quickly set out with a specific intent and, once it is attained, retreat back to safety behind their own lines. Wild intended to strike slowly. He planned on being gone several weeks, and after the column's passage, he expected to have rooted out the hidden enemy, as well as to have left a lasting impression on the local inhabitants about the wisdom of supporting the Union.

Wild's column camped the first night at Deep Creek. Etheridge and the men had marched nine miles. The next day, following the towpath by which draft animals pulled barges and other vessels along the Dismal Swamp Canal, the column marched twice the distance—another eighteen miles. That night, too exhausted to be exhilarated, Etheridge and another trooper pitched their tent on Ferrebee's Farm, outside South Mills, a community of some twenty houses.

The Dismal Swamp had given way to stretches of plush farmland bordered by tall, thick forests of pine and red cedar. Even in December, everything was green. Wild determined, perhaps without too much in-depth investigation, that the majority of farmers in the region sympathized more with the rebellion than with the Union. The marching order was eased and the men permitted to leave the road and forage at will. At that time of year, they got tubers mostly: white potatoes, parsnips, yams, a few late-ripening melons. When they returned to South Mills that evening, they also brought with them contrabands enough to fill seventy-five wagons.

The next morning, the guerrilla presence in the region was confirmed for Wild as his column, now nearly two thousand strong, was delayed at the River Bridge, which forded the Pasquotank on the way into Elizabeth City, an important commercial center on the Albemarle Sound. All that remained of the structure were the charred tops of the piles, jutting above the cold, flowing water.

The general had expected this sort of resistance and had resolved to meet it head-on. Gathering what information he could from locals who would cooperate but mostly from freed slaves, he discovered that a nearby resident was a member of the Partisan Rangers. Wild set a regiment of men loose on the man's property. They hauled the better timber from the house and barn to the river to reconstruct the bridge, burnt what was unusable, and confiscated the rest. Within six hours, the column was marching again toward Elizabeth City.

Without apology, Wild fought "total war" against the Confederate-sympathizing region a year and a half before Sherman popularized the expression in his famous March to the Sea through Georgia. "Finding ordinary measures of little avail," Wild would later report, "I adopted a more rigorous style of warfare; burned their homes and barns, ate up their live stock, and took hostages from their families." He meant to breed "disaffection" among the Rangers and drive them to join regular Confederate units or to "quit the business" altogether, as he put it. Understanding that guerrillas depended upon the goodwill of the local population, Wild also intended to galvanize Union support among the region's inhabitants, through terror if need be. He knew there was no better way to accomplish this than by occupying the area with a large number of armed black troops.

The general did show discretion toward loyal citizens. He published the names of all residents who supported the Union and distributed the lists to his subordinate commanders with orders to avoid harming their property, to afford them extra privileges, and to protect them from retaliation. But of the irregulars, he told his men, "General Butler intends to exterminate all guerrillas east of [the] Chowan River, and will use any means to do so."

The massive column of "sable soldiers," as a *New York Times* reporter named Tewksbury, who accompanied the brigade, called them, marched into Elizabeth City on December 9. The city had once been a thriving port, but its businesses had largely been deserted, its streets overgrown with grass. Store shelves were barren of stock. The only goods that could be had were those smuggled from Norfolk and available only on the black market. Rebel irregulars had looted the bank before the arrival of the column—its doors stood wide open, the interior gutted and abandoned.

Wild set up his headquarters at the home of a prominent local physician. The first night of the occupation, Wild ordered a gunboat that had joined the expedition to fire a volley of shots, a taunting warning to the enemy, announcing his arrival. His orders to his subordinate officers were the same he'd given Draper in Princess Anne County: protect all slaves who quit the plantations and join the column; guard any property they bring with them; if fired upon, hang the shooter and torch his possessions.

Draper rejoined the unit that night, having ridden from Virginia through much dangerous territory with just a single accompanying rider. Neither hell nor high water—and especially not the formalities of trying a Confederate guerrilla, which was what detained him at Fortress Monroe— would keep him from leading his men on this action. After the months of prejudice they'd faced within the Union ranks, he was anxious to have his soldiers prove themselves, not just to doubting Thomases in the army but to a skeptical nation as well. Draper also understood that his men were motivated to be on this raid, and he felt it his duty to be at their head.

The men of the Second had a stake here. Most came from the region or nearby, and they would be freeing family and friends. But there was a larger goal also. These men all wanted to make a strong statement about their unwillingness to see in bondage themselves, their families, or anybody who looked like them. Not a one among them had ever believed the propaganda about their infantile minds and their uncontrollable appetites, about their inherent ignorance and savagery, about their need for "governance." They now wanted to prove it to the slaveholders who'd conceived the lies about them and to the entire country, who had, apparently, believed those lies. Perhaps they wanted to show something to Colonel Draper, too.

For seven days, the African Brigade occupied the city. "Every man," Wild reported, "was constantly employed." The general "sent out expeditions in all directions, some for recruits and contrabands' families, some for guerrillas, some for forage, some for firewood, which was scarce and much needed." The Partisan Rangers "pestered" the units. Wild wrote:

"They crept upon our pickets at night, waylaid our expeditions and our cavalry scouts, firing upon us whenever they could." When the black troops countered, moving to flank the attackers, the guerrillas fled into the woods. On two occasions, Wild attempted to set ambushes to trap them, but both tries failed. All the while, Union boats shuttled confiscated goods and newly freed men, women, and children to the burgeoning camp on Roanoke Island. Etheridge and other natives of the island used the opportunity to send messages home with the refugees.

The presence of the armed freedmen terrorized local residents. Seeing the African-American soldiers played to their basest—and most fantastic—fears. One group reported to the *Raleigh Journal:* "The negro ran riot during the Yankee stay in Albemarle County. . . . On the streets the ladies of the place were jostled by the negro troops, and had to permit them to walk by their side and converse with them, on pain of arrest and punishment for insulting 'United States troops'!"

Wild and his subordinate officers reported the behavior of the men quite differently, and Tewksbury concurred. "Thoroughly obedient to their officers," the *Times* reporter wrote, "their conduct on every occasion was truly admirable." He did, however, confirm the unsettling effect their presence had on the locals. "The counties invaded by the colored troops were completely panic-stricken. Scores of families, for no cause but a guilty conscience, fled into the swamps on their approach. Never was a region thrown into such commotion by a raid before. . . . No sooner would the brigade enter a neighborhood than General Wild's quarters would be besieged by those wishing to take the oath of allegiance."

At week's close, the African Brigade prepared to leave Elizabeth City. Wild again divided his unit into columns, each one assigned to take a different route. Wild's group of twelve hundred men would head back to Virginia, via Indiantown. Another would be ferried to Powells Point, on a thin peninsula between the North River and Currituck Sound, and proceed north from there. Draper, leading a unit of men from the Second, including Etheridge's company, as well as detachments from the First and Fifth USCT, four hundred in all, would cross the Pasquotank River and "canvass" the lower region of Camden County for recruits and contrabands, rendezvousing with Wild two days later at Indiantown.

★   ★   ★

A heavy, cold rain fell all morning Thursday, December 17, as the various columns moved out. Wild went northeast, while Draper led his unit southeast on the Shiloh Road. The cart path was pitted with potholes, the mud soggy and difficult to march over. Etheridge and his men wore their wool overcoats with short cape, the collars up against the wind, but were drenched and miserable. And it was a foreboding countryside, with tall, dark bands of woods surrounding them.

By midday, the sun was breaking through the clouds, and before the end of the afternoon, the sky had cleared. At sunset, the regiment entered Shiloh, a community of twenty houses and a church. They hurriedly built fires at a crossroads near the church and cooked their rations. After eating, Draper posted pickets and ordered his men to retreat to the obscurity in and around the church. He had them keep the fires burning at the campsite, to "amuse" the guerrillas, he said, probably half in jest. There was little to fear. The Confederate irregulars had stayed largely in hiding during the occupation, picking at the black troops like gnats, arbitrarily popping shots and fleeing back into the swamps.

That night, Etheridge was awakened by a commotion and musket fire as a large group of irregulars opened up on the camp. Fortunately, the rebels mistakenly concentrated their aim at the area around the blazing logs, and in the meantime, Draper was able to rally the men and chase the rebels off. No one was injured in the attack, but Draper was forewarned: the irregulars were making a stand.

Friday morning, the regiment fell in, Etheridge calling his platoon to look ready and be sharp. The unit headed north up the Indiantown Road. As they marched, the "canvassing" for slaves continued. Occasionally, a soldier would break ranks and approach the colonel, tell him he was from the area, and plead for permission to go liberate a wife or a child, parents or siblings. The colonel sent out detachments of men—strength in force—to recover the families.

Near the small community of Sandy Hook, the Indiantown Road forked with the Dog Corners Road and approached a dense stretch of wooded swamp. From the trees, musket fire erupted. An ambush! The gunfire was heavy, from as many as two hundred men, and from several hundred yards distant. Etheridge and the others could hardly see a man for the darkness of the trees, but they were under heavy fire.

Draper shouted orders above the din of the successive volleys. *Return fire! . . . Aim at the smoke from their barrels!* . . . Etheridge and his men quickly executed the orders, dropping to the ground to make lesser targets while reloading.

Draper called to his side Captain Smith of Company I and Etheridge's superior, Lieutenant Joseph Longley, who was in charge of Company F until the recently dismissed Captain Ives could be replaced. Draper ordered Smith to attempt to flank the rebels in the woods to the left and directed Longley to move his men down a lane perpendicular to the road and flank the enemy from the edge of the swamp on the right. When within range, Company F was to charge the rebel position and drive the rebels from their position in the woods.

Longley yelled instructions, Etheridge and the other sergeants relaying them to their platoons. The company rose as one. They left their knapsacks on the ground, hustled down the lane for the swamp. The opposing fire was intense. Etheridge heard the distant snap then close-by whizzing of musket balls ripping the air. He heard the dull thump of lead striking flesh. Casualties fell.

For the first time, he witnessed the raw spectacle of war. These weren't the unearthly corpses of shipwrecked victims washed ashore months after their horrible deaths, the bodies broken by the sea and half-eaten by crabs. No. Leon Bembury, dressed exactly as Etheridge but for the sergeant's stripes, rolled on the ground, clutching his right foot, which had been shot through by a ball, blood staining his dark brogan slick. And long, lanky John Preston, one of the tallest men of his company, lay twisted on the ground, crimson coursing from between his hands as they tried to cover the gaping wound in his torso.

A log building stood beside the lane, a few yards ahead. Longley halted the men at its side, balls pinging against the walls opposite. The men clustered tightly together. None knew why they had stopped. Across the field, Etheridge could see the troopers of Company I, also stopped—they were in a thicket, not charging but commencing to fire. The lieutenant did not order them to prepare to move out. They all just waited there.

A company from the Fifth ran up to the cabin, and their commander, a captain, shouted orders, taking charge of both companies. Etheridge gathered his platoon around him. Colonel Draper himself ran up, yelling instructions. Here was the chance to prove themselves—charge the position! . . . "At the double-quick!" he yelled.

Etheridge had his men up and ready. They continued their push for the edge of the wood, the enemy fire pouring in. They fixed bayonets. Etheridge and the men picked their pace up to a dead sprint and screamed a murderous war cry, the air hot with musket fire, and as they neared the edge of the trees, the rebels turned and ran.

When the black troops reached the rebel position, they found the corpses of a few dead guerrillas lying in water and leaves, but it was clear that more had been hit. They searched for but could not identify the path by which the main body had made their escape. Draper joined them, and he and several men scoured the area for some sign of a trail. They could see only knee-deep water and thick woods, scrub brush and fallen trees.

The skirmish had lasted less than a half hour. Their first trial by fire. Draper had lost three men killed and eight wounded, but he and his men recognized the day had been a success. A sergeant from the Fifth remarked: "The men stood nobly and faced the cowardly foe when they were hid in the swamp firing upon them. They stood like men, and when ordered to charge, went in with a yell, and came out victorious."

With the wounded laid out in carts, the column proceeded onto Indiantown before the rebels had a chance to destroy the bridge crossing the creek. Draper left a detachment to guard the bridge and reached the settlement at dusk. On the way into town, the rear guard was attacked. Hearing the firing, the colonel ordered men to fall back to the position, but the rebels had already dodged into the swamps upon the approach of the reinforcements. They had killed another man.

Draper set up camp on the plantation of a Dr. McIntosh and sent out dispatchers to usher General Wild's column toward them. Hospital facilities were set up, the wounded attended to. One man died while a surgeon tried to save him. The colonel ascertained from freed slaves that several of the guerrillas resided in the community, so Draper sent his men out to torch their homes. Indiantown glowed orange on the deep Carolina night. By the time Wild arrived, little remained of Indiantown aside from Draper's HQ on the McIntosh place.

Locals reported to Draper that the rebels had lost thirteen killed and wounded in the fight at Sandy Hook. Draper had lost twelve. The next

day, Wild determined to root out the irregulars with his column, rein-
forced by units from the colonel's.

Draper's men were called out for review. Those who wished to stay
behind to guard the camp were asked to step out of the line; the detachment would be composed of the rest. Only thirty-five did, and these were
lame from the days of hard marching. Wild, on horseback, advised the
regiment, "We will be fighting at great disadvantage down in the swamp.
You lost a number of men yesterday and stand to lose a great many more
today. We need men to stay behind and take care of the camp. It would be
best, and no disgrace, to volunteer for this duty." None would. All wanted
another crack at the guerrillas. To fill the camp guard, Wild had to order
a detail from each of Draper's companies to remain behind.

With Draper's regiment in the lead, the column of black troops headed
back down the Indiantown Road. They caught glimpses of large bodies of
guerrillas, and Draper's advance guard was twice fired upon, but each
time, as the black troops charged their position, the rebels fled into the
swamp. Finally, Draper led his men into the woods after them. To the men
from Roanoke Island, the dense thickets and marshy soil were familiar.
After a vigorous search, the unit discovered a path: a series of felled trees,
lying end to end and zigzagging a route into the interior.

Draper took his men in. For a half mile, they wove their way single file
over the slick log trail, insect life and chirping birds the only sounds. Deep
inside the swamp, they came upon an island, the guerrilla camp. It was
deserted. Log huts and tents stood scattered around the small hump of
land. Campfires still smoldered, and Enfield muskets lay here and about.
The guerrillas had lit out just ahead of the troops' arrival.

The men searched the grounds, gathered anything of value: between
fifty and sixty new Enfield rifles (provided, Draper later found out, by
North Carolina's Confederate governor, Vance); a large quantity of
ammunition; clothing; provisions; and a roster of troops. The rest, they set
fire to. The roster was the prize. With it as a guide, Wild and Draper would
have a clear map of whose premises to fire.

The rest of the afternoon and all the next day, the expedition torched
the homes of guerrillas all over the countryside. Fires raged in Camden
County, over crops as well as houses and barns. They took one hostage, a
planter called Major Gregory, who served as commissary to the irregulars.
The column of troops proceeded toward Currituck Courthouse, a train of

contraband stretching more than a mile in length behind it. The houses they passed and left alone were shuttered closed. Tewksbury recalled that "a Sabbath silence brooded over the land." The raid was having its effect of leaving northeast North Carolinians with a distaste for guerrilla warfare.

Draper's detail reunited with the other columns at Currituck Courthouse, on the banks of the Currituck Sound. From there, Wild sent some of the confiscated property and freed slaves by steamer to Roanoke Island; other people, including the hostages, he directed toward Fortress Monroe—the sick and wounded by steamer, the rest, overland with an accompanying detachment of troops. Draper and his brigade, whose skill and tenacity against the guerrillas were obvious, were sent by boat across the sound to deal with the irregulars on Knott's Island.

Knott's Island, fourteen square miles of marshy outgrowth that straddled the Virginia–North Carolina border, was connected to the mainland by a short isthmus. Given its access to but relative isolation from the Union enclaves in southern Virginia, it was known to be a guerrilla stronghold. Wild instructed Draper: "Burn pretty freely." Before the end of the day, Tewksbury, who remained with Wild's column, reported seeing smoke rising from several locations across the sound, a sign of Draper's success.

When they were done on Knott's Island, Draper's column traveled north into Virginia. He was proud of his men. They had been tireless and marched well. Each man was disciplined and thoroughly obedient to his officer in every activity assigned him. Draper was most pleased with the courage and determination they'd shown. His men liked "nothing better than to be led into the presence of the enemy." "I am certain now, of what I always firmly believed," he later reported, "that the colored troops can be relied upon, in any situation of difficulty or danger." And the men were now thoroughly committed to their colonel, no matter the circumstances.

When the column reached the federal outpost at Pungo Point, Virginia, Draper along with a hostage he'd taken on Knott's Island—the daughter of a rebel leader—were invited to dine with the commander of the base, Lieutenant Colonel George Wead. During dinner, Wead surprised Draper, commandeering his sword and informing the colonel that taking the girl had been an outrage and that she would be returned to her family. One of Draper's officers, Lieutenant George Conant, happened by, burst in, and turned the tables on Wead. Conant and Draper, with their hostage in tow, hurried back to their own ranks, where Draper hurriedly organized the black troops. Wead likewise drew his men into battle array. The opposing units faced off.

The men of the Second prepared to wage war against other Union troops in defense of Draper. Here before them were troopers who embodied all those who had resisted the African Brigade, who had belittled blacks while they dug trenches, who had called them "boy" and ordered them to police their refuse. These men challenged their authority as—and their right to be—soldiers. A fight seemed imminent.

Neither commander called the order to fire. Draper, his men, and their hostage withdrew and continued their march toward their base camp.

Christmas Eve, Draper and his men returned to Portsmouth, a day after Wild had arrived in Norfolk. The nineteen-day expedition, the largest military action until then to be executed solely by black troops, had been a success. During the foray, Wild's African Brigade had burned four guerrilla camps, a score of homesteads of their sympathizers, and two distilleries; taken more than fifty guns, a quantity of ammunition, other equipment, and many horses; captured four boats engaged in blockade-running; and taken eleven rebel prisoners: six Confederate soldiers, four hostages, and one guerrilla, who was hanged. Plus, they freed some twenty-five hundred slaves, with four long trains marching to Norfolk overland, followed by two boatloads, and nine other boatloads sent to the freedman's camp on Roanoke Island. Of all the units involved in the raid, Draper's regiment saw the most action, and Richard Etheridge's Company F was in the thick of it.

The *New York Times* gave the raid front-page coverage:

INVASION OF NORTH CAROLINA BY GEN. WILD'S
COLORED BATTALION
Great Guerrilla Hunt by the Sons of Ham
(Price Three Cents).

Tewksbury concluded his long article:

It is the first [raid] of any magnitude undertaken by negro troops since their enlistment was authorized by Congress, and by it the question of their efficiency in any branch of the service has been practically set at rest. . . . It will have been seen that they performed in the enemy's country all the duties of white soldiers—scouting, skirmishing, picket duty, guard duty, every service incident to the occupation of hostile towns, and, best of all, fighting.

A company of the white cavalrymen, attached to the African Brigade as far as South Mills, also praised the determination and drive of the black troops. Had they had to follow them for any length of time, the cavalrymen claimed, it would surely have killed their horses.

The inhabitants of northeast North Carolina were not quick to forget the passage of the African Brigade. After the raid, General Butler threatened the locals with more "visitations from the colored troops" if they didn't help him drive the irregulars from the region. "You will never have any rest from us," he wrote, "so long as you keep guerrillas within your borders." In each of the counties touched by Wild's foray, the residents held public meetings and passed resolves to urge the governor to "remove or disband" the Home Guard.

On January 1, to commemorate the first anniversary of their emancipation, the Second along with three other regiments of black troops marched at Norfolk in full-dress military parade—"blacks in blue," wearing white gloves and with bayonets fixed. General Butler reviewed them in the public square, and a banner made especially for them by the black women of Little Washington, North Carolina, was presented to Draper's regiment. They had proven their right to wear the uniform, to fly their colors, to defend the Stars and Stripes and union.

4

Point Lookout

The Bottom Rail on Top

Wednesday, February 24, 1864: Clear and pleasant. Had a shower of rain last night. Yankees gave our division pants. For the first time in my life I have seen a Regt. of Negro troops in full uniform and with arms.

Thursday, February 25, 1864: Negro soldiers were put on post to guard us. Was there ever such a thing in civilized warfare.

—from the diary of Confederate prisoner Charles Warren Hutt,
Point Lookout, Maryland

Not all Northerners looked favorably upon the "success" of the raid. The *New York World,* in early February, condemned Butler for the action and called the companies of freedmen who made up the African Brigade "worthless to their owners, worthless to our government, and good for nothing in every aspect."

In fact, the general found himself under fire from several quarters for Wild's tactics. For Butler, Wild had suddenly become a political liability. Butler kept him in his staff, but limited his authority. He also decided to deflect attention from his black regiments for a time. On February 23, the

Second, redesignated the Thirty-sixth USCT, was transferred to Point Lookout, in the District of St. Mary's, Maryland, to serve as guards at the military prison there.

Point Lookout sat at the southernmost tip of Maryland, on a tongue of land that licked out into the Cheseapeake, bordered on one side by the bay and on the other by the Potomac River. The peninsula resembled the Virginia landscape they had just left. Salt marshes surrounded by thickets of pine and red cedar rolled northward to Washington, D.C.

Formerly a summer resort, in 1862 Point Lookout had been turned into a hospital. Hammond General had twelve wards, laid out like spokes on a wagon wheel, and a settlement sprang up nearby. Then, after the Battle of Gettysburg, the War Department established a prisoner-of-war camp on the land north of the hospital. Colonel William Hoffman, the commissary general of prisoners, planned to accommodate about ten thousand prisoners in recycled army tents. The first captured rebels began arriving in August 1863. By February, when the Thirty-sixth landed, eleven thousand Confederates crowded the prison compound, their numbers continuing to swell. By June, they would exceed fifteen thousand, and before the end of the summer, twenty thousand would be crammed into the space.

The main compound, called the Bull Pen, was laid out over twenty acres and surrounded by a fourteen-foot-high board fence with a platform walkway around the outside upon which the sentinels patrolled. From this vantage point, the guards could see the entire area, as the ground was level. Conical Sibley tents that each housed a dozen men were arranged two deep, back to back, along wide parallel streets, each tent opening onto one. The prisoners sarcastically called the principal passage Pennsylvania Avenue. Ten feet from the wall all the way around the compound was roped off and called the dead line. Prisoners were not to cross into it under any circumstances.

The men of the Thirty-sixth were among the first blacks to serve as guards of Confederate prisoners of war. From his loft above the Bull Pen, Etheridge watched them.

The prisoners were often poorly clad, some in rags, but despite complaints, few went hungry. All sorts of men were among the prisoners: sick and well; genteel Southerner and poor white trash; committed Confederate and those unfortunately caught at a sad intersection of time and geography. Many were but boys, some as young as fourteen. An eighteen-year-old might be a veteran of two or three years of battle.

During the day, the rebels milled about or set up stands on discarded crates where they sold all manner of goods: patches of cloth; rings they fashioned from scrap pieces of wood or tin; bone toothpicks. Mostly they sold foodstuffs, either made from their scant supplies or smuggled into the camp. Some of the savvy inmates would hang around the dead line looking for an opportunity to scuttle across and sell their wares to guards as souvenirs. Guards were forbidden to buy from the prisoners, so the rebels had to be careful whom they approached. Etheridge, a sergeant who wore his seriousness on his face, was not one to proposition.

Etheridge noticed an odd phenomenon that recurred toward the end of each day. Numbers of inmates would have to be led around by other men in the fading light. He learned from a medical officer that the brilliance of the sun reflecting off the white tents, the white sands, and the water, dusk to dawn, day in and day out, impaired some prisoners, temporarily blinding them as the sun set. Oftentimes, their sight wouldn't return until the next morning.

Among the prisoners were former neighbors, even former masters, of some of the guards. Etheridges, Doughs, and Midgetts figured among those held at Point Lookout. One trooper recognized his former master among a crowd of rebel captives and, calling him over, gave him ten dollars, a princely sum of money. Such friendly exchanges were rare, though, and Etheridge felt animosity toward him from within the Pen daily.

No matter their opinion on the rebellion, on captivity, on the czar in Russia, prisoners at Point Lookout shared one common sentiment: anger at being guarded by USCT. The arrival of the Thirty-sixth was humiliating for the Southerners. Whether they had owned slaves or not, each one considered himself superior to African-Americans. The rumor among them was that the Yankee authorities had assigned black guards for the express purpose of insulting and degrading the rebels, and most responded in kind. Prisoners talked openly of the vengeance they would seek out on blacks when they got home to Dixie. When, in March, just a few weeks after the arrival of the Thirty-sixth, the gun of one black sentry accidentally went off, shooting and killing another, Sonney Collins, the prisoners openly mocked and ridiculed the fallen man and berated the incompetence of colored troops.

The white Union troops assigned to the camp were not uniformly pleased to share duty with the USCT either. This seething mix of bad blood led to increased tension in the Bull Pen between Yankee and rebel, black and white.

General Edward Hinks, the officer in charge of the prison camp, had anticipated that tensions would arise with the arrival of the Thirty-sixth. A former state legislator from Massachusetts and protégé of Butler, Hinks supported arming freedmen, but he was concerned about former slaves having authority over whites.

A story went around camp of black guards taunting prisoners: "Looks like the bottom rail has got on top, now." One sentry was reported to have threatened a man whom he judged to be loitering too close to the dead line: "Get away from that fence, white man, or I'll make old Abe's gun smoke at you! I can hardly hold the ball back now." Black guards abusing their power was not Hinks's only concern. He also feared the opposite: that some blacks might be timid in executing their duties against the white captives. One guard, he was told, insisted on calling prisoners "master."

To forestall potential problems, Hinks insisted that strict discipline and observance of duty be the modus operandi in the camp. Colonel Draper took Hinks's principles one step further. His company commanders all had to be present each night at taps to assure lights-out and to guarantee order and quiet in the tents. During the day, the colonel expected them to maintain a presence in the USCT camp streets to police the conduct of their men.

The importance of routine and discipline to effective leadership was inculcated into Etheridge at Point Lookout. Etheridge was held accountable for the behavior of his men, so he held them accountable to him. Daily, he read to his platoon the revised regulations, which each sentinel was expected to know. And he tolerated no lapses of established order.

The Thirty-sixth took to life on the Point, where they were well supplied and had access to a sort of freedom few of the men had yet known, either in slavery or at Fortress Monroe. There were no more demeaning labor details. In their free time, the troopers crabbed in the salt marshes around the peninsula, bought goods in the commissary, began to learn to read and write in the library. But there was precious little free time. When the men weren't performing guard duty, they drilled.

By the early spring of 1864, the Confederacy was dying. The rebels had won a tactical victory at Chickamauga, but the autumn 1863 battle had been one of the bloodiest of the war. The South lost more than 16,000 men killed and wounded to the North's 18,500, and the Confederates could not sustain such casualties. In the months that closed 1863, Union forces under Grant won important victories in and around Chattanooga, setting the stage for Sherman to march through Georgia and cleave the Confederacy in two.

Draper realized that the fields of Virginia would be the next important battle site of the war. His challenge was to assure that the Thirty-sixth would be allowed to participate in the fight, not merely as raiders but as full-fledged soldiers in a campaign against regulars. In the short term, this meant his men had to continue to prove their worth in the field. Point Lookout, like Fortress Monroe, provided some good opportunities.

Although Maryland never seceded, St. Mary's County was much more sympathetic to the rebellion than to the maintenance of union. For all intents and purposes, St. Mary's County *was* the South. Many families had offered up fathers and sons to the Confederate army, and locals were known to smuggle supplies and military information across the Potomac to the rebels. This pleased neither Hinks nor Draper.

With General Hinks's sanction, Draper sent a detail of men into the county to seize seven thousand acres of land along the Patuxent River belonging to disloyal Marylanders. To equip the new farms, Hinks and Draper organized a short sortie into rebel Virginia. Draper marched his men across the forested hills beside the Nomini River, a peninsula rich with tobacco farms. As before, slaves quit their masters and joined the military train as it proceeded. The column stopped at the plantation of Joseph Maddox, a suspected blockade-runner. Draper arrested him and confiscated his tobacco crop. They proceeded on. That night, after the unit was fired upon from a cluster of farmhouses, a small body of Confederate cavalry took flight from the vicinity. A company set out after them. Unable to overtake the fleeing rebels, they set fire to the buildings. The next evening, with 177 boxes of superior Gravely tobacco—estimated to be worth forty thousand dollars—fifty contrabands, and their prisoner Maddox, the detachment boarded the steamer *Long Branch* for the voyage home. They had not lost a man or any matériel.

A dispatcher from the Confederate Signal Bureau sent a wire disparaging Draper and the black troops for their cowardice: "With a preponderance of negroes he would hardly venture a battle . . ." This man could not know that the colonel was not yet done with Virginia.

Prisoners at Point Lookout were not allowed outside their tents after lights-out except to relieve themselves, which they were permitted to do only at the "sinks"—washbasins used as portable toilets. On April 19, at around two in the morning, Mark Lisk, a private from Tennessee, slipped out of his tent to "do his business" nearby. As he squatted down, guard Irvin Willliams noticed him. Williams shouted for the prisoner to remove himself from there, which Lisk pretended to do, hitching up his britches. But when Williams began to move on, Lisk sat back down. Williams saw him. "What are you doing there?" he called.

Many of the prisoners suffered from chronic, sometimes uncontrollable, diarrhea. Yet when they left their tents at night for "imperative reasons," they complained of being "tantalized" with threats by the "insolent and brutal" guards. The sentries would call them over, they claimed, detain and harass them, keep them standing there while their bowels raged. On this night, Lisk, his insides writhing, decided he'd had enough. Defiantly, the Tennessean rose up, went to the space between his and the neighboring tent, and sat back down.

Williams, moving to a position where he was in view of the prisoner, again shouted for him to remove from there—warning number two. Guards were instructed to shout three warnings to a man caught out at night, and if the man did not obey, to shoot him.

Lisk retorted, "I am going to ease myself!"

Private Williams shouted one final time: "Get up, or I will help you up!"

When Lisk ignored him, Williams fired, hitting him in the right foot. According to Williams, Lisk "hallooed until they came and pulled him into the tent."

The minié ball from Williams's musket shattered the bone in Lisk's foot. It became infected, and Lisk died a short time later. The camp's chief surgeon, a Union officer, called the Lisk case a "reckless shooting."

Draper sought permission to conduct another raid into Virginia—as a release, as a distraction, as a way to show his men's merit and get them transferred to the front. On May 11, three hundred troopers from the Thirty-sixth, including Etheridge's Company F, joined a larger expedition sent to disarm and destroy Confederate torpedoes—land mines—along the Rappahannock River. The officers of Etheridge's company had all been insubordinate and been transferred; in their absence, Etheridge and the other sergeants led the men in the field.

The mission went without a hitch. The Thirty-sixth located and destroyed several mines, as well as the mill of the man responsible for making them. They also confiscated thirty-three head of cattle, twenty-two horses and mules, and some wagons for use at the contraband camps along the Patuxent. While marching in a skirmish line over the densely wooded hills between the Rappahannock and the Piankatank Rivers, a detachment of six troopers came upon a group of nine rebels. The two sides opened fire. A private from Etheridge's company dropped, shot through the left shoulder, but by the time reinforcements arrived, the Confederates were dead, dying, or ready to surrender. Despite this, the black infantrymen kept reloading and shooting. If not for the intervention of Sergeant Sylvester Price, who called an order to cease fire—once, again, and again—the men would have shot down all the rebels.

Weekly, Draper saw regiments, both black and white, shuttled through Point Lookout en route to the Virginia front. The Thirty-sixth was never part of those trains. In the meantime, two more prisoners were shot by sentinels.

Had his regiment been cast as lacking discipline? Might this be the reason they were overlooked?

Draper knew that, generally, his men were good, conscientious guards. But perhaps the shootings had, in fact, been purposeful and vindictive, a sign of strain that neared the breaking point. Perhaps the pressures were too much for the black troops to bear. Draper could not determine whether the men were abusing their power over their former masters or the former masters—captives, living in miserable conditions and resenting the new order—provoked the blacks to use force. One thing was certain: these incidents, justified or not, would mar the unit's record and keep them away from the front lines.

Draper pressed Butler to get his men into the fight, and in early June, the general gave him leave to lead them on another foray into Virginia. The raid began inauspiciously when, on the night of June 10, as the expedition was being ferried up the Potomac, the gunboat *Resolute* ran into the *Long Branch,* one of four transport steamers. No one was injured, but the men had to be conveyed to another steamer and the *Long Branch* sent back for repairs.

Draper was leading 475 men from the Thirty-sixth along with a detachment of 49 cavalrymen, en route to Pope's Creek, in the Northern Neck, on a mission to procure horses and farming implements for the contraband farms on the Patuxent. Their problems continued as, when the naval convoy attempted to land, the steamers found they could not get close enough to unload the cavalry horses. The animals had to be lowered by rope over the sides of the boats and swum to shore. The lengthy procedure gave local Confederate sympathizers ample time to spread word over the region of the landing.

Things went much as they had during previous raids. For three days, Draper's men, divided into two columns, canvassed the countryside from Pope's Creek to Warsaw Courthouse and back. Occasional potshots from guerrillas aside, the march was largely uneventful. The Thirty-sixth collected long trains of contraband and wagonloads of agricultural equipment, which were shuttled under armed escort to waiting transports on the Potomac. They found no horses. Though beyond the range of his field of operations, Draper learned of an abundance of them farther north and west, in the land around Occupacia Creek and Layton's Wharf. Taking more initiative than he had before, he decided to move the men to that region.

On the fourth day, instead of returning to the Point, he marched his men to Union Wharf, from where they would canvass the countryside on the opposite bank of the Rappahannock. They found the wharf destroyed, and Draper set the men to work rebuilding it so the transports could land. Lieutenant John O'Brien of Company C, against explicit orders to the contrary, gave three of his troopers permission to leave the regiment. They wanted to visit a house about a mile distant. On their journey there, they were attacked by a detachment of rebel soldiers. The rest could hear the firing from the wharf.

Colonel Draper immediately mustered a group of forty cavalrymen. With Draper at their head, they rode toward the shooting. Captain Joseph Hatlinger of Company E was instructed to follow with 150 infantrymen. The rest stayed behind to complete the wharf.

The cavalry came upon a body beside the road. Private Peter Wilson, one of the men O'Brien had let leave camp, had been riddled with musket fire, each of his feet also shot through with bullets. The rebels had continued to fire even after Wilson had fallen. A trail of blood leading into the woods testified to the fate of Henry Lee, another of the men. His body could not be found. The third was nowhere around. About a mile ahead, they saw a corps of Confederate cavalry.

Draper sent three cavalrymen ahead as an advance guard, to determine the size of the rebel unit, and cautiously moved his detachment forward. The three soldiers came back in a hurry, reporting some two hundred men in the Confederate line—five times their number. This hardly daunted Draper. He moved his men to within striking distance, the enemy clearly visible across the field, then ordered a charge, waving his sword above his head and leading his men toward the rebels. The rebels opened fire. As he came to within about sixty yards of them, Draper realized that he was all alone, save for his second-in-command, Captain Gibbs, and a few orderlies. He stopped his charge, turned his horse toward his men, ordered them to close up around him. Just then, the Confederates let loose a brash rebel yell. Upon this, the Union cavalrymen "turned their horses' heads to the rear," Draper later reported, "and ran for their lives."

The rebels, who proved to be significantly fewer than the two hundred reported, charged. Draper dropped to the ground beside his horse, and he and Gibbs yelled after the men to stop their retreat. A few did, but the majority were gone, tiny explosions of dirt kicking up beneath the batting hooves of the fleeing mounts.

Soon, Draper was "enveloped in the dust of the rebel pursuit," one orderly by his side captured, and another man, too. A third, dismounted, lit out toward a fence and was dodging into the woods. Draper, now entirely alone in a roaring sea of butternut gray, wisely "followed the crowd."

The rebels gave chase for three hundred yards, then, apparently surprised by their success, turned back and quit the field, raucously and full of swagger.

Draper returned to Union Wharf furious. The cavalrymen, a minority and secondary element of the larger unit, had brought disgrace on the entire expedition. Hatlinger's infantrymen arrived too late to "cancel the account," and the rebels won the day. Draper was resolved to avenge the afternoon's shame with his own men on the morrow. If the rebels could be engaged, the Thirty-sixth would do so.

Draper reminded his men of the date—June 17: the anniversary of the Battle of Bunker Hill—before marching two hundred troopers from the Thirty-sixth, along with thirty-six of the disgraced cavalrymen, back to the rebel position at Pierson's Farm. They found the rebels out in force. One hundred fifty cavalrymen had assembled there, supported by 450 infantry irregulars.

Draper immediately established an offensive position. He stationed his own cavalry in the woods, with orders to charge upon the call of the bugler. He ordered fifty troopers to conceal themselves in the trees. If the rebels, with their superior number, forced the cavalry to fall back, they were to rake the road with fire to cover the retreat. He led the bulk of his men, 150 in all, to the edge of the thicket and formed a line of battle, several ranks deep, five hundred yards across the field from the Confederates.

The rebels, meanwhile, hurried to erect a barricade across the road, to obstruct an anticipated Yankee charge. The Confederate commander, Lieutenant Colonel Lewis, expected the infantrymen to combine with the cavalry in an all-out assault. To his dismay, the colored Yankees did not charge. They opened fire from the distance.

With the first volley, men throughout the rebel line fell, some dead, others wounded, many screaming. Another volley came, and shortly thereafter, another. Lewis's men broke formation. Some returned fire, pell-mell. Others looked confused. Meanwhile, men continued to fall. At first in small groups, then in clusters, they broke for the woods. Lewis, as

Draper had the day before, rallied his officers to regroup his men. They screamed frantically after them, cursing them: "Come back! Come out of the woods!" By the fifth volley, little remained of Lewis's command.

This is what Etheridge and the other troopers saw. Colonel Draper had dropped twenty soldiers to the rear to form a reserve, then ordered the rest, in battle line, to fix their sights at five hundred yards. "Aim steady, men," Draper told them, "and fire at the bottom of the fence." They fired, dropped back to reload while the rear line fired, then moved forward, awaiting the order to fire again. Their aim was true. Above the roar from the thunderous volleys, they clearly heard rebels hollering in agony across the field. By the time they heard the rebel officers' curses, they knew they'd won the day. Draper led the men in "nine rousing cheers."

The following morning, the troopers embarked onto the transports for the return to the Point. In all, Draper and his men brought in 600 freedpeople, including some 70 recruits; 375 head of cattle; 160 horses—some fine enough to make cavalry mounts—and mules; and numerous plows, cornshellers, harnesses, cultivators, carts, and other farming implements for the contraband settlement on the Patuxent.

The mission was a turning point for Draper and the regiment. His merits as a field commander, one who was capable of taking initiative and making decisions, would finally be acknowledged. There could be little doubt that his men knew how to handle themselves in battle, not merely in detached skirmishes but in a tactical action, facing an organized, superior foe. "The gallantry of the colored troops on this occasion could not be excelled," Draper reported of the encounter. "They were as steady under fire and as accurate in their movements as if they were on drill." The black troopers had proved themselves to be disciplined, courageous, and ready to die for their freedom.

5

Before Richmond

In the Trenches

My old massa's come to town,
Cutting a Southern figure;
What's the matter with the man?
Lincoln's got his niggers.

We'll get our colored regiments
Strung in a line of battle;
I'll bet my money agin' the South
The rebels will skedaddle.

—*USCT camp song, to the tune of*
"Yankee Doodle"

After their tremendous success along the Rappahannock, Butler felt all the more pressed to have the Thirty-sixth transferred to the Army of the James. Colonel J. Wilson Shaffer, his chief of staff, came up with an idea by which to get Draper into the command. The strategists in Washington and many generals in the field still harbored misgivings about using African-American troops alongside white ones, in part because of their prejudices about the ability of black soldiers, but also because of the real racism that existed in white units toward the USCT. As a way to quell these fears and still deploy the Colored Troops, Shaffer suggested that Butler organize his USCT regiments into a separate, individual division, of which the Thirty-sixth would be part. The idea flew in the War Department. Segregation got the Thirty-sixth to the front.

In July 1864, Etheridge and the rest boarded naval transports, sailed past Norfolk and Fortress Monroe, then up the James River to Bermuda Hundred, a rail depot a few miles above Grant's base of supplies at City Point. After a month of drilling in which they learned tactical maneuvers and formations that they would need in front-line combat, the regiment moved forward. Thus began Etheridge's life in the trenches. This was where he and the other black troopers wanted to be, yes—to prove their willingness to fight for the right to equal citizenship. But after only a few days, it was easy to forget this.

Headquarters stationed the Thirty-sixth on the advance line. Here, two great armies had dug in and faced off. Tens of thousands of soldiers, men in faded dark blue or, just off in the distance, in butternut gray—everywhere. Draper's regiment were pickets whose job it was to be alert for troop movements in the opposing trenches and to hold the position as a first line of defense. Etheridge woke up daily to a sandwich of raw salt pork between two pieces of hardtack, then faced sniping, shelling, and taunting from an enemy within earshot.

From their first days in the trenches, the USCT were trophy targets of the rebel sharpshooters and artillerymen. The Southerners prized black blood over any other. One night, at a position along the line, Confederates called out to the white Union troops in the trenches opposite, forewarning them that they intended to shell the "smoked Yankees," as they called them. The rebels did so every morning thereafter. One USCT officer called it sheer "animosity toward the colored soldier." The Thirty-sixth held a position where they were under constant fire by the enemy. The men came to call it the Graveyard.

Thirteen troopers, nearly a third of the regiment's total deaths from enemy fire, were killed in the trenches that summer and fall by either sniping or shelling. Robert Hawkins of Company B was hit in the head; Edward Griffin of the same company got it in the neck. Both men died. During one two-week stretch, four men were killed from Etheridge's company alone. Ten days later, after a relative lull, a single shell got both Jonas

Capps and Ebon Hardy, privates under Etheridge. Hardest to swallow, though, was the death of Lawrence Midgett, a corporal in the company and relative of Etheridge's good friend Fields Midgett. Fields, Richard, and Lawrence had enlisted together. A rebel sharpshooter picked him off as he stood in the second line of trenches. He died where he fell.

And these were just the deaths. The number of men wounded in the rifle pits was not recorded, but an officer from the Sixth USCT, stationed along the line with the Thirty-sixth, remembered visiting the hospital and being surprised by the size of the pile of arms and legs in the rear of the amputation tent.

The sniping was the worst. The Thirty-sixth was prepared to give as good as it got, but opportunities rarely presented themselves for the men to return fire. Most often, they could only crouch in searing heat against the hard dirt walls of the trenches, feeling helpless as, all around them, life-long friends dropped screaming, clutching at shreds of cloth and crimson.

For the USCT, resentment from men wearing blue and occupying the same trenches as they did added to the danger. Though segregated in a division composed uniquely of USCT, black regiments still served side by side with white ones in the field.

Significant numbers of white troops, officers and enlisted men alike, held strong prejudices about the capacity of African-Americans to fight. Many openly expressed their lack of confidence in the USCT and their hesitancy to battle alongside them for fear that their cowardice and incompetence would cost the white troops their lives. Etheridge could hold no illusions about the very real risks that these hostile conditions posed for him and the rest. Just days before the regiment left Bermuda Hundred, news of what had happened to the USCT at the Battle of the Crater, along the line outside Petersburg, confirmed for him and the rest all their reservations about service at the front.

The plan of battle had been an ingenious one really. To break the stale-mate before Petersburg, Lieutenant Colonel Henry Pleasants from the Forty-eighth Pennsylvania, which was composed largely of coal miners (Pleasants himself was an engineer), proposed to dig a tunnel between the two lines, which, at his position, stood only five hundred feet apart. They would fill it with explosives and detonate the powder, then launch an assault on the sundered Confederate line. The plan was approved, with the USCT under Ambrose Burnside set to lead the attack.

At this point things began to unravel. The day before the assault, General George Meade, Burnside's superior, nixed the idea of leading with the black troops, even though they had spent weeks training for it. Meade feared political repercussions if something went wrong. Burnside protested, but Grant sided with Meade. Burnside had to shuffle his units at the last minute.

On the morning of the attack, the explosion blew a crater thirty feet deep and as wide and as long as half a football field. Nine companies of rebel defenders were thrown into the air. Two brigades of white Union troops charged, but as they had not been sufficiently prepared for the assault, they gathered at the crater rather than pressing forward to breach the Confederate line. By the time the USCT moved into the fray, the rebels' heavy defensive fire had pinned the Yankees down. The Confederates cut off the Union rear and intensified their shelling. Next, the rebels launched a fierce counterattack, and the poorly managed Union offensive broke, men fleeing helter-skelter to regain their own line. Many were trapped in the crater as the Confederates overran it.

The USCT were targeted and few spared. Just as at Fort Pillow, black troops were not allowed to surrender. "Take the white man, but kill the nigger!" swarming Confederates were heard to say. Though only a minority of the assaulting force, African-Americans made up 40 percent of the fatalities and more than a third of the casualties that day. During the battle, white Yankees were said to have been seen bayoneting black soldiers who were falling back from the Confederate charge. These men didn't want the rebels to seek retribution on them for fighting alongside USCT.

Was this the fate that awaited Etheridge? Jeering enemies in the line across the way and hardly less hostile ones in the trenches beside him? The twenty-two-year-old sergeant must have asked himself this question many times. At some point, he accepted that, in battle, as a black trooper, for him it was either death or glory.

In August, the USCT regiments began providing one hundred men a day to work on the canal at Dutch Gap, on the James, just west of Aiken's Landing. In trench warfare, all troops, black and white, had to constantly reinforce their position, digging trenches and constructing defensive parapets. The work at Dutch Gap was different, though. For the troopers of the Thirty-sixth, it felt like a return to labor details.

The inspiration to build the canal was General Butler's. After his failure to advance farther up the peninsula in May, the rebels had built up their river defenses along the winding James. At one five-mile bend around Trent's Reach, gun batteries and waterway obstructions completely blocked the passage. The base of this finger of land, though, at Dutch Gap, was just five hundred feet across. Butler devised a canal that would bypass the five-mile stretch of Confederate defenses. Digging began August 10.

It soon became obvious to the men doing the work that the canal was a mistake. The layer of topsoil gave easily, but underneath was hard, encrusted earth. Progress was slow. While the USCT and impressed black laborers (some of whom were brought from Roanoke Island) worked like mules to excavate the thousands of cubic yards of earth needed to open the way, the rebels subjected them to constant shelling, interrupting the work, destroying equipment, undoing gains made.

Etheridge might be supervising a unit of laborers when one of the watchmen, assigned especially for the purpose, would yell, "Holes!" The men would scramble for and crowd into the "bomb-proofs"—bunkers built into the embankments—until the shelling stopped. When they reemerged, dead and wounded lay half-buried under mounds of earth. The men would hustle those still breathing to small transports docked on the James, which would carry them to the hospital in the rear. Rare were the days that the boats were not ferrying men there. Soon, they came to call the Dutch Gap canal "Butler's Folly."

The black troopers rotated—three days on, three days off—between the trenches, Dutch Gap, and their reserve camp at Bermuda Hundred, where they could take short breaks from the strain of life at the front. But, in spite of this, tensions ran high in the regiment. Resentment was brewing between white officers and black troopers.

That month, Lieutenant Francis Bicknell of Company G shot and wounded Private Silas Hollis, allegedly for "stubbornness, disobedience of orders, and manifesting a mutinous spirit." Another trooper from the company, frustrated and mistrustful, deserted. Morale was sapped, and some of the black troopers increasingly questioned their officers. Like Judases, some officers in the Battle of the Crater had reportedly ripped the insignia from their uniforms so as not to be identified as part of the USCT. Among those of the Thirty-sixth, something seemed to have changed, too.

Major Theodore Read, the assistant adjutant general of volunteers, reported that the Thirty-sixth "seem[ed] unsteady and unreliable," but Thomas Morris Chester, a correspondent for the *Philadelphia Press* on assignment with the Army of the James, recognized something in the bearing of the men that he knew would stand them well in combat. Though hardly an unbiased source, Chester was a reliable one. The thirty-year-old Harrisburg, Pennsylvania, native was the only black correspondent to cover the war for a mainstream newspaper, and he made it a special point to follow the activities of the USCT. Among the regiments he observed, Chester focused particular attention on the Thirty-sixth.

"The 36th is a model regiment," he wrote, "and, wherever it has operated, it has been distinguished by the undaunted bravery of the men and the gallantry of its officers." Chester credited this to Draper and the discipline he demanded, and the journalist predicted that the regiment would "yet accomplish more brilliant achievements."

Chester also made a point to highlight the important role in the regiment played by the black sergeants, such as Etheridge. In one dispatch, Chester, commenting on a review of the troops, reported that, "in the 36th Regiment there were but three white officers present, the companies being commanded by the colored sergeants. . . . There is no lack of qualification in these sergeants to command their companies; in fact, many of them are superior in drill to some of the officers who are sent here to command them."

At twenty-two, Richard Etheridge was demonstrating the qualities of leadership that would stand him well throughout his lifetime. Etheridge and men like him kept their troopers in line and the command intact. Soon, in the chaos of battle, they would prove Major Read wrong and Chester right.

As August came to a close, the Thirty-sixth moved five miles away from Dutch Gap for picket duty at Deep Bottom, a position on the far right of Butler's line that the rebels had recently abandoned. Chester reported that, about this time, the hostilities between rebel and USCT subsided. At night, artillery still bombarded the trenches, taking occasional victims, but days were relatively calm. It was an indicator of a change in the war.

Union forces had cut the Weldon Railroad outside Petersburg, and supplies became increasingly scarce for rebels along the lines. Men from the Thirty-sixth could sometimes spy enemy pickets in the woods, hunting squirrels. Before long, the rebels were calling across to the Smoked Yankees, proposing trades. Though it was strictly forbidden (General Paine issued orders that anyone caught holding any sort of communication with the enemy be instantly shot), black troopers exchanged apples and hardtack for tobacco, the one side tossing their goods through the air to the other.

On occasion, a butternut would brave enemy fire, raise up high enough to be seen, and wave a newspaper over his head. This was a sign to exchange Southern news for Northern. The men of the Thirty-sixth were always anxious to get their hands on any information they could about the conditions of their families back home. For the rebels, it was word of the upcoming elections that interested them. The Union would elect a president in the fall, and the rebels knew that the North was tiring of a war that they perceived to be costly in lives and a stalemate in the field. They hoped a "peace man" who would be prepared to negotiate an end to the hostilities would unseat Abraham Lincoln. For the time being, though, the only peace was the begrudging one between the lines.

And it was a begrudging peace. The black troopers found constant reminders of whom they were facing. When the men of the Thirty-sixth moved into the position at Deep Bottom, they came upon some slave manacles that the enemy had left behind. "[T]wo pair . . . for the wrists," Chester wrote, "and one iron collar for the neck, which is fastened with a padlock, to which are several links of a chain to be attached, if necessary, to a similar necklace on another individual, by which means quite a number of men and women could be yoked together, single file, for any desirable length." Many of the troopers had worn similar contraptions. Should the "peace man" win the presidency, perhaps they might be forced to wear them again.

The news the rebels read in the Yankee papers in September turned their empty stomachs. General Sherman had taken Atlanta. With this defeat, they saw their hopes for a negotiated peace suddenly consumed and spiral away like the columns of smoke raging over the devastated city. Northerners now knew that the South, split in half by Sherman's army, would be beaten. They would reelect Abraham Lincoln, the man who had brought them to this point.

The Yankees also knew that Atlanta blew taps on Lee's army. Grant ordered Butler to engage the rebels on his front, preventing Lee from shifting them to support Grant's offensive in the Shenandoah. Benjamin Butler welcomed the order. It would be the opportunity he had looked for to act on his grander ambitions.

Butler formulated a plan for a three-pronged assault on the Confederate line. Not only would the Army of the James prevent the rebels from falling back to the Shenandoah, but Butler also planned to be the man to take the prized rebel capital. "[The] object," he instructed his field commanders, "is to surprise the Confederate forces in our front here and, passing them, to get possession of the city of Richmond."

His staff guarded the details of the plan with utmost secrecy. The troopers remained unaware that they verged on taking the offensive until the night before when, on September 28, orders came down the chain of command for the men to prepare themselves with three days' cooked rations and sixty rounds of ammunition, and to form up by companies. All those unfit for heavy marching were to be left behind, along with tents, camping equipment, and cooking utensils. The men of the Thirty-sixth quickly understood. These instructions signaled an impending attack.

Etheridge ordered his men into formation. They watched as regiment after regiment gathered at Deep Bottom. More arrived throughout the night, some marching across the Deep Bottom Bridge, and others sailing in by naval transport. Troopers billeted themselves as best they could and pondered the coming action. Rumors spread that they were forming to board naval transports bound for North Carolina, perhaps to attack Fort Fisher, at Wilmington.

The troop movements didn't settle until around 2 A.M. By then, all knew it was not North Carolina but Virginia—the formidable position before them—that they would advance upon. Twice before, the Union had attacked the redoubt at New Market Heights—both times unsuccessfully. Fourteen thousand men, twelve brigades, including one of artillery—some forty-one regiments—had congregated at Deep Bottom to attempt it again. Fifteen regiments were USCT. Colonel Draper headed the Second

Brigade, made up of the Fifth, Thirty-sixth, and Thirty-eighth. The Thirty-sixth, under Major Pratt, was 450 men strong.

Within two hours of bivouacking, company commanders moved through the men, rousting them from sleep, if any had been able to doze off at all. Tired but anxious, they formed up in regiments. At four, General Butler himself rode among them, confirming their suspicions. "This is an attack where I expect you to go over and take a work which will be before you after you get over the hill," the general told them. "You must take it at all hazards."

Butler noticed the nervousness among the men of the white regiments, "standing in line, flanked by colored troops." He'd expected this. He planned, in fact, to put it to rest once and for all.

Although the USCT were the least experienced division in the strike force—in fact, they were the least experienced of all Grant's seventeen divisions and had never fought together as a unit—and their commander, Brigadier General Charles Paine, was untested in the field at the head of a large body of troops, Butler chose to lead the attack with them. This would be the chance for the former slaves to prove themselves in battle. Butler wrote Grant, "I want to convince myself whether, when under my own eye, the negro troops will fight; and if I can take with the negroes, a redoubt that turned Hancock's corps on a former occasion, that will settle the question."

Now, he rallied the black troopers for the coming test. "And when you are over the parapet," he called to them, "your war cry should be 'Remember Fort Pillow!'" The men's ire rose. But they also understood the underlying message in Butler's words: that they must fight all the harder and avoid capture at all costs. The rebels did not take black prisoners.

The Thirty-sixth formed up between the Fifth and Thirty-eighth. Etheridge's company fell in. Draper's corps followed Colonel Samuel Duncan's Third Brigade of USCT. Colonel John Holman's First Brigade pulled up the rear.

The column marched up the incline of the Grover House Road past regiment after regiment of white troops. "Every man looked like a soldier,"

Chester wrote, "while inflexible determination was depicted upon every countenance. The officers as they went along the line, were impressed with an unwavering confidence by the martial bearing of the troops."

And the black troopers put their confidence in their officers. One, First Lieutenant James Backuss,* was excused from the fight because of lameness (one of his legs was shorter than the other), but he'd disobeyed orders to stay with the men and lead them into battle. It was men like Backuss who exemplified what was best about the white officers.

Still, fear settled in on most. "Seeing the elephant," battle-tested veterans called it—the feeling of terror and anticipation when soldiers prepare to go into the fight. Etheridge marched in line to the top of that hill to take a look at the elephant.

The brigade formed up in a field beside Ruffin's farmhouse, behind a stretch of woods. The sun had yet to show itself. A misty fog enveloped the land, and dew slicked the grass underfoot. Duncan's brigade—the Fourth and Sixth USCT, some seven hundred men—moved out into the wet darkness. They would be first to assault the Confederate position. It was five-thirty.

Before long, an explosion of howitzer and musket fire beyond the copse of trees cast a fierce gloom over the brigade. One officer described what all the Thirty-sixth heard: "The crash of small arms is terrific, a constant roll with the heavier discharges of artillery breaking in like the bass notes of some mighty organ." The fusillade persisted, a half hour, longer, and there was no drumroll pattering of return fire. Duncan's men were either pinned down or retreating, but they, like the two assaults before, had not reached the Confederate earthworks, the objective they had to reach before the order would be given to open up with their own guns.

Men stood around expectant. Others lay in the grass. All listened, anticipating the order to move out. They waited.

★   ★   ★

*He is alternatively called Backup in some records.

The distant firing finally stopped. Soon, groups of men, many organized around lieutenants, some around sergeants, still others by ones and twos, came falling back through the trees. Some dragged along wounded comrades. They were harried, frazzled, and significantly fewer than had gone out. Of the seven hundred men who had marched behind Duncan toward the heights, nearly four hundred were casualties in just forty minutes on the field. Duncan himself had fallen, hit four times. Three men carried him to the rear.

"It was a perfectly terrible encounter," one survivor moaned. "We were all cut to pieces."

As the Third Brigade fell back, orders came down the line to the men of Draper's column to prepare to move out.

Etheridge kept his men in line, moving them forward at a rhythmed pace. They entered a stretch of field—fire coming from the trees on the left—then into a wooded brake. The men of the Twenty-second USCT, from Holman's First Brigade, moved on the position on Draper's flank, driving in the rebel skirmishers. Draper's brigade proceeded on.

At a steep ravine split by a shallow creek, the order came to halt. Etheridge stopped his platoon. Others around did likewise. Batteries from the heights boomed ordnance at them. Some shells came dangerously close. Most fell harmlessly into the woods or beyond them in the field. Etheridge kept his men steady the long half hour it took for the entire brigade to regroup.

Draper ordered the regiments to form up, six companies wide, the Fifth leading, followed by the Thirty-sixth, then the Thirty-eighth. Etheridge led his men into position around their company's standard-bearer. The colonel, riding among them on horseback, shouted instructions prohibiting them from fixing the percussion caps on their muskets. They would be tempted to return fire and must not, he told them. Returning fire would break the momentum of the charge, and they would easily be exposed while aiming. This would be a bayonet attack. A full frontal assault.

Within minutes they were a Roman phalanx, three regiments deep, numbering thirteen hundred men. Etheridge called for his platoon to move out. They made their way through three hundred yards of young pines and thick underbrush, still under the barrage of artillery fire, then emerged out onto an open plain.

The sun had burned the veil of fog off the land. As the first men entered the field, rebels who had wandered out from their position to loot among the fallen scampered back over the works. Broken and bleeding bodies, the dead and dying, lay spilled everywhere, as though a giant hand from the sky had strewn them about like grains to nourish the earth. Muskets, shoes, cartridge boxes, haversacks—much was carried away. The pockets of the pants of some were turned inside out. Others had even had their clothes completely stripped off them, a symbolic act to deny them their status as soldiers, to deny that they had fallen as defenders of the Union, but had merely been an armed black horde, now dispatched by rightful men of arms.

The field was 130 yards wide, an open lane that dipped then rose toward the Confederate guns. Etheridge could see the imposing rebel position, 800 yards distant, up the slow-climbing slope. The rebel entrenchments were not at the summit but at the base of New Market Heights. There, a line of infantry crouched behind the parapet, looking down at the second wave of black troops to confront them this day; eighteen hundred Confederates manned the position.

Getting to the rebels would be no easy matter. The ground was swampy near the Confederate line. A stream necklaced the works, and just beyond it lay a wide strip of slashing—heavy trees, chopped down and interwoven, but with the branches left on, to tie up a body of men trying to pass through. Etheridge could see where pioneers, armed with axes, had begun the work of hacking a path through the mess, and he imagined that their own would attack where those others had left off. Beyond was a second line of abatis, this one, chevaux-de-frise: logs spiked with crisscrossed patterns of sharpened stakes. The rebel muskets, leveled at them from just a hundred yards past the latter line, would make it tougher going yet.

Orders came down the line, Lieutenant Backuss, other officers, shouting, "Move out! On the double-quick!"

Etheridge executed the order, also shouting out, "Forward! Double-quick!"

They charged, "with loud cheering," Draper later remembered. "[W]e started on a slow run," one officer from the Fifth recalled, "with arms at a right shoulder shift, the burnished steel bayonets gleaming in the bright sun."

The rebels opened up, first with grapeshot, then with fearsome canister: tin cans filled with cast-iron balls and fired from howitzers. The whistling shot scattered immediately upon discharge, cutting swaths in the ranks.

Men began to fall around Etheridge. Roderick McCoy. Simon Gaylord. Corporal Isaac Overton. Harry Hill got shot in the right ankle, and Pompey Simpson dropped, wounded but not dead. Etheridge called to his men to keep moving: "Forward, men! Charge!" Lieutenant Backuss limp-hopped along with the men, waving his sword above his head and urging them on.

The Fifth, ahead of them, hit the stream first, and before he knew it, Etheridge was sprinting into the water. It was deeper than it appeared. Etheridge had to wade to cross, then he scrambled up the opposite bank. But the men were all out of formation. They tried to re-form around the company standard, screamed orders overlapping screamed orders and balls zipping through the air all around. In the confusion, men began falling by the scores. The company colors dropped, but then another soldier picked it up. It dropped again. Lieutenant Backuss, calling the company to re-form on him, collapsed in a heap, the blue of his chest bleeding red. Etheridge, the other Company F sergeants, took up the call.

Perhaps now reinforcements from the other brigades should come up in support.

Nothing.

Then Etheridge saw some troopers, green recruits from the Fifth, cap their muskets and begin to fire. Others followed. Men around Etheridge dropped to a knee, capped their guns, opened up on the enemy parapet.

Etheridge saw Draper, hurried out of the saddle, the color all gone from his face, rushing up and down the line screaming instruction, but Etheridge could not hear it, and the men around him kept firing. Others crouched along the bank. Some even began slipping back.

The sergeant major, Henry Adkins, was then among them. He wasn't more than five feet six—and just twenty-one, a free black and former gardener from New York who'd sailed to Portsmouth to join the USCT and the fight—and his instructions were clear. "Form up on company colors!"

Etheridge repeated the orders. "Form up on company colors!" Others did, too. And Draper was among them: "Start the yell, boys! Start the yell!" So Etheridge did. As one body, the platoon and company and regiment swelled into one great cry to charge.

They scrambled through the slashing, following the picket path cleared by the pioneers, branches and bramble ripping and pulling at them. Here, like a great clap of thunder, the rebel muskets opened up, enfilading fire catching them from the right, the men all tied up in the entanglement and in a cross stream of hissing lead. Men fell. Etheridge and the USCT pushed on. Standard-bearers were shot dead, dropping the colors. Others picked them up, continued the charge.

They hit the second line of abatis—close enough to make out the features on the rebel faces. Lieutenant Gaskill, in front of the regiment, waving his sword above his head to lead them through, suddenly rolled on the ground, clutching the mangled remains of his arm. Nearby, Miles James, a corporal from Company B, dropped, too, his arm so badly mutilated it would require immediate amputation. But with his good arm, he loaded his musket, leveled it on the enemy position, and fired. A butternut disappeared behind the parapet. James did it again. Another rebel gone. Again and again.

A Confederate officer jumped atop the parapet. "Give it to them, my brave boys!" he called down to his men. James Gardiner, a private from Company I, far ahead of the regiment, rushed up onto the works at just that moment. Giving a yell, he shot the officer, then ran the man through with his bayonet to the hilt. The rest followed, racing up, over, and into the enemy line.

The rebels were running. They tried to form up on the summit of New Market Heights, but Draper's brigade pursued them there and took the entire hill. The Smoked Yankees had knocked the butternuts off their mountain. The Smoked Yankees were king.

Thomas Cook, the *New York Herald:* "Their charge in the face of the obstacles interposing was one of the grand features of the day's operation. . . . They never halted or faltered, though their ranks were sadly thinned by the charge, and the slashing was filled with the slain and wounded of their number."

Henry Jacob Winser, the *New York Times:* "To-day their praises have been on every tongue, and too much cannot be said in appreciation of their courage."

William Merriam, the *New York Herald:* "The behavior of the negro troops . . . was of the most gallant character. Who dare say, after this, that negroes will not fight?"

The *New York Times:* "The panic in Richmond is terrible."

The black troops formed defensive positions all along the heights. Butler, with his staff, had witnessed the entire assault from a position on a neighboring hill.

"As I rode across the brook and up towards the fort along this line of charge," he later wrote, "there lay in my path five hundred and forty-three dead and wounded of my colored comrades. And, as I guided my horse this way and that way that his hoof might not profane their dead bodies, I swore to myself an oath . . . that they and their race should be cared for and protected by me to the extent of my power so long as I lived."

When Butler reached the site of their victory, the men broke their ranks and swarmed around the general. The USCT rallied around his horse and cheered Butler.

Soon, news came to them that Edward Ord, the leader of another of the three prongs of the offensive on Richmond, had breached the line at Fort Harrison, taking the redoubt. Nothing yet of the third prong.

Draper's brigade lost four hundred and fifty men during the assault. Along with Duncan's losses, nearly one thousand black soldiers were killed, wounded, missing, or captured at New Market Heights. The Thirty-sixth counted twenty-one dead and eighty-seven wounded, including five officers. Etheridge's company suffered seven dead in the charge. Lieutenant Backuss, though gravely wounded, survived.

Fourteen of the sixteen Medals of Honor awarded USCT during the war were bestowed upon black soldiers who fought in the September 29 charge. James, the man who had picked rebels off the parapet after losing his arm, was one; Gardiner, who had topped the works and felled the Confederate officer, was another. General Paine, proclaiming that the men of the Thirty-sixth "behaved excellently in the assault," ordered the words *New Market Heights* inscribed across the company colors "for their gallantry in carrying the enemy works."

Butler decorated his field tent with the battle flags captured by his black troops on the heights, a symbol for all to see of the USCT victory. He had a medal struck with the words *Ferro Iis Libertas Perveniet*—"freedom will come to them by the sword"— and on the reverse side *Campaign before Richmond, Distinguished for Courage.* This he presented to nearly two hundred black troopers, identified by their commanders for acts of bravery during the assault.*

Butler also issued special orders recommending Draper for promotion to the rank of brevet brigadier general of volunteers "for incessant attention to duty and gallantry in action." President Lincoln approved it. Three officers, including Lieutenants Backuss and Gaskill, were promoted to captain. Two weeks after the battle, in an address to the Army of the James, Butler praised the black troops:

> In the charge on the enemy's works by the colored division of the Eighteenth Corps at Spring Hill, New Market, better men were never better led, better officers never led better men. . . . A few more such gallant charges, and to command colored troops will be the post of honor in the American armies. The colored soldiers, by coolness, steadiness, and determined courage and dash, have silenced every cavil of the doubters of their soldierly capacity, and drawn tokens of admiration from their enemies—have brought their late masters, even, to the consideration of the question whether they will not employ as soldiers the hitherto despised race. Be it so: this war is ended when a musket is in the hands of every able-bodied Negro who wishes to use one.

His political motives aside, Butler had become committed to African-American freedom, and he would have the doubting nation recognize it, too.

★   ★   ★

---

*The names of these soldiers have been lost to history.

Later in life, Butler would confess that the charge on New Market Heights had been superfluous. He had known the position would be abandoned once Fort Harrison fell, but sent the USCT to take the hill anyway, despite the potential cost in lives, as a way to prove a point. Butler martyred a thousand troops to prove what each of those troopers and each of his comrades in the USCT already knew: that they were men, with the courage, the foibles, the will to survive and to thrive, of men. Perhaps such sacrifices are not in vain but are the necessary steps that eventually lead toward meaningful change. It is hard to know what freedoms may or may not have been accorded freedpeople had they not laid down their lives on September 29 to prove their humanity to a disbelieving nation.

Some in the USCT were able to parlay their involvement in the fight into social and economic opportunities after the war's close. Etheridge was one of these men. Once he'd seized his chance to serve in the Life-Saving Service, he would not let it go, for himself, nor for those who would follow, without a mighty struggle. New Market Heights had been a terrible price to pay to give up gains so easily.

Although the offensive achieved Grant's objective of tying up the rebel forces around Richmond, Butler's goal of capturing the Confederate capital failed. The assault stalled at Fort Harrison, the opposing positions nearly unchanged. In October, the Thirty-sixth fell back to their old position on the line, doing duty in the trenches and at Dutch Gap. The routine of digging and shelling continued into November, most days in a chilling rain, but there was little movement between the armies as each side awaited the results of the coming presidential elections.

Though the soldiers of Draper's brigade were now all emancipated, the majority of them did not yet have citizenship rights and could not vote. The Fifth USCT, however, was composed mostly of blacks from Ohio who had been free before the war. Etheridge and the other new freedmen of the Thirty-sixth and Thirty-eight stood proudly by, cheering their comrades on as they lined up at the polls set up in the Union camp to cast their ballots. Rebels could only watch from their position in the trenches across the line. Lincoln won; peace was now only possible for the South through surrender or defeat.

Thanksgiving found General Wild in camp. Wild, now commanding a mixed brigade of white troops and USCT outside Petersburg, passed among his former African Brigade. He dined with Major Hart and staff, while the troopers enjoyed turkeys distributed among the ranks. The regimental bands played, soldiers sang, and celebration was the order of the day. Etheridge and the men relaxed.

Two days later, the picket post on the line at the Graveyard was attacked by artillery fire. Three shells hit home, killing two troopers, one from Etheridge's company, and wounding another. The explosion cast parts of their bodies into the branches of nearby trees. The official cause of death cited: "Blown all to pieces."

In December, Grant ordered Butler to capture Fort Fisher and close the vital Confederate seaport of Wilmington, North Carolina, the "last gateway" to the Confederacy. Butler, who himself took command of the expedition, bungled the attempt and failed to reduce the fort. At one point, he ordered a ship, loaded with 215 tons of powder, exploded in the bay. The detonation rocked the waters of the port, but had almost no effect on Fort Fisher. On December 27, Butler's unit returned to Virginia.

The press made light of the fiasco. "It is well that the progress of the war is so prosperous that we can laugh rather than cry over the Wilmington Expedition," *Harper's Weekly* reported; but for Grant, it was an opportunity to move against the politicking Butler. "In my absence, General Butler necessarily commands," Grant appealed to the secretary of war, "and there is a lack of confidence felt in his military ability, making him an unsafe commander for a large army. His administration of the affairs in his department is also objectionable." In early January, Lincoln, no longer bound by potentially dangerous political fallout, relieved Butler of his command and ordered him home to Massachusetts.

Many resentful white troopers sighed breaths of relief at his ousting, but the USCT felt otherwise. "As soon as the fact became known," Thomas Morris Chester reported from the Thirty-sixth's camp, "it caused a general feeling of depression among that class of persons who believe that the most vigorous means should be applied for the suppression of the rebellion. . . . One thing is certain, that the poor soldier and the humble contraband have lost a faithful friend, and the cause of the Union an uncompromising champion of loyalty."

It was generally thought—hoped, even—among Etheridge and the others of the unit that General Wild would take over command of the USCT, but Major General Godfrey Weitzel, Butler's second in the Army of the James, was put in charge.

The winter brought penetrating cold to accompany the continuing rains, and sometimes sleet and snow. Military operations were impossible in those conditions. It was chore enough to keep warm and well fed. For the rebels, under siege for seven months, food was particularly scarce. Hostilities even calmed at the Graveyard.

A cornfield partitioned the two lines there. But neither side let men from the other forage for supplies in it. In January, a separate peace was had. Some hungry rebels slipped out into the corn, hoping not to be fired upon. Instead, they came upon a group of USCT. Each side eyed the other, then coolly began to gather ears. Suddenly, a wild hog, in the field with similar designs on the corn, appeared in their midst. Both rebel and Smoked Yank commenced the chase, dropping the ears and scrambling after the pig. One rebel, in his haste not to let a prized feast get away, took up his gun and fired a shot after it. The ball whizzed by the head of one of the black troopers.

The black soldiers all froze an instant, ready to go for their arms. "Halloo, there, Johnny!" one said. "What do you mean by that?"

The rebels had given up the chase, too, waiting to see what the USCT would do. The one who'd fired replied, "I'm not shooting at you, but at that *other* hog."

Both sides broke into laughter, and the men continued the hunt. The rebels took the day—and the hog.

The journalist Chester reported: "Deserters are daily coming into our lines, whose loyalty is no doubt quickened by the chilling weather we are now experiencing." The end was inevitable and near. Most of the defenders in the Southern line knew this and now only sought a way to survive the fighting and maintain a measure of honor. One group, gathering corn in the Graveyard, wandered close to the pickets from the Thirty-sixth and asked if the black troopers might not come upon them with their muskets drawn so that they could surrender without appearing to be deserting.

*   *   *

During the last week of March, Lee's army, whittled to only 55,000 men (Grant had 115,000), launched one last-ditch offensive in the hope of breaking the Union line and clearing a path by which to unite itself with the remnants of General J. E. Johnston's Confederates in North Carolina. It was daring, but futile, and Philip Sheridan quickly quashed the assault. For Lee now, the only way to join Johnston was to abandon Petersburg and Richmond and run for it.

Just after midnight on the night of April 2, a series of explosions began in the rebel works surrounding the capital. One rocked the earth in the Union forts, jolting the Yankees stationed there. Before long, Union pickets could see fires lighting the dark in the direction of Richmond.

Draper rousted the Thirty-sixth and put them on the road to Richmond. The race was on. Every regiment wanted to be first to march on the fallen capital of the Confederacy.

Given their position on the line, the Thirty-sixth had a good lead. Etheridge and his platoon found Confederate positions abandoned as they passed, the bomb-proofs dark and empty, the trenches eerily quiet. "On to Richmond," the men joked. As they approached the burning city, jubilant slaves, now freedpeople, greeted them along the way. Then Etheridge and the others noticed columns of white Union troops advancing on the run toward the city.

A messenger caught up to Draper. He carried word from General Charles Devens of the white Twenty-fourth Corps: Draper's USCT were to step to the left of the road and allow the Twenty-fourth to pass into Richmond first. Draper acknowledged receipt, but turned to his men. "Forward," he called, "on the double-quick!"

Even today, historians still contest which troops arrived first, but Chaplain Garland White of the Twenty-eighth USCT, a former slave who had run away to Canada then enlisted in the army at the outbreak of war, claimed it was black troops. Thomas Morris Chester's testimony corroborates the chaplain's claim. "The gallant Thirty-Sixth U.S. Colored Troops . . . ha[d] the honor of being the first regiment," he reported. And of the units of the regiment, Chester wrote that Companies A and K reached the city first.

the *Harper's* correspondent on that front also credited the USCT, though he did not cite the specific unit.

The ironic justice of black troops leading the march on Richmond, the capital of the rebellion, was lost on neither journalist. The *Harper's* man reported, "It was fit that the old flag should be restored to the city of Richmond by soldiers of the race to secure whose eternal degradation that flag had been pulled down." As for Chester, he taunted the naysayers who would discount the USCT: "For marching or fighting, Draper's [regiment] is not to be surpassed in the service."

Blacks came out en masse to greet the Thirty-sixth's arrival. Once within the city limits, Draper lined his men up on the left of the road, as the message from Devens had instructed. He had his drum corps and regimental musicians play "The Battle Cry of Freedom" and "Yankee Doodle." Thus they greeted the Twenty-fourth.

President Lincoln arrived by boat on April 3. He toured the city, enveloped everywhere he went in throngs of jubilant freedpeople. One old woman wept. "I know that I am free," she said, "for I have seen Father Abraham and felt him."

The white troops of the Twenty-fourth were assigned provost duty within Richmond. The USCT occupied positions outside the city limits. Meanwhile, Sheridan led the pursuit of Lee's fleeing army. Lee raced for Amelia Courthouse to the west, from where he would resupply and travel by rail to join Johnston. Union cavalry attacked the rebel rear guard while General Sheridan tried to flank Lee's position. On April 8, at Appomattox Courthouse, the Yankees had completely surrounded what was left of the Army of Northern Virginia. Lee sent a note, wrapped in a white towel, to the Union lines: he would surrender.

Johnston surrendered a few days later in North Carolina. Richard Taylor, in Alabama, held out until May 4, and E. Kirby Smith, in the West, until May 26, turning over the last of his forces at Galveston. But after Appomattox, the war was effectively over.

★   ★   ★

Blacks everywhere, soldier and civilian, former slave and not, saw Lincoln as the "Great Emancipator." His death felt like a personal loss. "The warm imagination of this people cherished ABRAHAM LINCOLN as more than mortal," a *Harper's* editorialist wrote. "He dies; and in his death slavery doubtless seems to them again possible." The editorial went on: "As time passes they will learn that their cause is also ours. They will see that slavery, not LINCOLN is dead. For the work in which he was but the minister of the people, the people will fulfill to the utmost of sacred devotion."

Indeed, slavery was dead, and Richard Etheridge knew it. He had helped slay it. A stealthier beast—racism—lived on, and even though Etheridge and other blacks the nation over steeled themselves to confront it, they did not yet realize its protean faces, the unforeseen places it would expose itself, nor the color of its rage. Although he did not know it, Etheridge's struggle for equality had only just begun.

6

Armistice

Texas

Go now, black soldiers, to your houses, & become orderly,
sober & industrious citizens. . . . Do not create imaginary
wrongs for yourselves: be civil, polite, industrious, frugal, just &
religious, and you will prosper. Save your money, buy property,
and educate your children. If men speak disrespectfully of you,
be silent, if they taunt you, tell them you are free: if they menace you, tell them you are a man: but if they beat, oppress, or
strive to enslave you, resist. There are but two ways of maintaining freedom: by the bayonet & with the ballot. The Gov't
will give you one or the other, or both.

—*USCT regimental commander in a*
farewell address to his troops

May found the Thirty-sixth at Camp Lincoln, near Grant's field
headquarters at City Point, outside Richmond. Richard Etheridge, like
most of the men of the Thirty-sixth, had signed an enlistment of three
years. When the fighting ceased in April 1865, the men still owed Uncle
Sam another year of service. Most just longed to return home. In late
1864, the men had complained of feeling cut off from Roanoke Island and

asked that a member of the regiment be permitted to travel there to get news from their relatives. Leaves were granted, and some of the soldiers finally returned.

The refugee camp on the island had continued to expand after Etheridge's departure for the army. The thousand contrabands counted in the spring of 1862 had grown to 2,712 by January 1, 1864, and to 3,091 a short time later. Wild's December raid alone sent hundreds there. By the spring of 1865, some 3,500 African-Americans crowded the island, whose total population at the onset of war, white and black, had only been 590. In 1863, General John Foster, the departmental commander at the time, appointed the Reverend Horace James to be "Superintendent of Blacks" to deal with the refugee problem in North Carolina.

A Congregationalist minister, James had enlisted as the chaplain of the Twenty-fifth Massachusetts Infantry Regiment and had worked with the contrabands at Fortress Monroe. As a first measure, he established camps at New Bern and on Roanoke Island, but James had grand visions for the settlement on Roanoke. He wanted to establish a self-sufficient "African colony," patterned in the style of an idealized New England village. Claiming the unoccupied lands on the island's north end, he assigned one-acre plots to the families of USCT and other blacks employed by the government, as well as to the physically disabled. The lots were laid out in avenues—Lincoln Avenue, Burnside Avenue, Roanoke Avenue—which were intersected by narrower numbered streets.

The freedpeople immediately began building homes on the land. "So [z]ealous were they in this work," James reported, "as to spend, in many cases, much of the night in prosecuting it, giving no sleep to their eyes until they could close them sweetly, under their own dear roof-tree."

Though James did not recognize it, the freedpeople had been at this work of building a community well before his arrival. His vision facilitated their ability to accomplish their aims. James had a mill constructed with a steam-powered saw. Completed in spring 1864, it provided an abundance of lumber for the freedpeople to buy and use. Within a year, they had constructed 591 houses, whose value James estimated at over $44,000—"a sum large enough to have purchased the whole island three years ago," he boasted. They also built more churches, a hospital, and better schools than the one they'd originally put up. Teachers from the North, sent by the

American Missionary Association, began arriving in the fall of 1863 and, before long, numbered nearly a dozen.

Despite their industriousness and drive, the freedpeople still suffered from overcrowding and, as a result, from inadequate food supplies. Of the population, most were the aged and infirm, women with children, orphans. The able-bodied males were gone, enlisted in the army or impressed into labor duty for it. Less than 250 between the ages of eighteen and forty-five—prime working years—remained, and the majority of those present were "exempts on account of physical disability"—men wounded in battle or debilitated by illness or disease. Those women who could work did, as laundresses, cooks, and servants, but employment opportunities were scarcer for women, whether they were willing or not. A bad shad season in 1864 aggravated matters. The gardens on their plots of land helped some, but most families lived off government rations.

For all that his romantic vision expedited development of the settlement, James proved less effective at managing his human resources. One of his choices for two positions as assistant superintendent was a surprising one: a "copperhead"—a Northern Peace Democrat—named Holland Streeter. Too old to fight, Streeter had nonetheless volunteered to come South at the outbreak of war, expressing a willingness to serve in any capacity. Once assigned to Roanoke Island, though, he baldly admitted to the freedpeople, "There is not a particle of abolitionist about me." If anyone might have harbored doubts about his brash claims, they were soon dispelled by Streeter's actions.

Allocations from Washington were sparse during the war and policy toward the freedpeople uneven. Those employed by the government were often owed several months back pay. Some had never been paid at all. Streeter, who served as quartermaster, made no allowances for this. He cursed and berated freedpeople who reported to the ration house, demeaning them in front of others and sometimes physically expelling them from the property. The missionary teachers, powerless before the man, distrusted him and feared he had ill intentions at heart.

However, Streeter found plenty of allies among white Roanoke Islanders, many of whom resented the mushrooming black community and the bustling colony on the north end. He set up an underground market with some. He hawked rations intended for distribution among black families to private citizens, even selling quantities to local merchants and grocers, who would turn around and sell them back to the freedpeople. Streeter, who was also in charge of the mill, gouged blacks there, too, over-charging them for lumber.

Streeter was not the only copperhead among the occupying army. White soldiers regularly pilfered produce from the gardens and chickens from the pens of freedpeople. They played pranks and bullied them. Men from Hawkins's Zouaves kidnapped a group of blacks on the island one day and, with shears, cut their hair to make wigs for a minstrel show that the regiment was staging. On another occasion, some of the white soldiers came into one of the colony's churches, acting raucous and rowdy, and when the black minister challenged them, one put his pistol to the preacher's breast and threatened to shoot. The army higher-ups were hardly better. They ordered rounded up and impressed into labor duty twenty-five of the island's boys, some as young as twelve, trans-porting them to New Bern, without bothering to seek their families' con-sent.

When black leaders went to James about Streeter and the behavior of the white troopers, the superintendent dismissed their complaints. He claimed they were unfounded or just plain ignored them. In June 1864, Congress finally passed legislation to pay black troopers the same as white ones. In response, James cut rations to half the normal portion. The sol-dier relatives, he explained, should now be better able to take care of their families on the island. Though the wage scale was evened out, many USCT, like their relatives on Roanoke, were still owed back pay and had none to send home.

In March 1865, a group of frustrated freedpeople bypassed James to protested directly to President Lincoln and Secretary of War Stanton. They detailed the series of injustices they had suffered in the colony, con-cluding humbly: "we dont exspect to have the same wrights as white men doe we know that [we] are in a military country and we exspect to obey the rules and orders of our authories and doe   as they say doe, any thing in reason . . . but we are not satisfide with our Supertendent nor the treat-ment we receives . . . they taken us just like we had been dum beast."

Once it was challenged, James's attitude toward the freedpeople turned to sour racism. Indignant, he denied their charges, responding, "I look upon [the author of the letter], and others like him, as persons to be treated like children, who do not know when they are best used, and whose complaints should influence us but a little, while we do for them that which we know will promote their best good."

This was the news that the soldiers returning from furlough brought back to the men of the Thirty-sixth. William Benson, a black Outer Banker who had enlisted in the Thirty-seventh in December 1863, only to desert the regiment eight months later and steal back to the island, found his way back to their camp in Virginia and confirmed in great detail the sad developments at home.

The trials of having to lead men under difficult, sometimes life-threatening situations had forged Etheridge into a certain kind of man. He understood that he had a responsibility to his community, to stand up for them and not merely lie idly by while misery cropped up around him. Though he had no wife and no dependents in the colony, he took the lead in rallying support among the men of the regiment. Using Benson's testimony as a guide, Etheridge penned a letter to General Oliver Howard, the commissioner of the recently formed Freedman's Bureau (organized by the War Department to look after the interests of the former slaves), in behalf of the men of the Thirty-sixth.

"Genl," he wrote, "we the soldiers of the 36 U.S. Col Regt Humbly petition to you to alter the Affairs at Roanoke Island.

> We have served in the US Army faithfully and don our duty to our Country, for which we thank God (that we had the opportunity) but at the same time our family's are suffering at Roanoke Island N. C.. . . . There are men on the Island that have been wounded at Dutch Gap Canal, working there, and some discharged soldiers, men that were wounded in the service of the U.S. Army, and returned home to Roanoke that Cannot get any rations and are not able to work, some soldiers are sick in Hospitals that have never been paid a cent and their familys are suffering and their children going crying without anything to eat.

Etheridge reminded the general of the promises that had been made them about their wives and families being provided for, then informed him of the cut rations and the unpaid wages, "so the people have neither provision or money to buy it with. Consequently, three or four days out of every ten days, they have nothing to eat."

Etheridge did not in any way address himself "hat in hand" to Howard. It was not a former slave who was writing—not someone who didn't "exspect to have the same wrights as white men doe"—but an equal, with opinions and the drive to see the right thing done. He reported Holland Streeter's black-market activities without reservation or fear of reprisal. Etheridge went further, though, painting Streeter's true colors for his superior officer.

> Mr Streeter . . . is a througher Cooper head a man who says that he is no part of a Abolitionist.   Takes no care of the colored people and has no Simpathy with the colored people.   A man who kicks our wives and children out of the ration house or commissary, he takes no notice of their actual suffering and sells the rations and allows it to be sold, and our family's suffer for something to eat.

"Genl," he wrote, "perhaps you think the Statements against Mr Streeter too strong, but we can prove them." He also reported the abuses at the hands of the occupying army.

Etheridge's letter was not merely a cry of grievance, but was also a call for action. "Genl we the soldiers of the 36 U.S. Co Troops having familys at Roanoke Island humbly petition you to favour us by removeing Mr Streeter the present Asst Supt at Roanoke Island under Captn James." This, Etheridge proposed, would solve the problems on the island. He signed the letter "in behalf of humanity."*

Etheridge took the letter to Draper, soliciting the general's support and asking that it be forwarded up the chain of command. Draper did so, attaching a note of endorsement in which he appealed that the promises made his soldiers be carried out.

Draper had just hurried back from an early end to his own furlough when Etheridge approached him. Granted thirty days leave on May 13,

---

*William Benson's signature follows Etheridge's on the letter, though it is clearly written in Etheridge's hand.

1865, Draper had returned to Lynn, Massachussetts, to a hero's welcome. He was feted in the community and enjoyed a happy reunion with his wife of nine years and their four children.

As he'd left for Lynn, tensions were rising within the Union ranks. With the end of hostilities, the War Department began to demobilize volunteer units. As blacks had been excluded from service in the early years, the terms of enlistment of white troopers came up before those of the USCT. Large numbers of whites were being mustered out, suddenly "blackening" the army that occupied the defeated South.*

Southerners were none too pleased about this development. Armed blacks in military uniforms, the most blatant symbol of their vanquished way of life, now marched in columns through towns, patrolled streets on provost duty, publicly challenged white citizens who, just a few years before, had been their legal superiors. As if this were not disquieting enough, the black soldiers also sought out the former slaves, talking to them about their rights and assisting them when they felt they had grievances. The USCT was sowing the seeds of discontent among the labor pool, which, during this, the planting season, should have been working the crops, revitalizing the land, and beginning to restore the war-shattered economy. Southerners were outraged.

They found within the conquering army some who sympathized with their lot. General Henry Halleck, who took charge in Richmond, trumped up claims that black troops lacked discipline, were poorly officered, and were "altogether unfitted for the military occupation in Virginia," and he ordered all the USCT out of the city. Thus, Etheridge found himself at Fort Lincoln. Virginia had the largest slave population of any state before the war, and the black soldiers still had considerable contact with many. This created a potential for trouble that, in Halleck's mind, had to be forestalled. In May, Halleck devised a plan to have the USCT in Virginia removed from the state altogether.

Grant had recently sent General Sheridan with fifty thousand troops to Texas in response to the French invasion of Mexico during the Civil War. Grant wanted to make a show of force against the monarchists south

---

*Blacks made up about 11 percent of the Union army when the fighting ended. By the fall, with the large numbers of white volunteer regiments demobilized, the percentage of USCT jumped suddenly to 36 percent of the active forces.

of the border, and Halleck seized the opportunity. He attached the
Twenty-fifth Army Corps, composed of the USCT regiment, to the expedition for duty along the Texas-Mexico border. Draper was summoned
back just two weeks into his leave and ordered to ready his men to move
out for the desert Southwest.

A disgruntled group of men rose to reveille at Camp Lincoln on the morning of May 30, 1865, among them Richard Etheridge. Nothing had yet
been done—nor even promised—in response to the protest about the situation on Roanoke Island. Most of the men, including Etheridge, were still
owed back pay, as much as ten months' worth, so they felt all the more
impotent to help the black community back home. What was worse, after
two years of living in difficult conditions and trying times, fighting racism
within their own ranks as well as armed racists across the trench line aiming
to kill them, they were now being shipped even farther away, to the edges of
the Southern frontier, to a place none was from and none had ever been.

The regiment marched to City Point, where they boarded the steamer
Western Metropolis. Conditions aboard the transports were horrendous.
The troopers lacked proper and sufficient food, and much of what they did
have was rotting or already rotten. Sanitation was inadequate, so they
stewed in their own stench and waste aboard the seagoing vessel for fifteen
days. Men began to fall ill. They suffered from fever and seasickness. Comparatively, Etheridge and the Thirty-sixth were lucky; one regiment, the
115th USCT, lost an average of twelve men per day during the transit.

The *Western Metropolis* stopped at Fortress Monroe, Mobile, and New
Orleans before arriving at Brazos Santiago. The reception was less than
desirable. In the confusion and rush of Halleck's send-off, the army had
not made preparations to receive the USCT. There were no facilities to
accommodate them. The regiment, with little choice, made camp along
the beach, the tents of enlisted men pitched beside those of officers.

Brazos was a miserable outpost on the southernmost tip of Texas along
the Gulf of Mexico. The sun ruled over the land during the day, but the
coast was susceptible to violent storms. A gale blew through camp one
night, taking away or knocking over nearly every tent, and left the men
soaked and without shelter. Former Outer Banks fishers supplemented their
diets with fish from the Gulf, but with the unexpected arrival of ten thou-

sand troops, freshwater quickly became scarce and had to be rationed to one pint per man per day. Some troopers sold it at one dollar per mouthful.

In late June, the USCT regiments finally left the beach and trekked in clammy heat and through clinging mud to Brownsville for garrison duty. For those who had thought Brazos bad, Brownsville proved even worse. "[E]ven the most wretched hamlet of our most miserable districts of the north," one officer said, "would be perfection compared to this place." Here, the men were no longer on the water but at the edge of a stretch of desert plain. "The climate does not suit me," another officer wrote home, "and besides we are kept in constant fear of lying down on a venimous reptile or insect of some description."

For the black troopers, too—most of whom were from the lush agricultural lands of North Carolina, Virginia, Kentucky, or Maryland—Brownsville was a stygian badland of arroyo and rattlesnakes, cacti and pointless patrols in unbearable heat, far from home. Brownsville, like Brazos, was ill-prepared for their arrival, and the black troops were short of food. They lived on half rations, in anticipation of the arrival of a supply ship. When it came, it carried seeds, too late to be of use at that time of the year. Garrison duty was tedious. The USCT suffered many of the same complaints they'd expressed before: abusive officers; heat and disease; reports of mistreatment from their families at home.

Some, though, made the most of their experience, learning to read and write, honing artisanal skills. The Thirty-sixth had good officers and better sergeants. Etheridge remained a conscientious soldier. Lieutenant Colonel William H. Hart recommended him for promotion to regimental commissary sergeant, the departmental commander approved, and Etheridge took over quartermaster duties for the entire Thirty-sixth. He was not only a driven leader, he was an efficient organizer and record keeper.

In late August 1865, General Draper received word that he would be transferred from the corps to command the military post at Indianola. This was sad news. Draper, by his devotion to his men's inclusion and development, had been instrumental in helping them in their transition from slave to free citizen. No one exemplified this better than Richard Etheridge. Draper's departure would be as much a loss for Etheridge and the men of the Thirty-sixth as it would be painful for the general himself.

A few days after learning of the transfer, Draper, while riding outside the base with an orderly, suddenly fell from the saddle and lay stunned on the ground. His orderly quickly dismounted and went to his side. When he turned the general over, he found a hole, staining red over his back. The orderly had heard no firearms discharged, seen no other men in the vicinity.

He rushed Draper to the post hospital. The surgeon on call immediately attended to the wound. He found a minié ball lodged in Draper's spine. He called other surgeons in, had them examine the damage. After probing and much deliberation, the doctors all concluded that they could do nothing for the general. When Draper came to, they told him that, to their great sadness, his chances of recovery were slim. Draper replied, "Gentlemen, I am not afraid to die."

An investigation found the bullet to have been a stray, fired from some undetermined direction and quite a distance away. Probably from some trooper drilling.

Draper's family was notified, and his wife, Sarah, and mother, Hannah, immediately set out for Texas. On September 3, they arrived in New Orleans to the terrible news that three days before his birthday, Alonzo Draper had died. He was just twenty-nine.

None of the troopers of the regiment were able to attend the funeral in Lynn. Townspeople turned out en masse, though, including the mayor and other members of the city government. Several high-ranking army officers, including General Edward Hinks, Draper's commander and friend from Point Lookout, served among the pallbearers. Two companies from a local volunteer regiment escorted the procession. A hearse, covered in black cloth and garlanded with red, white, and blue silk, carried the casket. The Stars and Stripes lay draped over the coffin lid, as did Draper's hat, sword, sash, and belt. Two African-American citizens, substitutes for the mourning men of his regiment, led the horses that dragged the hearse.

A year later, in September 1866, as the Twenty-fifth Army Corps was being regrouped into the Ninth and Tenth Cavalries, the units that would later become famous as the "Buffalo Soldiers," the Thirty-sixth was mustered out at Brazos Santiago, Texas. Richard Etheridge and Fields Midgett did not try to reenlist. They hurried home to the Outer Banks.

7

Home

When a large school is inclosed the pressure of the fish against the seine [net] often lifts it from the bottom, and many pass under the lead-line; but failing to get out at the bottom, they rise to the surface and begin to jump over the cork-line with a rapidity that is truly surprising. Frequently a large part of the fish escape in this way, the air at times being completely filled with mullet. When the water is calm, boats are placed behind the seine to catch the "jumpers," these being completely filled in a few moments.

—*R. Edward Earll, "The Mullet Fishery"*

The Banks Etheridge and Midgett came back to had changed. The population of Roanoke Island had grown, with the settlement at Shallowbag Bay—once called Upper End or Dough's Creek—developing into a regular town. The summer cottages and hotels at Nags Head, destroyed during the war, had been rebuilt in larger number, and people from mainland cities such as Edenton and Elizabeth City crowded the beach late into the season. Investors from New England poked around the island with talk of establishing menhaden and mullet fisheries, and fleets of schooners, barks, and steamers—many hastily converted from warships to commercial ones at the end of the fighting—plied the waters of the sounds. The *Paragon,* sunk by her skipper at the outset of the fighting to avoid impressment into service, was raised and—"as good as ever," according to the captain's son—carried tar and other products between the Banks, New York, and Washington, D.C.

The African colony had changed, too. It was being wiped out, the freedpeople transported to farms and plantations inland.

Etheridge's letter of protest of the previous year had resulted in rations being continued for the families of soldiers; it, along with other letters of complaints, had also set in motion an investigation of Holland Streeter's activities. Freedman's Bureau men arrested Streeter for selling rations intended for freedpeople, tried and found him guilty of fraud and embezzlement. He was sentenced to three months hard labor and fined $500. Horace James, frustrated with the former slaves, interceded on Streeter's behalf, and the bureau reduced the penalty to merely the fine.

James had taken on the responsibilities of superintendent of blacks as an idealistic missionary with a vision. However, the onset of the period that came to be known as Presidential Reconstruction matched a change in his own attitudes. Though staunchly antisecessionist, Andrew Johnson, Lincoln's second who took over the presidency after the assassination, hailed from Tennessee and, soon after the end of the fighting, began to take measures to facilitate a speedy reconciliation between the North and the South. Johnson saw the maintenance of white supremacy in the former rebel states as the only way to assure peace. Policies favoring the established order over black franchise became part and parcel of his plan for renewal.

Johnson's reconstruction strategy included returning land to its original owners. Whites had only to sign an oath attesting that they were loyal to the U.S. government and provide proof of ownership to recover their property. Freedpeople, as a group, threatened the recovery of the South and, by extension, the well-being of the entire nation. Not only had slave labor been the backbone of the plantation economy, but their absence from the farms during four years of fighting and the possibility that, now emancipated, they might leave permanently, posed a serious problem. The president's policymakers deemed it best to return blacks to farming regions as quickly as possible, and James agreed.

Originally, James had staked out twelve hundred acres of abandoned and confiscated lands on the north end of Roanoke Island with the intention of selling it to the former slaves in small plots at a reasonable price. He was even prepared to buy it himself to see this land redistribution accomplished. As President Johnson's policies began to place obstacles in his way, James's vision shifted focus.

He became convinced that establishing the African village on the island was no longer possible and colluded with Freedman's Bureau efforts to break it up and relocate the ex-slaves inland, to the Trent River settlement, near New Bern. Established to be merely a temporary refugee camp, the Trent River settlement, like the one on Roanoke Island, had missionary schools, churches, a hospital. It was situated in the agricultural stretch called the Black Belt, and while, to James's thinking, the African colony on Roanoke depended on fishing and government rations to survive, the one at New Bern flourished and promised self-sufficiency. So well was it thriving, in fact, that the residents had recently formed a permanent town, renamed James City, after the superintendent.

Seeing blacks as of a sort and not individuals with particular lives and histories, James was prepared to indiscriminately remove all of them from the island. With their land gone, freedpeople on Roanoke Island were left homeless, their hospital and schools closed. James radically cut rations, and before long, large groups began being exported inland. In January 1867, the black population, once nearly 3,500 strong, stood at just 950. Many did not want to leave—some because they came from the island— but James made little effort to facilitate their staying. The African colony—indeed, the black presence in the Banks—seemed doomed to extinction.

The Roanoke Island blacks did not stand idle while James and the Freedman's Bureau tried to manipulate them like checkers on a board, and Etheridge, upon his return, fell in and became an active foot soldier in the fight for their right to stay. They penned letters protesting their removal from the plots of land that they had occupied and developed. They were rebuffed. So they offered to pay rent for the right to remain on their lots until they could find somewhere else on the island to live. They described themselves as fishermen, hunters of fowl, and "proggers,"* not farmers, and though homeless, evicted from property reclaimed by local

---

Progging was a local term for foraging for goods and supplies, such as lumber, that washed ashore.

whites, they demanded the right to live out their days in the place where they might "lay their bones to mingle with the dust of their childhood's home." Etheridge signed the petition, lending his name to the cause.

For native blacks and a few others bent on staying, the protest was successful. By the end of the decade, a community of three hundred remained on Roanoke Island, one hundred more than before the war. Some families banded together in groups and bought land. They called their neighborhood California.

In the first years after the end of the fighting, the federal government passed the Thirteenth, Fourteenth, and Fifteenth Amendments to the Constitution. The Thirteenth, proposed in Congress before the war's close and ratified by three-quarters of the states (including eight former Confederate ones) in December 1865, abolished slavery and involuntary servitude in the country. The Fourteenth, adopted in 1868, called for equal protection for all citizens, and the Fifteenth, ratified two years later, conferred universal manhood suffrage. These Civil War Amendments were written with the express purpose of making African-Americans equal citizens under the law of the land. Famed prewar social reformer Wendell Phillips boldly asserted, "We have not only abolished slavery, but we have abolished the Negro. We have actually washed color out of the Constitution." Phillips's optimism foretold a changing attitude in the North.

Presidential Reconstruction had been conciliatory in spirit. Under Johnson's administration, rebel states could be readmitted to the Union by merely accepting the Thirteenth Amendment and rewriting their state charters to account for the abolition of slavery. A group of Radical Republicans in Congress found the president's measures soft and opposed them. Their stance, more punitive in nature, gained support, and when Johnson continued to oppose them, the Radicals called for the president's removal from office. The resolution of impeachment failed by just one vote in the Senate in May 1868, but the event signaled a shift. Radical Republican policy would dictate the reconstruction of the South.

Upon his return to the Banks in 1866, Richard Etheridge did not go to his mother's house; perhaps President Johnson's policies had left her without a home for him to return to. Instead, he moved back in with his former owners. Neither he nor the Etheridges found anything odd in this. This event suggests that Richard's unique relationship to the family persisted after his return from Texas and service in the Union army. Whatever the nature of this relationship, Richard benefited from it.

Their land more or less intact, the Etheridges continued as fishermen and helped Richard establish himself in his endeavors. John B. had managed to retain his local prominence, and had even gained some standing. He and his brother Adam were each appointed a justice of the peace on Roanoke Island immediately after the war. During Reconstruction, John B. held other patronage positions in the local government. His position in the community probably helped Richard solidify his own.

Richard reacquainted himself with the waters of the inlets, sounds, and sea. Like most Bankers, he took up fishing and fowling, progging and crabbing, probably alongside John B. and Jesse T. early on, perhaps also with John's brother Adam and his sons—fifteen-year-old Patrick and fourteen-year-old Adam Jr.—as well as with Adam's son-in-law Edward Drinkwater.

Much as it is today, fishing was a risky business in the mid-nineteenth century. Storms wrecked skiffs, snatched away nets, and drowned men. The fish, many of which were migratory species, didn't always return each season, or with the same abundance. The flowing school of shad that coursed along the shoreline like a vein of silver ore might vanish with a gale. Some years, the water was so thick with bluefish it looked as if a person could walk across their backs; others, they just didn't run. Market value fluctuated dramatically. When the Etheridges were hauling in record catches, so, too, were the Midgetts, Austins, Baums, Daniels, and others. The result was oversupply and a glutted market. Prices fell to rock bottom, and all the hard work went for naught. Then there was the headache of getting the catch to market. Such was the life of an Outer Banks fisher.

Barter had long been the modus operandi in the Banks, but modern times were coming to the coast. John B. shared cash profits with family partners and began paying helpers with coin and notes rather than goods. Perhaps, as a former favorite slave, Richard worked deals with John B. for use of his schooner *Syntax* at a cut-rate price to carry his own takings. This would have helped him launch himself independently.

Richard lived with the Etheridges for a little less than a year, until May 1867, when he married the widow Frances Aydlett, whose husband had died eight months before. In 1870, Frances gave birth to a baby girl. They called her Oneida.

Northern capitalists with an eye to exploiting the abundance of fresh fish established processing plants and fisheries all over the coastal region. Less prominent fishers must have celebrated their coming. Now, these cash-poor men could run their catches to market themselves without having to rely upon more well-to-do Bankers who owned schooners to carry them for a fee. Speculators had explored Roanoke Island as a possible site to erect a plant, but when they did, suspicious locals sabotaged their gear, destroying their weirs.

Richard Etheridge, who was twenty-eight and three years married in 1870, played this new and uncertain game of a supply-and-demand economy. He was a novice, and for him, as for most Bankers, it took some getting used to. Though, as a former slave, Richard faced certain obstacles, he acquitted himself well. Just as it was for other freedpeople, his was the American Dream, only with a black face. He did not want the handouts that Horace James had accused blacks of begging after. Richard did not sue for the property that had been promised him during the war, though some Radical Republicans in Congress still demanded it be doled out. None of the island's blacks did. Richard Etheridge wanted to make his own way. He did not want to see his wife have to work in the homes of others, but strove to provide and create a life for them and the family they would raise.

In 1873, when he finally could, he bought land—two plots, one of fifty acres, the other of sixty-six—near California. The area was integrated, with whites owning lots adjoining his, and three black families—those of John Woodley, Julius Perkins, and Dempsey Baum—sharing an eighteen-acre parcel of Richard's sixty-six-acre tract. Richard's land bordered the Croatan Sound. For a fisherman, this was ideal. From here, he could easily set nets or launch his skiff, which he probably built himself. An industrious Banker using indigenous wood could craft in less than a month's time his own "kunner" (derived from the Native American word for "canoe")—thirty to forty feet long, with a shallow keel for navigating the sounds and a spritsail. Richard and Frances, like other Bankers, also raised crops: corn, potatoes, watermelons, some grain.

He invested himself in the black community, working with others to provide support and to capitalize on opportunities. In 1873, for one symbolic dollar against a tract of land as collateral, Richard loaned the freedpeople John and Eliza Meekins fifty dollars, with the stipulation that they pay him back in two years' time. It wasn't charity: Richard made a formal contract and charged them 6 percent interest. Just as he did not solicit handouts, he did not give them either. A little over a year later, the Meekinses had paid him back in full.

Richard rose to a leadership role in his community. As a war veteran, a former noncommissioned officer, he held a certain status among the freedpeople and felt a continued responsibility toward them. When Amanuel Etheridge, an illiterate former slave who, apparently, was not directly related to Richard, wanted to collect pension benefits for his son who was killed by a shell in the charge on New Market Heights, Richard served as his advocate. Richard composed the letters to the proper military officials and probably also accompanied the sixty-four-year-old Amanuel to Fortress Monroe to claim the money from the military disbursing officer.

Richard had no obligation to do what he did. He was merely rendering a service to a black neighbor in need. He was not alone in this. Other veterans, once they'd returned from the army, also became active and involved in the livelihood of the island's black community. This was true of former USCT across the South. Some who had taken on leadership roles went on to run for public office. Henry McNeal Turner served in the Georgia state legislature. Robert Smalls, of South Carolina, was elected to a seat in the U.S. House of Representatives. Richard, unlike most Roanoke Island vets, benefited from his relationship to the Etheridges. When he could, he used that relationship to assure that the larger black community also benefited from it.

Political redistricting at the end of the 1860s carved a new county, named after the first English baby—Virginia Dare—born in North America, from parts of the three that bordered the North Carolina sounds. Dare County included Roanoke Island and a large portion of the Outer Banks. Upper End on Shallowbag Bay, renamed Manteo (after one of two Native Americans transported to England by the European explorers who first came upon the region), became the county seat a few years later. Another settlement, a fishing village called Lower End, developed into a town and was renamed Wanchese (after the other Native American). About five hundred people lived on the island, with another five hundred living in small communities out on the beach in what was called Nags Head Township.

In 1873, John Wescott donated an acre of land on which to erect a courthouse. This was the site where the new landowner Richard Etheridge deposited his deed. The rewritten state constitution of 1868 guaranteed universal manhood suffrage, and Etheridge made voting-day trips from his house on the Croatan Sound to Manteo to cast his ballot. He had shed blood and seen it spilt for the right to do so.

The Good Hope AME Zion Church drew blacks from all over the island and around the Banks to hear the Reverend Andrew Cartwright's sermons. Cartwright, a former slave who had stayed on after the evacuation of the African colony, spoke often of emigration to Liberia. If Richard, Frances, and little Oneida sat in his congregation, Richard must have dismissed his resettlement rantings as poppycock. Here was home. He was an American. Richard, by his successes, was proving it every day.*

As commercial shipping continued to rise in the years following the war, the dangerous shoals off the Banks posed an increasing threat to lives and property. David Porter, the Admiral of the Navy, had, in 1852, dubbed the lighthouse at Cape Hatteras "the most important on our coast, and without doubt the worst . . . in the world." Congress appropriated $75,000 in 1867 to remedy this problem and better beacon the "graveyard of the Atlantic."

The federally sponsored project brought work to the region and dumped money into its economy. Construction finished in 1870, with "Mr. Hamilton's light" painted in distinctive black and white spirals. The

---

*Within a few years, Cartwright did relocate to the African nation.

Lighthouse Board also hired Bankers to restore the Bodie Island Light, once managed by John B. Etheridge and destroyed by the rebels during the war. It was painted in horizontal black and white bands to distinguish it from the one at Hatteras. That work was also completed the same year. The board then rehabilitated the Cape Lookout Light—laid out in black and white checkers—and set plans to construct another at Currituck Beach, to the north.

The federal government promised even more, long-term employment. Along the coast, highly coveted appointments were to be made for customs collectors, tax collectors, assessors, special treasury agents, and postmasters. For most, loyalty to the Union took precedence over qualification. Between December 1873 and December 1874, the federals would build and eventually staff seven Life-Saving Service stations to safeguard the coast. Positions would be limited, and local fishers, inlet pilots—just about everyone—clamored to get hired.

PART TWO

"National Calamity" or "National Crime"?

*The Life-Saving Service Founders
in North Carolina*

I N THE 1870s, PASSENGERS BOARDED THE STEAMER *Newbern* from Elizabeth City and crossed the sounds to arrive, three hours later, at the village of Nags Head. Lodgings at the Nags Head Hotel cost two dollars a day or twenty-five for the month. The hotel advertised "Bathing, fishing and gunning unsurpassed on the whole sea coast" and was equipped with its own livery, as horseback riding and fox hunting on the beaches were popular sports. Ladies and gentlemen from the upper crust dined on local seafood, fowl, and the house favorite, a soup made from diamondback terrapin. Mostly though, visitors came to take advantage of the "invigorating Sea-air, and the no less invigorating Sea-bath." Bands were hired to play the nightly hops, and the bar was heavily stocked with "London Dock Brandy, Pale Brandy, Holland and Schiedam Gin, Champagne, Madera, Sherry, Port and Claret Wines, and such like."

During the day, there were excursions to the enormous sand dunes at Jockey Ridge, which rose from the maritime forest like the back of a sleeping dragon. Sportsmen trolled at Oregon Inlet for drum or cast in the surf for pan-sized sea trout. Many chose to just lounge on the hotel's piazza and read. The closest newspapers, from Elizabeth City, made for good reading, describing shipwrecks, the relative merits and shortcomings of creating an inlet at Nags Head, as well as happenings in the counties along the inland sounds.

People from the mainland were a general nuisance to Bankers. They trolled into nets, grounded on shoals, or otherwise risked their lives in boating practices whose safety left much to be desired.

Richard Etheridge was never a guest at the Nags Head Hotel. A hardworking fisherman and inlet pilot, he spent most of his days with his feet firmly planted on the decks of schooners and skiffs. The smell of mullet, it seemed, would never leave his body. Plying the Roanoke Sound, he could see the Nags Head Hotel lit among the hummocks, and no doubt he rescued a mainlander or two from embarrassing, if not life-threatening, situations.

Real disasters, the ones claiming lives and valuable cargo, were occurring in the surf all along the Outer Banks. Bodie Island Light, as it swept over the Atlantic, the sounds, acres and acres of yaupon flats, and sand dunes, warned sea captains of the dangerous shoals, but the brightest light for coastal shipping along the Outer Banks was the coming of the United States Life-Saving Service.

8

The Life-Saving Service in North Carolina

The results of the few years of its existence, and particularly those of the past year, demonstrate the usefulness of the Life-Saving Service. The great things it cannot fail to accomplish in the future will force it permanently upon the notice of the public, and it is destined to stand in the front rank of philanthropic institutions of the country.

—*Sumner Kimball, General Superintendent, in the*
Annual Report of the Operations of the
United States Life-Saving Service, *1872*

Shipwrecks have been occurring off North Carolina since European settlement of the New World. For nearly three hundred years, ships grounded on the shoals, pitchpoled in the enormous breakers, encountered sudden knockdowns outside Cape Hatteras, or simply disappeared from the gray, heaving sea without a trace. While men and women carved a new country out of the North American frontier, fighting the Native Americans, the French, the Spanish, the English, and each other, almost no effort was made to save the countless mariners, merchants, and passengers who found themselves clinging to the tattered shrouds of shipwrecks.

Massachusetts first tried to provide an organized effort to assist stranded sailors in 1785, when the Massachusetts Humane Society established a system of unmanned boathouses and shelters for shipwreck victims. In the event of a disaster, the local townspeople were offered rewards if they used the supplies stored there to rescue the shipwrecked. There was no training, other than what these coastal men had gained from their association with the sea as fishers, and the system quickly proved inadequate. The volunteers lacked leadership, and after a time, the unattended equipment itself became rust-ruined and unreliable.

Finally, in 1847, Representative William A. Newell of New Jersey, who had himself survived a shipwreck, successfully lobbied Congress for money to set up shore-based lifesaving houses in the style of those built by the Massachusetts Humane Society. These first federal dollars secured equipment for only the New Jersey coast, between Sandy Hook and Little Egg. The following year, Congress began to allocate funds for "houses of refuge" along the Massachusetts, New Jersey, Long Island, and Great Lakes coasts. They were stocked with lifesaving equipment and supplies such as blankets and food to help stranded seafarers survive. Unfortunately, the unmanned houses of refuge were no more efficient than the earlier ones had been, and many of the buildings soon became weathered shacks to be either rebuilt or abandoned.

Congress remained stingy, with a faction of politicians clinging stubbornly to the idea that U.S. lifesaving efforts could be modeled after the British organization, which was strictly volunteer-based. Then, the *Powhatan* came ashore off New Jersey and two hundred people perished. In 1854, on the heels of the disaster, Congress passed a bill that employed keepers to maintain the existing stations. Still, in the event of a disaster, volunteers had to be assembled to form a crew. These first keepers were often political appointees—a further problem—more adept at receiving favors than taking a seat in a surfboat. Enormous losses continued, often right before the lifesavers' eyes, sending cries of complaint and shame throughout the nation as well as calls for reform.

Though the origins of organized lifesaving are rooted in the experiments and efforts of the Northern coastal states, for decades untold numbers of ships had been coming ashore on North Carolina beaches. The *Henry,* the *Horacio,* and the *Islington* all foundered in the winter of 1820. The elegant steamship *Home,* which sailed right into the terrible "Racer

Storm," was one of sixteen wrecks recorded in 1837. Grounded just one hundred yards off Ocracoke, the *Home*'s shipmates realized they had only two life preservers on board. Ninety souls perished in the surf.

The *Pulaski* in 1838, the *Congress* in 1842, and the French bark *Emilie* in 1845 were all victims of the shoals off the Outer Banks. And the toll continued to mount. The *Mary Anna,* the *Ocean,* the *Magnolia.* During some storms, such as the brutal gale of July 24, 1850, that took five vessels at Diamond Shoals alone, miles of beach would be strewn with debris and bodies. Just how many lives were lost during this period can never be known.

The alarming loss of life off the Outer Banks prompted Congress to allocate funds to station surfboats at Bodie Island, Ocracoke, and Wilmington in 1852, for use by volunteer crews. Despite the great need for more, North Carolina lacked the political influence for appropriations comparable to those allocated to New Jersey and Massachusetts.

In the late 1850s, a small majority in Congress finally acknowledged the need for a publicly funded organization of well-trained lifesavers to safeguard against maritime catastrophes and to respond when trouble struck. The outbreak of the Civil War delayed their efforts, but in 1871, amid continued debate, the United States Life-Saving Service (the LSS) was born as a branch of the Revenue Marine Service of the Treasury Department. The age of volunteerism was over.

The first wave of stations were concentrated along the rocky coasts of New England, but in 1874, seven opened for service along the Outer Banks, in what was designated the Sixth District. Each was situated about fifteen miles from the next, with stations at Jones Hill, Caffeys Inlet, Kitty Hawk, Nags Head, Oregon Inlet, Chicamacomico, and Little Kinnakeet, the southernmost outpost. This left the wildest, most dangerous stretch of the coast, the windy span at Cape Hatteras and its outlying shoals, without any lifesaving facilities.

The task of the newly formed service was to staff the stations with local fishermen who could assist in rescuing mariners in the event of a disaster. The chief of the Revenue Marine Service, Sumner Kimball, a thirty-six-year-old lawyer and shrewd administrator from Maine, took a special interest in the LSS. Arguably, Kimball's vision, more than any other factor, shaped the character of coastal lifesaving in the United States.

In a short time, from 1871 to 1878, Superintendent Kimball was able to convince a skeptical Congress and the voting public that supporting a national corps of civilian lifesavers was both fiscally and politically wise. In a brilliant move, he hired William D. O'Connor, a former writer for the *Saturday Evening Post* and longtime friend of the poet Walt Whitman, as his assistant secretary. A forerunner of the modern PR man, O'Connor, who had the gift of the pen, was charged with preparing Kimball's annual reports. His vivid depictions of rescues captured the popular imagination and won over public opinion to the virtues of the service.

To regularize service from crew to crew, Kimball published *Regulations for the Government of the Life-Saving Service of the United States,* a uniform set of guidelines that were easy to interpret. The forty-five-page book detailed all necessary practices in a simple, illustrated manner, and one was issued to every keeper along the coast.

Despite good intentions, the first seven Tar Heel stations, undermined by organizational as well as logistical flaws, were no match for the wrath of the Atlantic. To begin with, Congress had allotted only enough money to keep stations open from December to March. The stations sat padlocked and empty during the greater part of the year. The building, equipping, and staffing of new stations invigorated the economy, but generally, dedication to the service was largely lacking in its early years. The keeper's position was a year-round job for which he earned two hundred dollars, but surfmen were paid just twenty dollars per month and received no benefits. They would often quit during the bluefish runs in February and March, when they could earn as much or more with less risk.

Some of the first North Carolina and Virginia stations were manned by "checkerboard crews," composed of both black and white surfmen. As many as nineteen African-Americans were listed on the rosters of District Six stations in the 1870s. Many of these men were hired only temporarily, and most were assigned to the lowest ranks, the numbers five and six positions on the duty roster, or as substitutes. They often had to take on a station's domestic chores, usually as cook. When a ship came ashore, the black lifesavers were expected to perform all the duties of a surfman. Richard Etheridge first served on one such crew at Bodie Island in 1875.

In rare instances, as many as three black surfmen would be hired for a single station, and with the comings and goings among crewmen, some of them reached higher-ranked positions than their white counterparts. At the Nags Head station in 1875–76, the inspecting officer discovered that the keeper had hired his own brother as his number one man. Kimball strongly discouraged familial relationships within the stations. The brother was discharged, and George Reed, an African-American, was hired in his stead. Reed joined two other black surfmen already serving at Nags Head, and the crew became half black. As the number one man, Reed was next in line for the keepership. But in an area where slavery had been abolished barely a decade before, it was widely known and expected that white surfmen, despite inexperience, would leapfrog over blacks when it came to earning the respectable position of keeper. A new keeper came in and got rid of the black surfmen altogether.

Although public opinion of the Life-Saving Service would change drastically over the forty years it operated in North Carolina, the duties of surfmen remained largely the same. A crew's most important responsibility was to ensure the safety of vessels passing between their and neighboring stations. With only seven stations along the Carolina coast, though, patrols, which were done on foot, spanned twelve to fifteen miles. This distance was unmanageable, too long for one man to cover. Lifesavers had trouble keeping a close account of all passing shipping over the length of their beat. The long, treacherous marches also took their toll on patrolmen. Some surfmen constructed lean-tos or shacks along their routes where they could stop and warm up, further hindering the efficiency of patrols.

When a surfman sighted a wreck, the time to get back to the station to muster the crew and to return to the scene proved exceedingly long. Many of the stations were without draft animals, so surfmen had to pull the half-ton beach cart filled with their lifesaving equipment through wet sand, often in violent weather. It could take several hours to arrive on the scene of a wreck. Lifesaving involved the arduous task of setting up the "beach apparatus" and pulling mariners in on a line, one at a time, or the back-breaking and dangerous feat of launching a surfboat into the breakers and rowing it to the wreck. The lengthy distance the crews traveled made these already exhausting tasks more exhausting still.

To make matters worse, the service in North Carolina was wrought with corruption from the outset. Although national in scope, the problems of political favoritism and nepotism ran rampant in the South after the Civil War, especially on the local level, and the service in the Outer Banks was not exempt. Today, North Carolina boasts some of the Life-Saving Service's most memorable and dramatic rescues; during those first years, however, lifesaving on the Tar Heel coast left much to be desired, to the extent that skeptics resuscitated the lingering doubts about the wisdom of a federally funded service of civilian lifesavers.

9

North Carolina's Lifesaving Woes

The buildings were found neglected and dilapidated, the apparatus rusty or broken, portable articles had been carried off, the salaried keepers were often living at a distance from their posts, some of them were too old for service, others incompetent, and the volunteer crews were in a quarrelsome temper with each other and the coast population.

—Harper's Weekly, *February 1882,*
on the early Life-Saving Service

Positions in the Life-Saving Service were made by appointment. Keepers were nominated by district superintendents and approved by Sumner Kimball. The keepers themselves hired and fired their own crews from among area watermen. Superintendent Kimball insisted on drawing crews from the local population, which was acquainted with the region's tides, weather, and wind. He also intended for these men to represent the new civil service positively in the eyes of the local community, establish good rapport, and institute lifesaving as a community responsibility. In practice, though, many keepers and surfmen who were not up to snuff found their way into the North Carolina service.

In 1875–76, just a year after the first Outer Banks stations opened, a board of examination commissioned by Kimball to inspect the country's stations toured the district. Of the seventy-nine lifesavers who had been appointed, the board rejected fifteen, including four of the seven keepers. One of these keepers was a teacher, another a blacksmith, and neither had any knowledge of the sea. A third was judged physically unable to perform lifesaving duties and "displayed a shameful lack of courage when ordered out with the surfboat." At one station, only two competent men were found in the entire crew. The most dubious appointment of all was the district superintendent, the region's chief officer, Charles Guirkin. A member of an Elizabeth City banking house and former town commissioner, he held the patronage position of postmaster and was steeped in politics, but had little experience with lifesaving and the sea.

John Guthrie, a Civil War veteran, succeeded Guirkin as district superintendent, but conditions hardly improved. Stations were haphazardly run, patrols were often neglected, and lifesavers sometimes quit their stations for long periods.

The Life-Saving Service officials blamed the problem on "petty local politicians, whose aim was to subordinate the service to their personal ends; their methods being to pack the stations with their own creatures, without slightest respect to use or competency." Kimball recognized that the problem of political favoritism plagued "nearly every new district," but he made a point to call attention to the extent to which the problem existed in Districts Five (which comprised six stations, from Cape Henlopen, Delaware, to Cape Charles, Virginia) and Six. Calling it the "demoralization of 1876," Kimball explained that "[a]ny public establishment seems to be regarded by [the local politicians] as something which may be turned to their personal account and prostituted and polluted for their petty ends."

During the political turmoil of Reconstruction, the new federal jobs in impoverished Dare County must have seemed fertile ground for area politicians attempting to gain footholds. The promise of government jobs was one way by which politicians hoping to win elections could secure blocs of followers. Political patronage could be an especially important tool in counties where the Republican/Democratic electorate was evenly divided and the newly enfranchised black vote might determine the outcome of the election.

Dare was one such county. While its neighbor, Currituck, was solidly Democratic, Dare was hotly contested and could go either way. In the 1870s, nearly half the county's population voted Republican, and about 10 percent of it was black, most concentrated in the area around Roanoke Island. In an environment such as this, political appointments could play a pivotal role in attracting swing votes.

The LSS in the Outer Banks was closely tied to the Republican Party, and many area lifesavers were active in local politics. Edward Drinkwater, the keeper at Bodie Island, chaired the Republican County Convention of 1876. Nominated that day were, for sheriff, Marcus L. Midgett, who would soon be appointed a station keeper, and, for register of deeds, Joseph W. Etheridge, who had served in the state's General Assembly from 1868 to 1871 and who would be appointed district superintendent of the Sixth District in 1878. Etheridge, in his application for the super-intendent's position, was described by one referee as "the most prominent and influential Republican in his County."

Area Democrats certainly believed the service to be an organ of the Republican Party and berated the "Brindle Tails," as they called the party's players, for their supposed kowtowing to the black vote. "Mars Joe," the Democratic *Elizabeth City Economist* charged, referring to Joseph Etheridge, "loves darkness, and retires amid the shades of night to harness into line his colored brothers." Etheridge was active for the Republicans in the African-American community of Roanoke Island, speaking at churches and before crowds of black Bankers.

Drinkwater's political involvement did not mean that he was guilty of making improper appointments at his station. In fact, Drinkwater, who'd served in the Union navy during the rebellion, was judged one of the few first-rate keepers during the LSS's first year in the Outer Banks. The dis-trict superintendent had reported of his station: "House and contents in good order. I take pleasure in recording Keeper Drinkwater's attention to Signals, as well as to his general duties as Keeper." Drinkwater enforced discipline among his men. Still, it is probably not coincidence that many of them were Republicans.

Drinkwater was also one of a limited number of keepers who enlisted blacks into their crews. Most of the African-Americans who served in

North Carolina stations in the 1870s were hired into only a few stations—mainly into ones in the vicinity of Roanoke Island, where the majority of the Outer Banks' blacks resided—and by a few specific keepers. During his five years as keeper at Bodie Island, Drinkwater hired five different black men. He had at least one on his roster each season, and more often, two. Richard Etheridge worked under Drinkwater in 1875.

The African-Americans hired, whatever the circumstances, were quality watermen. Four of the five would serve for at least a decade, and two would become keepers. Three of Drinkwater's five, and six of the ten African-Americans hired into the four stations in question—Bodie Island, Pea Island, Nags Head, and Caffeys Inlet—were Civil War veterans. All were active in the black community. Nevertheless, given the prevalence of patronage in the district and the stature of these men among blacks on Roanoke Island, their appointments probably had political undertones.

In Richard Etheridge's case, he and Drinkwater also shared a connection to the prominent Etheridge household. Drinkwater was married to John B. Etheridge's niece, which probably helped Richard Etheridge get on the Bodie Island crew.

In other cases, because of nepotism, unqualified men found positions in North Carolina stations. Two of the seven keepers examined in 1875–76 had hired their own sons; two others had hired brothers. Of these four surfmen, three were rejected, two for "general debility." The one not rejected was transferred to another crew.

Lifesaving in North Carolina was not in a total shambles. Kimball reported a "pleasing contrast" in 1876–77 to the demoralization of the year before. Successful rescues did occur, but not always in the most expedient or satisfactory manner.

The British bark *Tinto* came ashore at Pipers Hill, four miles from the Caffeys Inlet station, on Christmas Day, 1876. The surfmen spotted her, but after pulling the beach apparatus through four miles of wet sand, the crew could not successfully land a rescue line across the wreck. Meanwhile, the seventeen Scottish sailors, freezing to death, helplessly watched from their vantage point aboard the disintegrating ship. Fortunately, Keeper Malachi Corbell had thought to haul along the surfboat.

Like the beach apparatus, the surfcart weighed a half ton. Though exhausted from hauling the heavy equipment over the soft beach, the crew was able to launch their boat into the angry surf. In the station's log, Corbell described the survivors' reactions to the crew's belated arrival: "many of them <u>very</u> unruly."

The Sixth District counted many good lifesavers in its ranks, but finding good keepers among them proved to be a challenge. Corbell was certainly a capable surfman. The recipient in 1875 of a Silver Life-Saving Medal for his rescue of two black fishermen, he had succeeded Willis Partridge as the keeper at Caffeys Inlet after Partridge was judged unqualified for duty. Once in the position, however, Corbell misused his authority. At least one of his surfmen was a political appointee and incompetent in the surf. Corbell was also caught appropriating government property for personal gain.

The problems in the North Carolina stations set Kimball's service on a course that would jeopardize the very existence of the LSS. Four maritime disasters occurred in rapid succession from 1876 to 1879 off the Outer Banks to which keepers and their crews responded in a questionable manner. Two would put the Life-Saving Service as a whole on trial in the eyes of the nation. All four would impact upon Kimball's own evolving views on the needs of the service, an evolution that would lead to the appointment of Richard Etheridge.

THE WRECK OF THE *NUOVA OTTAVIA*, MARCH 1, 1876

Information has been received this a.m. that an Italian bark, name unknown, in ballast, came ashore 20 miles north of here on the night of the 1st inst. . . . 6 bodies have been recovered and 9 are still missing.

—*Observer, Kitty Hawk, March 3, 1876*

At sunset, the surfmen of the Jones Hill crew could see her off the coast: a bark rolling and pitching in the thick weather and heavy seas. All day, they had watched schooners push by in the freshening winds. There was nothing out of the ordinary about this bark. Darkness fell and her white sails vanished.

The Jones Hill station had the advantage of being directly adjacent to the new Currituck Light. With the lighthouse and the lifesaving station so close, a small community had sprung up. Fishermen and beachcombers alike knew the men in the stations, and their children played together on the sound side of the island, in the calm, brackish waters. Patrolling surfmen always had the comfort of that great sweeping lens to guide their way. On this chilly March evening, the beacon revealed the same bark as seen earlier, this time dangerously close to the breakers.

Just after dark, the bark struck a shoal north of the station.

In the event of a disaster, the keeper had to quickly decide which method to employ, the mortar and shot or the surfboat. The Jones Hill crew had been graded poorly in the use of the cannon by LSS officers. In fact, they had damaged the apparatus trying to execute the drill for the officials. Even though the bark was well within its range, Keeper John Gale decided against attempting the rescue cannon. He ordered his surfmen to haul the surfboat to the scene of the wreck.

Hauling heavy equipment across Currituck Beach was not easy. The area was particularly flat, so much so that an ordinary storm left tidal pools several inches deep for as much as a mile inland. The soft beach made for bad traveling, especially when hauling the cart.

The crew, consisting of Gale, Spencer Gray, Lemuel Griggs, Lewis White, Malachi Brumsey, Jeremiah Munden—a black surfman—and George W. Wilson, a local on the beach that night who had volunteered to fill in for an absent crew member, arrived abreast the wreck and launched their surfboat. Men from the lighthouse, local fishermen, and their families on the beach reported seeing the surfboat clear the breakers "beautifully" and, by the boat's lantern, saw her come under the distressed vessel's bulwarks. The lifesavers maneuvered to the lee side of the wreck and tied up to her with a whip line. Everything seemed to be going as planned.

Then, breaking the chilly night came the sound of horrified men. From shore, witnesses watched the glimmering light of the surfboat's lantern go out. Between the rhythm of breaking seas, men could be heard calling for help.

Four oars washed up in the surf. Then, the surfboat, keel up and empty. Next, the body of Surfman Brumsey came ashore, rolling at the feet of the beachmen.

Most of the events of the night had to be pieced together later. The ship turned out to be an Italian bark, the *Nuova Ottavia*, with thirteen passengers. Keeper Gale, three surfmen, and five Italian sailors were quickly drowned when the panicking Italians rushed the boat. It capsized and spilled the men into the icy, debris-strewn surf.

Some surfmen and sailors were able to swim back to what remained of the *Ottavia*, where they waited for assistance. The crowd on the beach hauled the beach apparatus to the site, but, untrained at using it, were unable to land a line across the wreck. They burned dozens of rockets and fired the mortar until sand choked the vent, but none of them knew what else to do.

For more than twelve hours, the survivors held fast to the remains of the ship, until the next afternoon when she completely broke apart and sank below the waves, taking the rest of the men with her. Only four Italians managed to survive, by clinging desperately to a piece of wreckage that eventually washed ashore.

Undeniably, Gale and his Jones Hill crew were committed to saving lives and did not lack courage. Their actions, however, demonstrated the tragedy of their inexperience. Gale's decision to use the surfboat instead of the mortar and shot, which would have saved the sailors without risking the surfmen's own lives needlessly in the rough sea, became the talk along the coast. Perhaps Gale decided to go after them in the surfboat because of the position of the wreck or for fear of its imminent breakup. Still, he should not have allowed his men to launch without first putting on their cork life belts. Beachmen who transported the corpses to the station, temporarily converted into a morgue, must have been struck by the irony of those seven unused belts hanging from hooks.

Nearly two weeks after the disaster, the keeper of the Caffeys Inlet station recorded in his log: "The Body of Jeremiah Munden has been found [and] Buried By George Scarboug. Munden was one of the Surfman at Station no. 4. His Body is Burried near Paul Gamills Hill." Munden's corpse was a tragic reminder to area lifesavers of the terrible danger of their chosen line of work and of the consequences of errors of judgment.

For the lost surfmen's families, there were few answers and no government pensions. The Italian authorities sent money in compensation, which, when divided among the seven families, came to just fifty-five dollars each.

A year and a half later, two more disasters would strike the North Carolina coast, disasters for which the entire lifesaving organization would prove ill-prepared.

THE WRECK OF THE USS *HURON*, NOVEMBER 24, 1877

> The United States man-of-war steamer *Huron* struck two miles north of Number 7 station at 1:30 A.M. The foremast and main topmast have gone. The steamer is a total wreck. Assistance is needed immediately. The sea is breaking over her, and several bodies have already washed ashore drowned. The number on board is about 135. No Cargo.
>
> —*Signal Service dispatch, Kitty Hawk, November 24, 1877*

The U.S. warship *Huron* had left Hampton Roads on Friday, November 23, 1877, with 132 men on board to survey the coasts of Cuba. Storm signal flags had flown over Norfolk since the twenty-first, and wind gusts at Cape Henry were forty miles an hour. The whole Chesapeake was latticed with windblown foam. From the deck of the warship, sailors could see the roofs of Norfolk, the chimney smoke arching in the wind. Red-painted sea buoys jolted on their chains as the *Huron* pushed past them.

Superstitious mariners recalled the saying that it was bad luck to go to sea on a Friday, and there was almost no naval activity that morning but for two schooners scurrying in from the fury of the Atlantic and the 175-foot *Huron* heading out into it. Captain George P. Ryan, a promising young commander, had asked for a delay in the voyage but was denied. As he navigated the ship toward the mouth of the Chesapeake, the Atlantic heaved and buckled outside the protection of the capes.

Rough seas and a thick fog had settled in, hampering visibility. Ryan chose to take advantage of the currents flowing south and close to shore. Rounding Cape Henry, the 541-ton warship encountered mountainous swells. Most of the shellbacks went belowdecks to their berths, but officers and navigators bent over charts topside, hoping for a break in the weather.

The *Huron* was unique in so many ways. She was one of eight warships built between the Civil War and 1882. Powered by both sail and steam, she was one of the last ships to be built of iron. With iron plates five-eighths of an inch thick in her hull, she was one of the strongest ships in the world. Her four-bladed propeller, which was twelve feet in diameter, pushed her at speeds of up to ten knots. With her full complement of sails aloft and a thin trail of smoke coming from her stack, she had a regal air about her as she inched passed Currituck Light and into the final hours of her career.

After Currituck Light was Bodie Island Light. The dense fog and rain made it impossible to see anything. The *Huron* labored up twenty-five-foot faces and bucked deep down into their troughs. Ryan, with a stack of charts before him, remarked that their present course ought to give them plenty of sea room. Uneasy at the size of the seas, the captain decided to remain at the helm until the *Huron* cleared Hatteras.

During the night, between eight and midnight, the crew killed the engines several times to take depth soundings. All was well—they had fifteen fathoms beneath them. At 1 A.M., officers suddenly discovered there were only ten fathoms between the *Huron* and the bottom. Terrified, they sounded the alarms. Four bells rang out, and the captain ordered the engines forward, but it was much too late.

The ship grounded violently. At first, the officers thought that they had struck a submerged wreck or, as the men shaken awake in their berths below believed, another vessel. Lookouts spotted an ominous sight, the North Carolina shoreline, obscured by an assault of giant, broken combers. The ship had foundered on the outer bar off Nags Head beach. Captain Ryan, who had thought their position to be eight miles offshore, cried, "My God! How did we get in here?"

Seaman Daniel Devoy recalled, "The thump of the ship when she struck, awakened me, and as soon as possible I went on deck. . . . The water washed up the port side and over the forecastle, and I clung onto the iron railing like grim death." Other men witnessed their comrades being killed by falling spars or knocked off their feet and swept away by angry seas.

Military men to the core, the survivors maintained their sense of order. Belowdecks, engineers kept the boilers going in hopes of reversing the engines and backing the ship off the shoal. Others climbed the rigging and cut the sails, while some stumbled along the wave-swept decks and tried to jettison the heavy guns. Ryan ordered the ship's cutter launched, but with a damaged hull, it quickly sank.

Soon, conditions aboard the ship began to deteriorate. Seawater, pouring into the hatches, filled the hold, and the ship listed over at forty-five degrees. The pitch of the vessel and the crashing waves forced men overboard, sometimes as many as twelve at a time.

The summer before, in port of call at Charleston, one of his officers had forewarned Ryan of this. Lieutenant Arthur Fletcher had been overcome with nightmares of the *Huron*'s going down with her crew and had approached the captain with his frightening premonition. "I don't want to go to sea with this hanging over me," he'd said. Ryan dismissed Fletcher's fears, but before leaving port, Fletcher had gone absent without leave. And here they were, not sinking, but pitched on a shoal and coming undone.

Ryan went to launch a lifeboat, a desperate attempt to call on help from shore, but the ship rocked with the violent onslaught of waves, and he was crushed between the boat and the iron plates of the *Huron*. His broken body washed overboard.

A light on the beach gave the survivors hope.

A milky sunrise, November 24, found the remaining crew lashed to the rigging, clinging to the chains, huddled on the forecastle, waiting for assistance from the beach. Gusts up to sixty-eight miles per hour and the frigid sea furthered their agony. The floating debris seemed to drift seaward, and survivors believed the same currents would whisk them away to their deaths if they tried to swim for shore. They had seen movement on the beach. They decided to wait for help to arrive.

They waited in vain. It was still one week before the beginning of the lifesaving season. The Nags Head station, located just two miles away, was unmanned and padlocked.

The fishermen whose light they'd seen during the night assembled on the beach, but no one among them dared to break into the station. They feared they lacked official permission. Even had they broken the lock, none was trained to use the equipment.

They did not stand idly by, though. Forming a human chain, they waded out into the undertow and plucked the sailors who were washed overboard out of the violent wash.

As the morning wore on, giant breakers demolished the ship piecemeal. Each crashing wave took more men to their death. Peter Duffy, second class fireman, later reported, "I was washed overboard twice, but got back to the ship each time. The third time I was washed over too far to get back, and swam for shore. After swimming for some time I was hauled out by some men on the beach." Duffy was one of the lucky few.

Although some managed to make it to shore, 98 of the 132 sailors drowned. By the time the keeper of the Nags Head station, B. F. Meekins, had been notified and was able to summon a crew to the scene of the wreck, all that was left for the lifesavers to do was comfort the few survivors and collect the dead.

In the ensuing days, bodies washed up as far away as Currituck Beach, some twenty miles north of where the *Huron* had struck. The ship's bowsprit drifted ashore with four corpses still lashed to it. Most of the bodies, disfigured and damaged, had to be identified by their tattoos.

The tragedy did not end there. On November 25, District Superintendent J. J. Guthrie arrived at the scene aboard the wrecking vessel *B&J Baker* to attempt to recover a sum of gold on board the *Huron* and salvage what was left of the ship. The *Baker* and several navy steamers were forced to lie offshore most of the day, as the seas were still rough. In the afternoon, Guthrie, the *Baker*'s Captain Stoddard, and a crew of men launched a boat and proceeded toward the beach. Two hundred yards from shore and a hundred from the wreck, a wave caught the boat and shot it forward into the surf. Life-Saving officials observed that "the steering-oar broke in the hands of the helmsman, and a breaker twisted the surf-boat broadside on, and, catching it on the crest of the waves, threw it bottom upward into the air ten feet. All the crew were thrown into the sea." Stoddard, Henry Brooke, an editor of the *Virginian* newspaper, and a seaman managed to cling to the boat and make the beach. Guthrie, however, was lost, along with the four men at the oars. The death count of the *Huron* disaster rose to 103.

*   *   *

Reporters, rushing to the beach to cover the scene, found a detail of gravediggers working nonstop in the dunes, and thirty-four haggard survivors trudging away from the makeshift cemetery. All that remained visible of the *Huron* was a section of the bow breaking the surf at low water.

It was hard to fathom how a warship, designed for battle and described as the strongest in the fleet, could be reduced to wreckage in just a few hours. Rumors emerged over the orders to take the *Huron* to sea with storm signals flying and in weather that was bound to be "dirty." Were storm warnings only for the public? Did the higher-ups consider delaying the voyage? Was the *Huron* as seaworthy as they said she was? Editorialists flirted with the idea that the navy was partly to blame, but focused their wrath on the other government organization: the Life-Saving Service.

East Coast newspapers, whose correspondents had witnessed the *Baker* debacle, denounced the LSS for allowing such an unnecessary loss of life. A column in the *Virginian* explained, "Had the station in the vicinity of which the *Huron* struck been properly manned and in efficient working order, there is little doubt that many, perhaps all of the lost might have been saved from the wreck." Another column from the same paper asked, "If our vessels and our merchants are expected to navigate the coast the year round, why in the name of common sense are the means intended for their assistance limited to one-half year?" And a third challenged, "The loss of the *Huron* and her crew [was] well termed by our contemporary, the *Landmark,* a national calamity—another such occurrence would be a national crime. We call upon the administration and Congress to take steps as to render it impossible. Let them divert a few dollars from the stolen and wasted millions to the salvation of human life on our coast."

Before the Life-Saving Service could respond to its critics, tragedy again struck on the beaches of North Carolina.

THE WRECK OF THE *METROPOLIS,* JANUARY 31, 1878

At 6:05 steamship *Metropolis* struck on Currituck Beach, three miles south of Currituck Light. 248 persons were on board; 50 swam ashore. No assistance from Life-Saving Stations.
—*Signal Service dispatch, Kitty Hawk, January 31, 1878*

The 198-foot steamship *Metropolis* was no stranger to the Outer Banks. During the Civil War, she had been a Union gunship and had served in the 1862 Battle of Roanoke Island. Then named the *Stars and Stripes,* she was one of the first federal ships to pass through the inlet at Hatteras. Grounded on one of the Pamlico's hidden shoals, she had shelled Confederate positions along the thick coastal underbrush of Roanoke Island. After the battle, her sleek silhouette could be seen patrolling the North Carolina sounds until the end of the fighting. After her military career, she was outfitted to be a merchant ship and renamed. Originally built in Mystic, Connecticut, in 1861, her papers were altered to shave nine years off her age.

The *Metropolis* had been hired in December 1877 by the Seaboard and Roanoke Railroad Company to carry light cargo between Norfolk and Wilmington, North Carolina. On her voyage to Norfolk, however, she bogged down. Leaks in her hull dumped seawater several inches deep into the engine room. Her engines were too small for her size, and her pumps were unable to gain on the leaks. She slunk into Norfolk Harbor fifty-six hours later under tow from the naval tug *Pinta.* Her contract was promptly canceled, and she was sent to Philadelphia. Deemed unseaworthy, she seemed at the end of her career.

Surprisingly, a month later, the Collins firm of Philadelphia chartered the vessel to transport workers and cargo to Brazil, where the company had won a bid to construct a railroad. The newly fitted *Metropolis* left Philadelphia with 248 people on board: 215 laborers, 20 saloon passengers, and 13 crewmen. Her cargo consisted of 250 tons of coal, 500 tons of iron rails, and 200 tons of stores.

Rough weather struck the ship soon after departure and dogged her all the way down the coast. The laborers, mostly Irish tradesmen unaccustomed to being at sea, became sick as the ship pitched and rolled in the Atlantic. A strange "jarring" sound in the hold—the iron rails, improperly stored, pitching and shifting with the movement of the ship—made even those who had been to sea ill at ease.

The vessel could have waited out the storm in Norfolk Harbor, but instead, the ship's master, J. H. Ankers, had the crew press on, dumping buckets of coal overboard to lighten the ship's weight. One worker estimated that the bucket brigade tossed fifty tons into the sea.

Lightening the ship brought some reprieve, but the shifting rails continued to bang against the hull. Before long, the seams of the ship were leaking so badly that water in the shaft alley was two feet deep. Engineer Jake Mitteager discovered a leak near the rudderpost that all but sealed the vessel's fate. Water continued to rise in the hold, the engines strained, the pumps stopped, and the *Metropolis* rolled heavily with each swell.

Suddenly, a towering wave broke over the ship, taking with it the smokestack, seven lifeboats, the after-mainsail, and the steam whistle. Freezing seawater in the engine room extinguished the coal fires. The ship lay dead in the water.

Just two months after the *Huron* disaster and only twenty-five miles north of the spot that had claimed her, the *Metropolis* lay distressed off the North Carolina coast. Through the thick fog, Captain Ankers saw a brief beam of light, which he knew to be Currituck Light. He had no choice but to order the remaining sails set and head for the breakers, where he could beach his ship and hope that lifesavers would see them.

High tide helped the ship skip the outer sandbar and slam into the inner one. Believing they had struck land, the passengers gave out a cheer. As the sun climbed up out of the sea, they realized that their ship was still surrounded by violent surf. They were close enough to see the telegraph poles rising from the dunes, but still too far out to swim to shore.

They came up with a plan. Deciding that their best chance for survival was to land a rescue line on the beach, six men set out for shore in the last remaining lifeboat. Tossed across the field of broken seas, sometimes bow first, sometimes leading by stern, the lifeboat somehow managed to get through the raging surf. Their success did the other 242 passengers no good. In the chaos of the moment, they had forgotten the line.

As did many locals, N. E. K. Jones always went to the beach after storms in hope of finding cargo and valuables washed ashore. Accompanied by James Capps, a young trapper, Jones was first to see the vessel in the breakers. Already, debris was in the surf and corpses were on the beach. The older man sent Capps to a neighboring house to get help.

Swepson Brock had been hunting in the marsh near his house when he heard "peculiar cries" coming from the beach. As he listened, Capps arrived to report the wreck. On horseback, Brock dashed to the lifesaving station, pausing abreast of the wreck and waving his hat to let the survivors know help was on its way.

The nearest lifesavers were those of the star-crossed Jones Hill station, which had lost its entire crew in the *Nuova Ottavia* disaster. The new keeper, John G. Chappell, a Currituck farmer and bluefisherman, had been the absent surfman, gone after supplies that fateful night two years before. Chappell instructed his men to pull the heavy beach apparatus to the site, four and a half miles away.

Even by Outer Banks standards, patrols out of Jones Hill were remarkably arduous because the distances to the neighboring stations were so great. The north patrol consisted of a sixteen-mile round-trip over dunes and tidal creeks; the south patrol was twelve miles over expansive tidal flats. Men who patrolled these beaches faced miles of trudging in wet sands and as many as eight hours of exposure to the elements.

Brock arrived at eight-thirty and reported the wreck to Chappell. With the medicine chest across his lap, Chappell dashed ahead on the station's only horse. Here and there en route, he was forced to stop to resuscitate survivors he found in the surf.

His crew completely exhausted themselves pulling the cart through the wet sand. They had only traveled a mile and a half in the first two hours. Finally, a local, John Dunton, arrived with a horse. "They were worn down, it being a bad beach to travel," Dunton later reported. "I hitched on to the cart and was glad to do so. We arrived at the wreck about 12 o'clock."

Some six hours had passed since the *Metropolis* had come ashore. Many of the seafarers had already been washed overboard. Those who remained clung feebly to the wreckage.

Chappell and his surfmen set up the beach apparatus and fired a line out, but the mariners were unable to secure it. It washed overboard. The second shot was perfect, falling into the fore topsail yard. A sailor made his way to the line, but inexperienced with lifesaving techniques, he did not know to pass it under the wire forestay. While he was hauling the tackle aboard the wreck, the rescue line, passing over the wire, frayed and snapped. The shipwrecked victims watched helplessly as the tackle, not an arm's length away, fell back into the sea and swept northward with the current. Chappell went to attempt a third shot, but realized his powder flask was empty. Although the station was well supplied, only enough had been brought for two rounds.

Swepson Brock stocked black powder at his nearby residence. He ran after it. It was quick-burning stuff, though, used mostly for fowling guns, not lifesaving. As there was no time to send someone back to the station for more powder, Chappell decided to try Brock's.

The crew fired twice more. Each time, the projectile parted from the lines.

Without mortar or reliable powder, the beach apparatus was useless to the lifesavers. They had not brought the surfboat. It lay idle back at the station, over four miles away.

Chappell, in a cumbersome Merriman "life-saving dress," twice tried to swim a line out to the wreck. He had practiced this several times, but never in breakers like these. Unable to get past them, he had to be pulled to safety by his crew before he drowned.

The remaining survivors aboard the fast-crumbling *Metropolis,* seeing this activity on the beach, realized that no assistance would come from the lifesavers. With the rigging collapsing around them, they began to swim for shore, singly and in groups of three or four. Few had life preservers. They floated on doors, pieces of wreckage, barrels. Chief Engineer Joseph Lovell waited by the wreck until about 4 P.M., when it was clear the lifesavers were not going to save them. "I said to the man above me, 'Give me a chew of tobacco to give me courage.' He did so and laughed." With a door as a raft, Lovell drifted ashore a half mile north of the wreck.

Many were not so fortunate. Scores were killed, battered by wreckage in the surf, while others simply drowned in the freezing waters. Those who were able to reach land were pulled ashore by lifesavers and local residents. Chappell and his crew, forming a human chain, waded out into the breakers to retrieve some who were too exhausted to stand.

Other area lifesavers began arriving, among them Malachi Corbell, who dragged a man from the sea and resuscitated him. Even Brock's retriever, a noble Newfoundland dog, saved a life. Plunging into the surf, the dog brought to shore a half-drowned man.

Large burning piles of wreckage warmed the survivors while brandy and food were passed out among them. Signal Service operator William Davis arrived from Kitty Hawk, spliced into the telegraph lines, and was able to tap out an eyewitness report to Washington. "State of affairs this morning terrible," he transmitted. "Dead bodies lying along the beach for a distance of 2 miles." Reporters, familiar with the area after the recent *Huron* disaster, descended on the Banks in droves.

★   ★   ★

Mangled and misshapen corpses, grim messengers from the sea, continued to wash up on the beach for several days afterward. In all, 85 of the
Metropolis's passengers and crew died. The 163 survivors swam or were
washed ashore with almost no assistance from the lifesavers. Captain
Ankers, who was wrenched from the surf by the Jones Hill crew, reported
of the rescue efforts: "Had [the lifesavers] come properly prepared, nearly
everyone could have been saved. From my experience here with lifesaving, I consider it a farce."

Ankers and the *Metropolis* owners shared in the blame, but negligence
and poor decision making on the part of the lifesavers played a significant
role in the enormous loss of life. Although the investigating officer labeled
Keeper Chappell "personally an excellent man, and . . . also a skilled surfman," he concluded that Chappell had been guilty of "inexcusable
neglect."

In two months, 188 lives and more than a half million dollars in property
had been lost off North Carolina. Even more than in the case of the
Huron, the public outcry that followed the *Metropolis* disaster churned
through the national press. Some castigated the owners of the vessel for
their decision to put such a well-traveled steamship at sea with such an
enormous cargo. "In England," cried an editorialist from the *Landmark,*
"they hang men for such crimes." Mostly, though, the *Metropolis* disaster
was blamed on the lifesavers and the shortcomings of the LSS.

Harper's Weekly ran an illustrated article as the issue's cover story, and
the *Times* of Philadelphia, the ship's port of departure, detailed the "terrible picture of death" at the site of the wreck. Rumors that mailbags were
robbed and trunks broken into shocked the nation and cast Outer Bankers
in a nefarious light. Journalists even reported that locals had robbed the
bodies of their clothes. Lifesavers and locals at the scene were ridiculed as
unprepared and negligent.

Editorialists chided the wicked impact of political appointments, particularly among keepers, whose duty it was to properly prepare and super-
vise crews. Some coastal voices agreed. The *Virginian* criticized the LSS's
political involvement and called for the whole operation to be handed over

to the navy. "It begins to be painfully clear," charged the *New York World,* "that the terrible loss of Human life which attended the shipwreck of the *Metropolis* on the North Carolina coast Thursday must be attributed directly to the inefficiency of the Life-Saving Service."

The attacks were leveled not only on the Life-Saving Service but also on Congress. The *Virginian* published several articles, one that included a chart demonstrating the unmanageable distances between Outer Banks stations, and passed blame onto the national legislators for their miserly policies. "They knew that the stations were too far apart to render prompt assistance to the shipwrecked, they knew that they were inefficiently manned [and] unsupplied with means of conveyance along the beach. They left a half dozen men to drag mortars miles over the sand, while scores of human lives perished in the rigging and amid the waves."

Before the season came to a close, on February 21, a German bark ran aground at Hatteras, some distance from the nearest station, and all sixteen of her crew were lost. It was a pitiful exclamation point to end a disastrous lifesaving season.

Congress spent the spring debating the future of the LSS. The Senate summoned John Sherman, the secretary of the treasury, to explain its failure in North Carolina. Sherman, using Superintendent Kimball's reports, defended the Outer Banks surfmen for their courage and appealed for appropriations with which to expand the service along the Tar Heel coast and to lengthen the active season.

Critics in the Senate, though, were not calling for the abolition of the service, but rather questioning the wisdom of using a civilian corps of men for the titanic responsibility of lifesaving. Senator Aaron A. Sargent, a California Republican, argued that only with "proper military discipline" could surfmen and keepers be made to perform reliably and efficiently, and he presented a bill that would make lifesaving a responsibility of the navy.

Representative Washington C. Whitthorne, a Tennessee Democrat who introduced the bill in the House, explained that the Life-Saving Service "has now grown . . . into a large service, but it has ceased to perform the high offices that was expected of it, because it has been more or less under the influence and control of politicians and of local influence." He argued that "the purpose [of the bill] really was to make the service more efficient, by a thorough discipline and a thorough organization of this large body of men. . . . [W]e have a large number of men educated at the public expense [at the Naval Academy]. . . who might readily take charge of the whole subject. Here you have the light-house service and the Coast-Survey service under the control of men educated in the Naval Academy. Why not place this life-saving service under the same control?"

Spurred by the lifesaving debate, other legislators introduced plans for an inland canal that would connect the Chesapeake Bay to Wilmington, North Carolina. Ships could travel via a chain of waterways, avoiding that treacherous stretch of coast between Cape Henry and Cape Hatteras altogether. But this plan proved too costly.

In a speech more than ten thousand words long, Representative Samuel Cox, a New York Democrat, argued against Whitthorne and for the Life-Saving Service Bill, H.R. 3988, a substitute to the Sargent bill. Without denying the existence of problems with appointments, Cox deflected blame away from Kimball and his personnel and placed it on organizational flaws that resulted from inadequate funding. "Incompetent persons may get into the stations," he explained, "but the examining boards prevent them from staying there." The real problem, according to Cox, lay elsewhere, and the Life-Saving Service Bill would address these needs in a way that transfer to the navy could not.

H.R. 3988 would make the Life-Saving Service its own autonomous agency, a first cousin of the Revenue Cutter Service (the RCS), and would authorize the establishment of thirty new stations—eleven of which would be built in the North Carolina district, increasing their number to eighteen. This would reduce the distance between stations from twelve to about six miles. The bill provided for the upgrading of lifesaving equipment and techniques and doubled the annual salary of keepers, from two hundred to four hundred dollars. It also authorized the assignment of RCS officers to serve as assistant inspectors in each district. Importantly, the length of service of surfmen would be increased to eight months, from September 1 through April 30.

"Where there is sufficiency," Cox argued, "there is efficiency."

The summer after the *Huron* and *Metropolis* disasters, Congress passed H.R. 3988. Kimball had won a victory, but his problems were not yet solved.

10

The Reformation of the Sixth District

Impress upon the Keepers and crews in your district on your visits to their stations, the gravity of the responsibility which rests upon them as the guardians of the good name and destiny of the Life-Saving Service and the importance and necessity of constant vigilance and fidelity in the discharge of their duties.

—Imperative sent from LSS headquarters to the
assistant inspector, Sixth District, September 23, 1878

Where vacationers at the Nags Head Hotel had swum the summer before, the twisted iron hull of the *Huron,* too heavy to be pulled from the surf, broke the surface of the sea at low tide. To avoid being called yellow, boys ventured out to the spot where so many had lost their lives the year before, the boldest ones diving to the wreck for a closer look. At night, wait staff clanged the *Huron*'s bell, bought at auction, to summon visitors to dinner in the hotel's dining room. Charged by stories of recent shipwrecks and the tragedy of lost lives, the summer of '78 took on a new feeling of adventure, and conversations concerning the LSS burned each night long after the bonfires had turned to embers.

That summer also brought the sound of hammers and saws to the

Banks as workers labored in the searing sun to raise eleven new stations. These new buildings, placed at six-mile intervals, would create jobs for the ragtag fishermen who peopled the coast and, many hoped, give Outer Bankers a chance to redeem themselves. As the workmen toiled along the strand, in Washington Sumner Kimball puzzled for solutions to his personnel problems in North Carolina. A lack of experience may have been responsible, in part, for the questionable decisions made by North Carolina lifesavers, but still John Chappell's "inexcusable neglect" and other similarly inappropriate actions had to be accounted for if service was to improve. The public had latched onto the image of lifesavers fumbling with equipment while bloated corpses washed ashore.

Kimball knew that over time the expansion of service in the district would right the wrongs. Such had been the case along the coast of New Jersey, where, in the early years, corruption had nearly ruined the service. Pragmatically, however, given the public scrutiny of Tar Heel lifesaving, Kimball needed immediate solutions to staunch the wounds caused by the recent disasters.

The strength of the new legislation in combating political wheeling and dealing rested in the service of Revenue Cutter officers. District superintendents were prime candidates for patronage problems. These were local men named by the secretary of the treasury, who himself was a political appointee. Revenue Cutter officers, on the other hand, were accustomed to discipline and military organization. As outsiders, they were also less likely to be susceptible to the will—or wiles—of area politicians.

In the fall of 1879, Kimball sent Revenue Cutter lieutenant Charles Shoemaker, a Union veteran who in 1876 had successfully overseen the reorganization of the New Jersey district, to team with another officer, Second Lieutenant Frank Newcomb, the man recently assigned as the assistant inspector of the Sixth District. The two cast long shadows along the beach as they toured the stations and drilled keepers and their crews. As Northerners, independent of local political pressures, Newcomb and Shoemaker soon came to understand the machinations of the service in North Carolina.

The reports they sent back showed that the criticism leveled against the Carolina service had some credibility. Negligence of duty was still rife, despite the recent lambasting in the press. Assistant Inspector Shoemaker cited five of the eighteen keepers he'd inspected for being guilty of grossly improper service, referring to two of these men as "imbeciles." Of one, Shoemaker reported to Kimball, "if life had been lost [during his tenure at the station] he would have been entirely to blame, and the service suffered accordingly as a result of his wretchedly imbecile course."

Newcomb uncovered another keeper who had broken into and stolen the alcohol from the medicine chest. "Fire-lighting"—the unlawful shooting of waterfowl as they raft on the water after sundown—was common throughout the district, and some keepers absented themselves from their stations for days at a time for this lucrative pursuit. Even more seriously, though, Newcomb reported to Kimball that night patrols, an essential duty of surfmen, had more or less been neglected throughout the district.

For the Northern inspectors, the problem in the Banks was not a lack of competent watermen. Both had encountered plenty of skilled surfmen. "Owing to the general failure of the shad and blue-fish fishing in this vicinity," Shoemaker observed, "the service has its pick of the best men along the beach and they are gradually accustoming themselves to discipline and subordination, although it is something entirely new to them." The problem was the inability of some station keepers to resist the abuse of power. They did not always hire the best men available—some of them having received their own appointments by questionable means—nor did they always enforce order and a strict adherence to duty.

In the worst cases, keepers enlisted men who had no business in the service. One of the "imbeciles" Shoemaker referred to had hired two surfmen whom the inspector described as "cowardly." These men refused to "embark [in a] lifeboat in medium surf." At Caffeys Inlet, Malachi Corbell had hired a man who proved unable to keep stroke with the other men while drilling in the surfboat and who, Newcomb reported, was "generally known throughout his neighborhood, as a worthless, lazy, good for nothing fellow." Newcomb would discover that both Corbell and this surfman had ties to an area politician and that Corbell was using his position to advance the politico's cause.

Shoemaker concluded his fall 1879 report: "In another season it is to be hoped that this district will compare favorably in nearly every aspect, with the other L-S districts." When four lives were lost under dubious circumstances in the wreck of the schooner *M&E Henderson* off Pea Island that November, Shoemaker and Newcomb found themselves pressed to root out the source of the persistent troubles before large-scale tragedy again struck in the Outer Banks.

By all reports, the night of November 30 was moonlit and clear, the wind fair. Keeper George C. Daniels of the Pea Island station reported that Leonidas Tillett, who had just returned from the south patrol, had seen from his position on the observation deck a figure staggering along the beach. Tillett first took him to be a fisherman, but then noticed that the man was not wearing a hat. Native Bankers always covered their heads to protect themselves from the sun or the biting winds at night. Tillett notified Daniels. Daniels mustered the crew.

The exhausted and freezing man turned out to be a sailor washed ashore. The only information that the lifesavers were able to get from him was "captain drowned, masts gone." Daniels reported that they carried the ragged sailor to the station and left him under the care of the station's cook. Then they began combing the beach for other survivors.

Daniels and his crew discovered hundreds of yards of debris washed upon the shore. The trail of rent planking led them to the source: the 397-ton schooner *M&E Henderson,* lying keel-up in the surf, decking and wreckage tossed well up the beach. Her cargo was phosphate rock, and the white lumps littered the shore. No living souls were to be found. A little later, the Pea Island crew encountered a fishing party that reported having come across another castaway sailor, whom they were succoring at their camp. A third sailor was soon discovered. In his report, Daniels claimed to have resuscitated both these men.

Upon investigating Keeper Daniels's report, Lieutenant Shoemaker immediately noted some irregularities. First, the inspector could not explain how Tillett, who had just returned from the south beat on what was reported to have been the "clearest and brightest" night, had failed to remark either the debris from the ship or any of the other sailors. On clear nights, ships are easy to spot; their sails silhouette against the glimmering swells, their red and green kerosene lamps appearing as cataracts on an empty canvas. Near Hatteras, thirty miles south, a surfman had spied the schooner offshore, making her way north. Why had Tillett not noticed her?

That he did not see her as she approached the beach suggested that the patrolman was either careless in this vital duty or was not where he swore he was on the night in question. Shoemaker's further inquiries uncovered a series of problems, not only with the wreck report, but with the running of the Pea Island station in general.

Keeper Daniels, it was learned, frequently left his station at night to go fire-lighting with other area surfmen. Shoemaker suspected that he had been absent for a time on the night the *Henderson* came ashore. Shoemaker also found out that not only had Surfman Tillett been negligent that night, but that Daniels had borne "false witness" to protect him, and that another of Daniels's surfmen, Charles Midgett, was unqualified for duty. Under questioning, Midgett himself admitted that he was incapable of performing the tasks demanded of a surfman.

As the investigation continued, more evidence came to light suggesting that Daniels had abused his power. The inspectors learned that the fishing party was chiefly responsible for having saved the shipwrecked sailors. Shoemaker interviewed the fishermen and discovered that Daniels had not only embellished his report of his crew's involvement, but that he had also neglected to mention that they had forgotten the medicine chest when setting out to the wreck. Daniels had had to dispatch a surfman to return to the station for the chest, two and a half miles away.

To make matters worse, during the investigation, Daniels was bullying surfmen into covering for him. District Superintendent Joseph W. Etheridge wrote Shoemaker that "the Keeper of Station 17 [Pea Island]— Has been using his influence directly or indirectly to get Jesse B. Etheridge #1 Surfman in Said Station to testify falsely in [the keeper's] behalf in regard to said Etheridge's absence on the same day that the wreck came ashore." On the night before he would be questioned, William C. Bowser, a black surfman who had served under Daniels the previous year, sent a confidential letter to the keeper that fell into Shoemaker's hands:

> Sir, I would like to no just what kind of a tail you are going to tell a bout the charge of firelighting I want to no what you are going to do I am ordered down there to morrow   I suppose on that I think we had better tell the truth that we went one time on the Beach as agreed many knows it and we should get ourselves foul most   likely let me hear from you to night. yours truly W. C. Bowser

Under questioning, Bowser told the truth: in the past, he and Daniels had quit the station during the active season to fatten their billfolds. The evidence was overwhelming. Daniels had no other choice but to admit his guilt, acknowledging that he had neglected his duty as keeper.

Inspectors Newcomb's and Shoemaker's discoveries tempered the wholesale enthusiasm that Representative Cox had adopted in arguing the Life-Saving Service Bill. Incompetence and neglect persisted, and unqualified or otherwise unreliable men continued to find their way into North Carolina stations, many into positions of authority. Had the *Henderson* been a large vessel carrying numerous passengers and a sizable cargo such as the *Huron* or *Metropolis*, who knows how many would have been lost to the waves? The *Henderson* affair was a call to action.

For Shoemaker and Newcomb, the chief problem in the district was the lack of reliable keepers. Keepers had to demonstrate not merely ability but also responsibility for the service of their crew. They had to properly prepare their men and enforce discipline. It is telling that a decorated keeper such as Malachi Corbell, who was the first North Carolinian to be awarded a lifesaving medal, would, just four years after receiving it, be dismissed from the service for politicking and mismanagement.

The inspectors would address the problem station by station. The *Henderson* affair gave them an opportunity to resolve it at Pea Island. Newcomb and Shoemaker formulated a plan by which to restructure the internal organization of the crew. To begin with, they recommended that Sumner Kimball discharge Keeper George Daniels as well as surfmen Tillett and Midgett. Under normal circumstances, the number one surfman would assume the keepership of the station for the remainder of the season, but both inspectors avowed that conditions in the district were far worse than normal, and they urged Kimball to take more radical action.

On more than one occasion during his fall tour, Shoemaker had found the cooks or lower-ranked surfmen, some of whom were black, responsible for the only semblance of reliable service that he had encountered. "Such as are surfmen," he wrote Kimball, "[blacks] are found to be among the best on the coast of North Carolina." Newcomb had made similar observations. A letter written jointly by both inspectors recommended that African-American Richard Etheridge, the number six surfman at Bodie Island station, be appointed the new keeper of Station 17, beginning service as soon as possible.

Newcomb, the originator of the idea, wrote: "Richard Etheridge is 38 years of age, has the reputation of being as good a surfman as there is on this coast, black or white, can read and write intelligently, and bears a good name as a man among the men with whom he has associated during his life. . . . [T]aking him all in all, [he] seems to be a superior man for the position."

Shoemaker agreed, adding that, despite his race, Etheridge was "considered to be *one* of the best, if not the best surfman on this point of the coast." He had met Etheridge, and there was something about him that shined. He could read and write, an important criterion for keepership, but there was more: he was sharp, dedicated. Shoemaker, a former military man himself, could see by his bearing the evidence of Etheridge's days as a sergeant in the war, could imagine him leading men up a grassy knob toward a blistering Confederate battery, could imagine him driving his men into the maul of pitching breakers. Newcomb concluded the recommendation: "His Station will be a credit to the Sixth District and to the Life-Saving Service."

Both Newcomb and Shoemaker had considered the risk involved and stood by their proposal. Shoemaker, the ranking officer, followed up in a letter to Kimball: "I am aware that no colored man holds the position of Keeper in the Life-Saving Service. . . . I have given this matter as careful consideration as I am capable of, and have tried to weigh every argument, for and against its adoption, and I am fully convinced that the efficiency of the service at this station, will be greatly enhanced by the adoption of my recommendations as above set forth."

In a surprising and unprecedented decision, Kimball approved the inspectors' recommendation.

11

Segregation for the Good of "Progress"

Keeper Austin of this station would prefer a white crew if choice were left to him. My object is to get rid of the mixed crew.

—*Telegram, Assistant Inspector Frank Newcomb to Sumner Kimball, General Superintendent, USLSS, January 22, 1880*

Nⁱew Year's Eve, 1879. The end of a turbulent decade. The dawn of a new one.

That morning, the lookout atop the Bodie Island station called down to the keeper, Marcus Midgett, that a ship was in distress beyond the northern bar. Midgett rushed from his quarters, up the twisting, narrow stairs onto the roof, and across the widow's walk to the surfman's side. Doubtless, Richard Etheridge and other crew members congregated around the second-floor window to get a view for themselves.

Keeper Midgett immediately spotted her. She looked to be a small vessel, single-masted, and was a mile, maybe a mile and a quarter, out, north of Oregon Inlet. The surf was heavy. Midgett, like all good Bankers, had learned to read the coast before he had script: the intricate seams of channels; tidal currents swirling; waves raking the sandbars offshore. The sloop did not appear lodged on a shoal, she shifted with the sea, but her bow faced the breakers, and she was taking a beating. Midgett called down for the men to ready the surfboat. It was 10 A.M.

The crew donned their cork vests, harnessed themselves to the boat carriage. Two men swung open the boatroom doors. Etheridge took his position beside the boat cart, the leather strap hitched over his shoulder and across his chest. The crew dragged the carriage to the water's edge, unhitched themselves from it, and launched the boat into the heavy surf. The first strokes were always the hardest. Once they'd cleared the breakers nearest the beach, the keeper would steer a path through the broken surf. Etheridge and the other crewmen concentrated on their only task: to keep a steady stroke. Forty minutes later, the surfboat reached the sloop, landing at her stern. Keeper Midgett hailed the vessel.

She was the *J. R. Smith*—headed for Jacksonville, Florida, her skipper told them. Port of origin: Philadelphia. The sloop carried two passengers and a crew of three, including the skipper. They all looked frazzled. The skipper explained that, while passing Oregon Inlet, they'd been obliged to drop anchor to keep from being swept in by the strong current and washed ashore or grounded on a shoal. He did not know how to get clear of this mess.

The lifesavers could not board her there, it was not safe, but they would guide her into the inlet. Midgett hollered instructions. They should weigh anchor and turn her stern toward the breakers. Keep off the bar, if possible. If not, they would get her off. Just beyond the bar was the entrance to Oregon Harbor.

The skipper did as he'd been told, and the sloop came through the rough stretch. Once past the bar, a member of the crew adept at piloting boats—perhaps Etheridge, since he was raised on the waters here—brought her safely through the inlet. The skipper "returns thanks to the service," Midgett reported in his log. For a vigilant, rigorous keeper such as him and a disciplined crew, it was just a day like any other. So smoothly did the rescue go, they might have been drilling with the boat instead of defying the ocean, saving lives.

One month later, on February 1, 1880, the district superintendent arrived at the station, called for Richard Etheridge, and the two headed south, toward Pea Island. Keeper Midgett reported matter-of-factly: "Richard Etheridge absent to take the oath of office + take charge of Station 17."

Each of the men in the Bodie Island crew, some of whom he'd served with since Drinkwater was keeper, watched him go. Among them: African-American William Bowser.

No sad fare-thee-wells accompanied Etheridge's departure from Bodie Island. Some of the crewmen had probably resented serving alongside him and Bowser because of their race and were happy to see the one gone. The circumstances of his leaving, though, must have rankled them as much as, if not more than, his membership in the crew had. Keeperships were much sought-after, and many aspired to the position, including Midgett's number one surfman, Adam Etheridge. Adam, John B.'s nephew, had put in his candidacy for a keepership, once one should open. One had, in place of George Daniels, and a black man had gotten it instead. The resentful surfmen wanted Richard Etheridge and the other blacks gone, but would rather have seen it accomplished under other circumstances.

The feeling of the crewmen at Pea Island about the appointment was clear: when, with the district superintendent, Richard Etheridge entered the station to take the oath of office, the white crewmen—Leonidas Tillett, Charles Midgett, Llewellyn Cudworth, and Jesse B. Etheridge, the brother of Adam from Bodie Island and another nephew of John B.'s—prepared their departure. Not one of them would suffer the indignity of serving under a black man.

Jesse Etheridge appeared particularly unhappy. Under normal circumstances, he, as the number one surfman, should have been put in charge of the station for the remainder of the season. When new candidates were reviewed, he would have been at the top of the list for promotion to the permanent position. Seeing himself passed over must have angered Jesse, much as it had his brother Adam, when, eleven months earlier, Marcus Midgett was selected over him to succeed Edward Drinkwater as keeper at Bodie Island. But for Richard to be the person for whom Jesse was bypassed added insult to injury. For Jesse, serving under Richard would mean subordinating himself to a man who, in his childhood, had been a family slave. That idea was particularly unpalatable.

Also passed over was another aspirant from the Etheridge family:

Patrick. Etheridges served in crews up and down the Banks, most in positions of authority—Adam and Jesse, Patrick's younger siblings, both held jobs as number one surfmen—but Patrick had had trouble getting on in a station altogether. Their older sister Josephene had married Edward Drinkwater, and Patrick had lived with them for a time. Yet though it was clear that Patrick sought a position and was capable, Drinkwater, who employed several African-Americans, had never hired Patrick. After the keeper's transfer, Marcus Midgett let Patrick on as a substitute, and Patrick spent short stints in the crew, but Midgett, too, never employed him in a permanent position on the duty roster.

Recognizing himself to be one of the most skilled and daring watermen along the coast, Patrick did not always bend easily to authority. With the added scrutiny on Outer Banks lifesaving, from both within the service and without, hiring Patrick was a risk, one that neither Midgett nor his own brother-in-law was willing to take.

However these men felt about Richard Etheridge, one thing was certain: all resented the Northern inspector Newcomb coming in, shuffling things around. With the close of Reconstruction three years before came an end to what Southerners saw as Northern tyranny—the national bureaucracy's imposition of its will over local custom. Few whites would see a return to large-scale federal intervention without putting up some resistance. In the Life-Saving Service, appointing keepers was the district superintendent's job and no one else's. The district superintendent, a local political appointee, need not even consult the assistant inspector, if he preferred not to.

In fact, the district superintendent, Joseph W. Etheridge, had spoken against the black keeper's appointment. He opposed the hiring of blacks altogether.

Of all people, Joseph Etheridge was the least likely adversary of black service. During the war and immediately after, J. W. Etheridge had championed black equality. He'd joined the Union army during the fight and served as an officer. Afterward, he became an agent for the Freedman's Bureau. Horace James described him as being "thoroughly with us in respect to Northern ideas, even to the extent of free Negro suffrage." In 1865, running on the platform of "negro suffrage," Etheridge carried two counties in the race for the state convention and, in 1868, was elected on the Republican ticket as a legislator in the only North Carolina General Assembly ever to seat a Republican majority. They were a progressive, reformist assembly and included twenty black legislators; among other measures, they guaranteed public education for both black and white children and even tossed around the idea of woman's suffrage. Etheridge served four years. If J. W. Etheridge disapproved, it wasn't a matter to take lightly.

Specifically, his charge, as district superintendent, was to recommend keepers. He also had some say in whose names would line the duty rosters of stations and whose would not. As the civilian head of the district, J. W. Etheridge was accountable directly to Kimball and, through his various duties, served as an intermediary between the community and the service. His role consisted, in part, of interpreting the feelings and communicating the interests of locals to the bureaucrats in Washington, of making sure the federal authorities didn't overstep their bounds and upset area customs and traditions.

The district superintendent never doubted Richard Etheridge's qualifications for the job, nor those of any of the black surfmen. He was not anti-Negro. Conservatives, in fact, scorned his "negrophilia." But he *was* a native of the region, and he knew his neighbors. He knew that, in 1880, just three years after the end of the unpopular Reconstruction, putting a black in a position that too many white men wanted was a risky business in the Outer Banks of North Carolina.

He reported to Kimball that he had already "thoroughly canvassed" the subject of blacks in the service with the assistant inspector who had preceded Newcomb, a Revenue Cutter officer who had also apparently entertained the idea of elevating blacks to higher positions in the stations. "[A]fter mature deliberation, I stated my opinion," J.W. informed Kimball, "and he yealded and come to the conclusion *I was right.*"

Newcomb, on the other hand, ignored the district superintendent's admonitions. Assistant Inspector Shoemaker, too. Both insisted that appointing Richard Etheridge was the right thing to do.

Superintendent Kimball had waffled. Kimball had recognized early on in his tenure at the head of the branch that, if he aimed to realize his goal of establishing a professional, civilian lifesaving apparatus, the service had to ensure the cooperation and much-needed support of each region's watermen. The LSS bent, and sometimes altogether ignored, regulations and policy when the rules came into conflict with local conventions or popular inclinations.

Kimball usually paid particular care to leave staffing up to his district superintendents. When J. W. Etheridge reinstated a keeper who had hired cronies of his political party, some of whom were unqualified for service and whom Newcomb had urged dismissed, Kimball acquiesced to the district superintendent's wishes. Yet in the Pea Island affair, he hesitated before heeding Joseph Etheridge's counsel.

In mid-January, two weeks after receiving Newcomb and Shoemaker's proposal, Kimball summoned Shoemaker to Washington to confer with him. The recommendation went against Kimball's better judgment, but he knew Shoemaker to be one of his most reliable men, and he wanted a tête-à-tête before taking action. When Shoemaker fell ill and couldn't travel, Kimball further put off making a decision. After finally meeting Shoemaker and more careful deliberation, Kimball concurred. "In view of the report of Lieutenant C. F. Shoemaker," he wrote on January 28, "Keeper George C. Daniels, formerly of Station No. 17, has been removed and Richard Etheridge appointed in his stead."

For Outer Bankers, it was Reconstruction renewed. Joseph Etheridge recognized this. Though, as a former "scalawag," he must have applauded the brash move someplace inside himself, he also understood that it might portend disaster. With the decision now made, he did not wait on Newcomb—perhaps to lend a belated vote of confidence to Richard Etheridge, perhaps in defiance of Newcomb's challenge to his authority. He set sail for Bodie Island on the date prescribed to direct the changes himself, without the Northern official.

On February 2, the day after Joseph Etheridge administered the oath of office, Frank Newcomb returned to his base in Elizabeth City, where official word from Sumner Kimball awaited him. Newcomb understood full well that the decision to appoint Richard Etheridge would be unpopular, and he wanted to be on hand for the changes, as a show of authority or perhaps in case of trouble. He planned to depart immediately, but bad weather kept him grounded in Elizabeth City for two days. When it finally broke, he set sail in the Revenue Cutter sloop *Saville* down the Albemarle Sound to Manteo. He intended to pick up the district superintendent and continue on to Pea Island. He did not know the induction had already taken place.

Whatever apprehensions he might have felt about the coming encounter at Pea Island, even greater questions must have tugged at Newcomb's mind as he sailed down the sound. First and foremost, how would Richard Etheridge acquit himself as keeper?

In another world, Richard would have been the obvious choice. North Carolina crews lacked discipline and a familiarity with the military style that was so necessary to provide proper service. A veteran such as Richard Etheridge seemed ideal. Other military veterans, though few, had performed well as keepers. Etheridge himself had received his early lifesaver's training under one of them. Etheridge was not just a superior surfman, he was also a leader in his community, respected by both black and white. His race aside, he was, without question, the best choice.

The fact remained, though, that Etheridge would not be taking over the way any other keeper might. Southerners increasingly resented blacks, particularly in the tough political and economic times of recent years, and stories of racial strife were rife throughout the South. The Ku Klux Klan had made its appearance in North Carolina around 1868, after Republicans advancing Radical Reconstruction policies had taken over the state. For nearly a decade, night riders had terrorized local populations opposed to their socially conservative ideas, with blacks as favorite targets. In one notably heinous incident, the Klan murdered a black woman and her five children, killing one by "kicking its brains out with the heel of his boot."

Though Ku Kluxers had been active up in Norfolk and in the counties across the sounds, the Klan had yet to rear its hideous face in the Outer Banks. Locals swore the region too tightly knit, the people different from those on the mainland, but Newcomb understood that Outer Bankers, like other Southerners, were willing to take extreme measures to see their will done. Who could know what obstacles might be thrown in Etheridge's way?

And much was at stake, for both the LSS as well as the young Revenue

Cutter officer Newcomb. Reputations. Efficiency in the crews. The future of the entire civilian lifesaving apparatus might be imperiled if scandal arose over the changes at Pea Island.

When Newcomb arrived at Manteo, the district superintendent greeted him with the news that he'd arrived three days late. Joseph Etheridge had even more bad news for the assistant inspector: the four white Pea Island surfmen were presently also in Manteo, "declining to remain at the station under a colored keeper."

An angry Inspector Newcomb called the men in and, in his own words, "reprimanded them all severely" for deserting the station and leaving the crew understaffed. The men asked Newcomb about their employment status—what would be done with them?—and he responded that he was of a mind to telegraph Washington right then for authorization to discharge them on the spot. He did not, though. Instead, Newcomb sent them home, telling them he would let them know the service's disposition toward them.

In fact, Newcomb, though peeved by their rashness, had anticipated just such a response—albeit, one following proper protocol. He wrote Kimball that "owing to their early training and feelings it was not to be expected that they would remain at the station under a colored Keeper." The assistant inspector had counted on their refusal to work under Richard Etheridge to set in motion the second part of his and Shoemaker's plan for revitalizing the district.

Appointing Richard Etheridge keeper was merely a beginning. "My object," Newcomb explained to Kimball, "is to get rid of the mixed crew." He and Shoemaker proposed, and Kimball approved, a plan to juggle personnel between stations and staff Pea Island uniquely with African-Americans. This was the recommendation the Northern inspectors had deemed "essential to the welfare and efficiency of the Service": segregating black service at Station 17.

The reason for the segregation at Pea Island was simple: to put black lifesavers into one station as a way to go on including them in the LSS. Black surfmen numbered among the district's finest—Shoemaker himself had attested to this after his fall 1879 tour. Establishing a station run and manned by them would guarantee they continued to be hired in the Outer Banks, which, after the district's first seasons, was becoming increasingly less likely.

Although two of North Carolina's first seven stations were staffed by checkerboard crews, many whites had resented from the start the presence of the black lifesavers. Service meant living in close quarters with one another for eight months of the year, and many white surfmen did not want to serve alongside African-Americans. They had tolerated it in the early years, but now, integrated crews had become unpopular. Newcomb knew firsthand of this distaste among white lifesavers. Keeper Daniel Austin of the station at Caffeys Inlet, who had inherited two black surfmen when he took over the crew in midseason, expressed to Newcomb his preference for a white crew, "if choice were left to him." The Northern inspector understood that Austin was merely voicing a sentiment that was becoming apparent throughout the district.

As many as nineteen blacks had served in the district during the 1870s. In 1875–76, twelve black men served in four different locations, although only ten stations were commissioned at the time. One-fifth of the sixty positions that season were filled by African-Americans. By 1880, when Richard Etheridge took charge at Pea Island, the number of stations in the district had increased to eighteen, yet only six blacks had found spots on duty rosters. Before the enactment of civil service rules in the Life-Saving Service, keepers had tremendous latitude in determining who would fill their crews, and as the ambitions of Reconstruction increasingly faded from view, white keepers quit hiring black surfmen.

Only a few of them, primarily those active in Republican politics, had employed blacks in the first place. All the black surfmen working in the district in the 1870s served in one of five crews and were enlisted by five specific men. Marcus Midgett, Richard Etheridge's last keeper, did not hire him at Station 16. Edward Drinkwater had, as well as four other black lifesavers, while he ran the Bodie Island crew. After Drinkwater's transfer in March 1879 to Station 2, however, he never took on another. Malachi Corbell, Daniel Austin's predecessor at Caffeys Inlet, had hired African-Americans Lewis Wescott and Joseph Case. Corbell was discharged not long afterward, but when he was eventually reinstated and made keeper at Wash Woods in 1882, he did not enlist any others.

Although one-quarter of all the black men who worked in the district in the 1870s served under Drinkwater at Bodie Island, Midgett and his eventual successors never hired one. Daniel Austin did not hire African-Americans either. Midgett and Austin were not exceptions. Keepers who took over for men who'd previously hired blacks did not do so in filling their own crews. M. W. Etheridge had three blacks on the Nags Head roster in 1875–76, and the following season he hired one. After he was replaced by B. F. Meekins in July 1877, no more blacks served at the Nags Head station.* This increased antipathy toward integrated service did not merely stem from an unease about living alongside African-Americans. More was at play.

Although the LSS continued to expand along the Banks, getting jobs, especially keeperships, remained competitive. More often than not, the blacks hired proved themselves to be good surfmen, capable of the most important responsibilities within crews. Even though, uniformly, they occupied the lowest rungs, these men showed themselves to be qualified to eventually climb the ranks to positions of command; this possibility posed a threat that ambitious white surfmen could not ignore. The case at Cape Henry station best illustrates this.

In 1875, a passing assistant inspector judged the entire crew of the station to be insubordinate, and five of the six surfmen were replaced with black men. As punishment? Perhaps to humiliate the ungovernable white lifesavers? It is unclear. The hastily organized crew performed well, leading their keeper, Jay D. Edwards, to boast that they were "faithful" and "active," and "if an opportunity had required [they] would have proved themselves worthy of the trust imposed upon them." During the next season, however, when one had to be promoted to replace a stricken Edwards, Frank Creekmore, the only white among them, was chosen. At twenty-four, Creekmore was the youngest member of the crew by five years or more, but he skipped ahead from the number four position, passing over three blacks, including the number one surfman, George Owens. This appears to have been a deliberate attempt to avoid promoting an African-American.

---

*Additionally, four other black men served in crews in Fifth District (Virginia) stations in 1875. Two were gone in 1877, and by 1881, the other two had followed. Later, in 1882, John and Robert Smith would be hired by Dunbar Davis at the Cape Fear (N.C.) station. Robert would leave the service the next year, but John stayed on until after the formation of the Coast Guard in 1915. This case was exceptional.

At forty-four, Owens was Creekmore's senior by two decades and respected for his ability. Despite this, when Creekmore himself fell ill during the following season and had to be replaced, Owens was again passed over, this time in favor of William Henley, who was not even part of the crew. That February, Owens's "sound physical condition," "good ability," and "intelligen[ce]" rated him higher during examinations than every other lifesaver in the station, including Keeper Henley. Nevertheless, he was judged not to be keeper material. The following season, Henley chose to not rehire any of the blacks. Owens never served again.

Unlike District Superintendent J. W. Etheridge, Assistant Inspectors Newcomb and Shoemaker spoke for the good of the LSS broadly with little regard for local feeling. Both were steadfast, devoted officers, neither the sort of man to take his responsibilities lightly. For them, charged as they were with overseeing the revitalization of the Outer Banks stations, the likelihood that North Carolina's black lifesavers would be eliminated from the service promised dire consequences for a district already plagued by too many poorly run crews. Appointing a black keeper, then, might offer a solution to the problem of white keepers refusing to hire these skilled watermen.

This is not to suggest that Richard Etheridge was hired merely because of the color of his skin. On the contrary, were he not the man he was, the Northern officials would not have been willing to risk upsetting the area's racial conventions to appoint him. They did not want just any black man. If so, they might have hired William C. Bowser, Etheridge's black colleague at Bodie Island. Bowser could read and write to keep the log, was a skilled waterman and a good surfman. Or William B. Davis: he had been a decorated sergeant of the USCT. They might have recommended some other military veteran; at least seven of the first African-American surfmen had fought during the war. No, Richard Etheridge stood out, not only among the black lifesavers but among all of the Outer Banks surfmen—enough for Kimball to judge the risk worth taking. Still, he *was* black. For Newcomb and Shoemaker, that fact was significant.

Although it might seem surprising, even paradoxical today that many whites, North and South, progressive and conservative, viewed segregation favorably in 1880, it does, in fact, make sense. The Compromise of

1877 that put Rutherford B. Hayes in the White House marked the end of an era. The Civil War and Emancipation were remembered as moral and just sacrifices made by the nation to right the wrongs done in the name of slavery, but Americans considered Reconstruction an example of the federal abuse of power.

While the period had been experienced by blacks as a time of promise, it was for much of white America one of anguish. Reconstruction had come to be seen as a sad era when a handful of Radicals in Congress tried to force a biracial democracy on the defeated South. This resulted in chaos, strife, and eventually violence. Regardless of a person's feelings about the immorality of slavery, the country as it was known before the war was turned on its head when 6 million freedpeople became equal citizens. The persons who only a few years before had been slaves—just three-fifths a man before the law—were an enigma to most; they were much talked and written about, but hardly understood and rarely accepted. Their "place" in society, before circumscribed by the restrictions of their bondage, forever changed—for better or worse, none yet knew—the day the shackles were struck from their ankles and wrists.

No longer bound to the farms, many freedpeople just up and left, or threatened to, in the hopes of finding relatives or communities away from the sites of their enslavement. The South, in ruins after four years of fighting, had to contend with the unsettling question of who, in their absence, would work the land, grow the precious cotton, rice, and other cash crops upon which the region had supported itself. The threat of a black exodus also infected the mind of the working-class North. Would the migrating freedpeople vie for the limited industrial jobs above the Mason-Dixon Line? No one could predict.

Black franchise seemed as great a threat as their newfound mobility. The new citizens would vote, but how, and for whom? Whites, North and South, mistrusted the black voting bloc and angrily wondered if this mass of people, generally considered ignorant and intellectually inferior, would be allowed to determine who ran the nation and the terms upon which it would be run. Would the former slaves, in fact, elect some of their own to positions of power? Whites from sea to sea feared the uncertain shape of things to come and saw newly freed blacks as the source of this social chaos.

The end of the Radical revolution came joyfully to many, for it promised a return to order. The economic depression, lingering since 1873, seemed a more pressing issue than civil rights and race relations in the South. In the most disputed presidential election in the country's history, moderate Republican Rutherford Hayes gained the White House in 1876 by a margin of just one electoral vote on the promise of a return to "wise, honest, and peaceful local self-government" in the South. People read this as a pledge to quit the heavy-handed and costly federal interventions that the Radical Republicans had imposed in the name of equality for African-Americans.

Whereas programs begun during the war and expanded during Reconstruction advocated a strong federal government to protect the rights of all citizens, Hayes, a Union army veteran who had opposed the abolition of slavery, quickly put in place "let alone" policies that favored "home rule." He began by immediately initiating the removal of the occupying troops from the South. He even went so far as to nominate an ex-Confederate for a post in his cabinet. A Republican official from Kansas bitterly summed up the changes: "The policy of the new administration will be to conciliate the white men of the South. Carpetbaggers to the rear, and niggers take care of yourselves."

As the social climate in the South—indeed, in the nation as a whole—veered away from the strides made during Reconstruction toward a more tenuous racial ground in what was coming to be called Southern "Redemption," segregation did not have all the negative associations that would become synonymous with it in the twentieth century. "Whites only" water fountains; tired black domestic workers forced to give up their seats in trolley cars for boarding white businessmen; one-room, ramshackle schoolhouses just down the lane from freshly painted, well-supplied ones reserved for white children—these were not yet the images associated with segregation. Many, Northern liberal and Southern conservative alike, saw it as a forward-thinking response to the societal upheaval that they believed characterized the postwar South.

There began to be talk of a "New South," one in which blacks and whites would share equal citizenship—equal facilities, equal opportunities, equal schooling—but in separate spheres. Henry Grady, editor of the *Atlanta Constitution* and a leading spokesperson, was merely voicing the popular opinion of the day when he wrote in the national forum *Century Magazine:* "The assortment of races is wise and proper, and stands on the platform of equal accommodation for each race but separate." The Reverend Atticus Haygood, president of Emory College and author of *Our Brother in Black: His Freedom and His Future,* a book that received much acclaim in the North, preached the same sermon. Even Thomas Wentworth Higginson, a leading abolitionist and supporter of John Brown who had served as a colonel of the USCT during the war (the film *Glory* would be based upon his 1870 *Army Life in a Black Regiment*), trumpeted this evolution in race relations. In the *Atlantic Monthly,* he applauded the developments he had witnessed firsthand during an 1878 trip to South Carolina and declared that he believed the need for federal intervention had passed.

Though his view smacked of paternalistic racism, Haygood rightly perceived a common attitude among African-Americans at the time when he described a "mutual desire and willingness for separation." Many blacks also favored segregation, if not in principle then pragmatically in their day-to-day lives.

Slavery had been an affliction that had lasted 250 years, its justification based solely on their African ancestry. But although blacks were finally free, whites continued to lord over, denigrate, and abuse them merely because they were black. Sharecropping bound poor blacks to the land, much as they had been during slavery. African-Americans had the ballot, but the Ku Klux Klan and other terrorist vigilantes ran wild in the Southern night, beating black leaders, intimidating black voters, rigging elections, and murdering anyone who stood up for the rights of the freedpeople. Terror forced many to avoid the polls altogether. Soon, men who promised a return to prewar values began to be voted into office.

Former rebel general Wade Hampton, during his 1876 run for governor of South Carolina, toured the state with an entourage of hundreds of armed "Red Shirts," who rallied whites to his campaign while, during the night, they bullied anyone opposed to him. Hampton and his cronies did not fear federal intervention. The new presidential policies promised to let the states alone to run themselves. In neighboring North Carolina, in the wake of a wave of Klan violence, white Tar Heels elected former Confederate governor Zebulon Vance, first to a seat in the U.S. Senate, then, in 1876, following Hampton's lead, to the governor's mansion. Soon, legislation favoring civil rights, written during Reconstruction, was rewritten or struck from the record.

To blacks, the message was clear. Thousands of "exodusters" left the state for Indiana, Illinois, Kansas, or the "Indian territory" of Oklahoma. Those who stayed did not pine for integration—to mix with whites, to eat beside them or marry their children or send their own to school beside white ones. They merely wanted equal opportunities and fair treatment. Equal access to jobs and equal pay. Equal education for their young. Black teachers. Blacks in positions of authority over black workers. Protection from discrimination and violence.

James W. Hood, one of the delegates who had reworked the North Carolina constitution in 1868 to include blacks, summed it up best when he said, "I do not believe that it is good for our children to eat and drink daily the sentiment that they are naturally inferior to whites, which they do in three-fourths of all the schools where they have white teachers." Hood did not favor *legislating* separation, but in his daily life, he made a point to practice it.

In a world seemingly in chaos, segregation seemed a modern approach to managing complex and increasingly conflicted race relations. Both Newcomb, a social progressive, and Shoemaker, a pragmatist with only the efficiency of the service in mind, favored segregation as a way to revitalize the Sixth District. Newcomb was so committed to the value of black surfmen and the idea of segregated service that he later recommended that the proposed New Inlet station, which was scheduled for construction between Pea Island and Chicamacomico, also staff a black keeper and crew.

As for Sumner Kimball, the general superintendent, just two years removed from the heated debate over whether to incorporate his Life-Saving Service into the navy, he realized that he could not afford to discharge capable surfmen merely because of their race. Neither did he want to risk the decreased effectiveness of any particular crew because the presence of blacks within it created tensions. Even though he harbored deep misgivings about taking any action that would alienate the service from the surrounding community, Kimball ultimately agreed with Newcomb and Shoemaker that the move was essential to the welfare of the entire service.

★   ★   ★

Newcomb kept Kimball apprised by telegraph of his progress in installing the segregated crew at Pea Island. First, Richard Etheridge's former black colleague from Bodie Island, William C. "Bill Charles" Bowser, was transferred to the station and joined William B. Davis and William Daniel, black lifesavers who'd been hired by George Daniels and who remained after the white lifesavers' desertion. The station was half-staffed.

On February 5, Newcomb set sail north to pick up Lewis Wescott and Joseph Case, the two blacks from Daniel Austin's Caffeys Inlet crew. On board the *Saville* with him were Jesse B. Etheridge and Leonidas Tillett, whom Austin had consented to accept into his crew. As per Kimball's instructions, the assistant inspector had given Tillett a severe browbeating for his negligence on the night the *Henderson* had come ashore and warned him that any future slipups would not be tolerated. The surfman was happy just to be kept on.

As for the other two white Pea Island crewmen, Llewellyn Cudworth reported to Marcus Midgett for duty at Bodie Island, in place of the departed Bowser. Newcomb discharged Charles Midgett because of his poor qualifications.

Much as it had on the voyage to administer the oath of office to Richard Etheridge, the Outer Banks weather betrayed Newcomb on the trip north. "Slick cams"—glassy, calm water with the absence of wind—made for slow going, and by the next morning the *Saville* had only traveled as far as Kitty Hawk, still twelve miles from its destination. Newcomb stopped at the LSS station there and sent Tillett and Etheridge overland. He wired for Austin to send his two men down. He also telegrammed Kimball, perhaps a bit impetuously, that the transfers had been "perfected to-day."

At noon on February 7, Lewis Wescott arrived alone. Joseph Case had been absent from the station—gone home, Newcomb was informed, "on account of sickness in his family." The assistant inspector sent word for Case to report to Station 17 as soon as possible, then he and Wescott set sail south. The light winds again resisted their progress. The *Saville* did not land at Pea Island until the next morning.

To round out the crew, Newcomb instructed Richard Etheridge to hire two men of his choosing, one, temporarily in place of Case, the other, to fill the empty space on the duty roster. First, the new keeper recruited George Riley Midgett, with whom he had served in the Thirty-sixth. Midgett had been a Reconstruction-era justice of the peace and was highly regarded in the black community. Richard made him the number one surfman. As a sub for Case, Richard hired waterman Henry Daniel, William Daniel's brother. With this, the first black crew was set at Station 17. Caffeys Inlet and Bodie Island stations, which before had "checkerboard" crews, were now all-white.

That Sunday, February 8, Joseph Case returned to Station 10 and informed Keeper Austin that he was refusing the transfer to Pea Island. He told Austin that he wanted to retain his place in the Caffeys Inlet crew.

Case's pronouncement, though perplexing, surprised neither Austin nor Newcomb. As early as mid-January, when rumors had begun to spread of the proposed changes for the district, both Case and Wescott had voiced resistance to the move down the coast. The two disgruntled surfmen penned a letter of protest together that they sent to Sumner Kimball, appealing the order.

> *Dear Sir,*
>   *. . . If we are removed from this station it will greatly inconvenience us both, as we will then be 40 or 44 miles from our homes while we are now only 3 or 4 miles from our home where we can visit our familys between the sun's.*

During the active season, they complained, furloughs would be all but impossible. Also, they enjoyed serving under Keeper Austin and thought that he was "very well satisfied" with them. Apparently, neither man knew of Austin's displeasure at leading a mixed-race crew. Kimball informed Newcomb of the surfmen's protest.

Case was a good surfman. He had assisted Malachi Corbell in the 1875 rescue of two fishermen that had earned Corbell a Silver Life-Saving Medal, the first such honor awarded a North Carolinian. Case's resistance, however, did not fit in with the assistant inspector's plan, nor with the station keeper's wishes. "I did not propose to consult Case and Wescott in the matter," Newcomb responded to Kimball; "they can be left [at Caffeys Inlet] and we can still get a colored crew at No. 17." The simple fact, however, was that Austin did not want them. With Sumner Kimball's approval, the changes moved forward as proposed. Newcomb instructed Austin to discharge Case from the service, which Austin promptly did. Then, Newcomb notified Richard Etheridge to hire Henry Daniel permanently.

Ten days after dropping off Wescott, Newcomb returned to Pea Island to assess the crew. He drilled the men, running them through procedures and regulations thoroughly. They fired the mortar and set up the beach apparatus. They launched the surfboat, practiced resuscitating the apparently drowned; each man rattled off his particular responsibilities to the inspector. Newcomb, perfectly satisfied, reported, "I found them, on the whole, fully as intelligent and competent to perform their duties, as any crew in this District, with the same amount of training."

Richard Etheridge, much like Newcomb and Shoemaker, welcomed the segregation at Pea Island. His men, largely, felt likewise. Here was a place in which they could take pride. Here was a place they could call their own without the fear of random, sudden dismissal if the keeper changed or the political climate deteriorated. No longer would Etheridge nor any of the others be subordinate to less experienced, less qualified surfmen merely because of their race. Here, Etheridge was in charge, and each man would have the possibility of attaining a rank commensurate with his skills and performance. Here they had their equality—equality of pay and of working conditions, under a man who, like each of them, was invested in seeing that equality maintained.

A new day had dawned in the Life-Saving Service. The black surfmen suspected—and, in fact, some actually knew—that trouble was brewing just beyond the horizon, but for the present, Pea Island was President Lincoln's promise fulfilled.

12

Fire on the Beach

My judgment has been against colored Keepers and colored crews entirely, and if every man had gone threw with what I have + knew what I think I know, they would agree with me. The Keeper of this station was competent but the idea was, He is a negro.

—*District Superintendent Joseph W. Etheridge to Sumner Kimball, General Superintendent, USLSS, June 2, 1880*

Trouble was brewing on the beach. The day Inspector Newcomb arrived on Pea Island to run the crew through their first drill as a unit, some of the men seemed unsettled, ill at ease. Lewis Wescott approached the inspector. "Please give me my discharge," the surfman tersely asked. "I wish to better my condition."

Newcomb wasn't totally surprised. Wescott, like Joseph Case, had resented and resisted the move from the start. Keeper Etheridge, though displeased, informed the inspector that he had another man ready, if need be, to take Wescott's place. Newcomb wired the news to Kimball for final approval.

Newcomb completed his inspection tour of the district by the end of February and, from his office in Elizabeth City, sent his report to headquarters. Most crews, as with Pea Island, had shown well. There was the problem of the pillaged medicine chest and missing brandy at No. 9. That same crew was guilty of fire-lighting. Newcomb and the district and general superintendents would have to decide how to handle the problem. There were also equipment shortages in the stations. All needed one-and-a-half-inch ropes, some needed life belts, and others needed rubber tarpaulins to protect their outfittings from the rain. The seven original stations required painting, and all the new ones had poorly constructed chimneys. Newcomb made it a special point to inform Kimball of the latter. He thought them unsafe and warned that the buildings were "liable to be burned down any time."

A few weeks after submitting the report, Keeper Daniel Austin of the Caffeys Inlet station informed Newcomb that one of his surfmen, Walter Harrison, had been absent without leave for ten days. Austin vouched for him, but Newcomb had had run-ins with him before.

Harrison was the surfman who had fared so poorly upon Newcomb's initial inspection tour of the district and whom Newcomb had called "a worthless, lazy, good for nothing fellow." Newcomb's inclination had been to dismiss him then. Since, he'd learned of Harrison's connections to the local Republican machine and was convinced that the man held his position in the service purely for political reasons. With this latest transgression of LSS regulations, Newcomb wired headquarters for permission to have him discharged.

A month later, Newcomb received correspondence from Superintendent Kimball asking that he reply to charges made against him in a letter sent to headquarters, a copy of which was enclosed.

The letter, from Joseph Case, accused Newcomb and his "mear tool" Daniel Austin of playing politics and using the *Henderson* disaster to advance Newcomb's personal agenda of filling the stations with Democrats. "For prejudice he discharged the Keeper Daniels [formerly, of Pea Island] I am satisfied for no other reason than that he was a Republican," the letter charged. "I was discharged from the service," it continued, "because I was a colored man and a republican."

Accusing Newcomb of "carrying on a reign of terror," the letter continued:

everywhere, [Newcomb] has made a party question of the Service. . . .
he has taken all the power from the Supt. [Joseph] Etheridge and he
hates all of Etheridge's friends in the Service and out. But loves his
enemies which are Democrats. . . . Lieut. Newcomb had his plans
arranged with Austin to remove Walter S. Harrison, Lewis Wescott
and myself in the very first of the season because we were taken in by
Capt. Corbell. . . . Austin prefered a false charge against Walter S. Harrison and discharged him from the service and put a Democrat in his
place for nothing only because he was a Republican and taken in by
Capt. Corbell.

Case openly admitted to Republican patronage in the Outer Banks
stations, explaining, "J. Martin owes his seat in Congress to certain republicans that was in the L.S.S. last season who has been removed; one of the
prime moovers was Malichi Corbell who was unjustly charged by
Democrats." And Case raged, "Now I want to know if this kind of treatment is going to be winked at by the higher tribunals," predicting a defeat
of the Republican Party in the county if action was not taken to stop Newcomb and to redress the injuries he had already inflicted.

Perhaps what hurt Newcomb most was the charge that he was racist,
targeting black surfmen because African-Americans were "not calculated
to demand [their] rights."

Another letter, whose author refused to sign his name but was
"reported to be a reliable gentleman," made similar charges that Newcomb pandered to local political forces. Newcomb did not sit on the matter long. He responded, not so much in defense of his name, but to root
out the source of the problem before political forces undermined his
authority in the still-fragile district.

Talk of Newcomb's troubles was the order of the day all over eastern
North Carolina. Dare Democrats knew that Republicans ran the show
among LSS personnel, and they reveled in the chaos among the county's
Republicans and their minions in the service. The *Elizabeth City Economist* seized the opportunity to chide the party: "Surely our republican
managers here and hereabouts are hard up for clothes lines to hang the
bloody shirt upon, if the street rumors that reach our ears be true, about

their efforts to make capital out of the management of the 'Life Saving Service.' We hear that they are making a big cry whenever Lieut. Newcomb removes or appoints a keeper or a surf-man in the Service, and howl through the wilderness, that he is tainted with democracy and perhaps not 'truly loyal.' " The newspaper concluded, "Fact is our cousins are either very greedy or want a United States officer to make no appointments without consulting the bellows blowers and wire pullers of the party and making himself the mere puppet, football and mouthpiece of a ring."

Newcomb sought neither the Democrats' defense nor the Republicans' approval. He aimed to see that Outer Banks stations ran efficiently and by the rules. Like the editors of the *Economist*, the assistant inspector also knew the Republicans had tremendous influence in the district, but he recognized that the Case letter was not merely a case of political in-fighting. Local lifesavers were attacking him and his authority. He knew where to begin looking to unearth the source of the troubles.

To begin with, Newcomb doubted that Case was the actual author of the letter. He knew Case to be illiterate. Even had he dictated the letter, someone else would have had to have helped compose it. In addition, this did not sound like the same man who had, a few days after refusing the transfer, stopped by the inspector's office in Elizabeth City.

Regretful of his decision, Case had sought Newcomb out to explain his situation. He confided that a group of local white Republicans— among them, Malachi Corbell and Walter Harrison—had approached him and urged him not to accept the transfer. These men told Case that it was merely a plot to get all the black lifesavers in one place, from which they would all be kicked out of the service. Case could easily have made the move; he owned no property and could have settled his family on Pea Island. The men had convinced him not to.

Newcomb, now wondering if Case alone had been the target of this underhanded manipulation, traveled down to Pea Island. As he imagined, Wescott had also been approached, but not only him. Richard Etheridge was also assailed with the same misinformation.

This was a deliberate campaign of intimidation to trick the black surfmen into quitting the service. Republican keepers, men such as Corbell and George Daniels, had been responsible for first hiring African-Americans into the LSS. Now, they'd turned against them. Perhaps they wanted to use the black lifesavers to undermine Newcomb's authority. Or, perhaps it was racism, pure and simple: blacks in inferior positions on the duty roster had been fine; now that one wore a keeper's coat, they posed a threat.

As Newcomb returned north to Elizabeth City, rumors reached him that Walter Harrison openly boasted of having authored the letter in Joseph Case's name. Newcomb transmitted all that he'd learned in a nine-page letter to Sumner Kimball, denouncing Harrison and Corbell for their roles in the forgery and troublemaking. Newcomb described Corbell as having "been a source of considerable annoyance . . . during the past season." Since his firing (by Kimball upon the recommendation of New-comb's predecessor, for mismanagement and stealing government property), Corbell had, according to Newcomb, "used every opportunity to stir up discord and lessen [Newcomb's] authority over the keepers and men in the District." Corbell lived in a house he had built beside Station 10, and Newcomb observed that it would be "desirable [and] advantageous to the Service" that he be evicted from the property.

Newcomb felt no need to justify himself against the charge of playing politics. "I do not propose to do the dirty work for any political party," he wrote, "neither do I propose to allow anyone to use my name for the purpose of making political capital." If headquarters did not feel satisfied with his integrity, then he urged them to investigate the matter. His recommendations for Pea Island had had nothing to do with politics, he claimed. In fact, if they had, he explained, local Republicans should have been pleased with the changes, as the vast majority of African-Americans in the county were Republicans, as were the black surfmen themselves. "At any rate," he added, "not one Republican has, to my knowledge endorsed the appointment of a colored man to the keepership of a station."

To close, Newcomb expressed his regret over the chicanery that had cost Case his job. "Case proved himself to be a first class surfman," New-comb wrote, "and Keeper Austin did his best to persuade him to consent to be transferred to no. 17."

Satisfied with Newcomb's response, Kimball let the matter rest. Corbell and his cohort were out of the service and exposed. Order appeared to have returned, with Case the only casualty of the moves in the Sixth District.

*   *   *

At Pea Island, storms came and went, darkening the hull of the recently wrecked *Henderson*. For the men, life went on as before. Richard Etheridge had convinced Lewis Wescott to stay. Daily, the keeper ran his crew through the paces: doing patrols; drilling; and maintaining the station house in top shape. On the last day of April, Etheridge dismissed the black surfmen for the season. They were free to return to their families on Roanoke Island and resume their other occupations. Like all keepers, he periodically returned to the locked station to assure that all was well. On Saturday, May 29, three days after one such trip, the building caught fire and, with a light ocean breeze stoking the flames, burned to the ground.

News spread fast along the Banks. Richard Etheridge immediately boated back across the Pamlico to find that little remained: the bricks from the chimney and scorched beams of the boat ramp; charred ironwork from the house properties made of metal; a stack of firewood beside the stable, just beyond the flames' reach. The outhouse, standing intact west of the ruins.

"I picked up the gun and 10 shot," Etheridge reported, "and the axles of the boat Carriage and hand cart and a few other articles, and deposited them in the Privy."

That same day, District Superintendent Joseph Etheridge also visited the site. Thoroughly unsurprised, he communicated the sad news to both Kimball and Newcomb, announcing that he suspected foul play. "There are two ways to account for this. I am rather of the opinion I shall be able to trace the burning close to some one." He went on to say, "From certain circumstances I am a little suspicious of some parties."

Newcomb, for his part, was outraged. Although he'd had firsthand experience with the racial bias that existed in the Banks, he never suspected, upon making his recommendation to appoint Richard Etheridge, that his efforts would result in so violent an act, particularly considering that Etheridge, a native Banker of some repute, was one of their own. Etheridge and his surfmen were lifelong neighbors. Some were former slaves.

Sumner Kimball's response was both prompt and strained. He telegrammed Newcomb: "Report here in person immediately."

★   ★   ★

Newcomb and Joseph Etheridge spent the summer of 1880 trying to restore order in the troubled Sixth District. They met at Joseph Etheridge's office in Manteo in mid-June and laid out a plan of action. Kimball, perhaps hoping for what would seem the lesser of two lamentable findings, had ordered Newcomb and Etheridge to begin by ascertaining "if there was any neglect or misconduct on the part of the employees or the Keeper at the station." The investigators began by pursuing this line of inquiry.

The two officials arranged to meet Richard Etheridge and three of his men at the charred ruins of the station. They interviewed the keeper and one surfman and quickly exonerated the crew of any responsibility for the fire. Richard Etheridge claimed that all flammable materials had been properly cleaned and stored when the crew left the station the month before, explaining in detail the method used; he also said that he had not lit any matches during his visit of May 26, three days prior to the blaze. Given what they'd seen of Keeper Etheridge's running of the crew and the evidence in the rubble, there was no reason to doubt him.

A more likely candidate than negligence was the station's chimney, which Newcomb had reported to be unsafe. But the chimney, too, was quickly dismissed as a possible cause. Given the absence of fire of any kind for several days preceding that fateful night, the investigators deduced that the blaze could not have originated there. An incendiary device must have ignited the flames. If neither the keeper nor his men had lit it, then who did?

Word up and down the beach, from Kitty Hawk to Chicamacomico, corroborated the district superintendent's suspicion that the fire was the result of arson by a person or persons who lived near the station. Arson was not without precedent in the region. Just the summer before, a similar incident had occurred in Virginia. Station 10, located on Cobb Island, burned just three days before the surfmen were due to report for duty. The investigating officers had immediately recognized that the fire had been no accident. The black powder used to shoot the rescue cannon—ten pounds of it—had mysteriously been removed from the station before it caught fire. The investigators concluded that the arsonist was familiar enough with the contents of the station to know to remove it and avoid the resulting explosion, which might have put his life or those of neighbors in jeopardy. The leading theory was that a local man whose wrecking enterprise had been hurt by the presence of the LSS had lit the flame. Although the principal motivation in the case was believed to be economic, the investigators noted that the Cobb Island station was the only one in the district that still had a "checkerboard" crew.*

With the details of this event in mind, Newcomb and Joseph Etheridge set off for Chicamacomico and Kinnakeet to gather testimony from other locations first before questioning Bankers who lived near Station 17. They interviewed several people. Most believed the fire to be arson, and all roundly condemned it. Asked why they thought it was set, the interviewees called it a case of individual spite.

Newcomb and Joseph Etheridge's inquiries revealed that three parties had been on Pea Island the day of the blaze, one from Chicamacomico, another from Kinnakeet, the third from Roanoke Island. That those groups had been there was not in the least suspicious. Pea Island was a popular spot for progging and fowling. As the investigators reported, "Parties are continually scouring the beach in all directions, hunting terrapin, fishing, shooting, looking for wrecked stuff, etc. In this manner, many of the 'bankers' . . . get their living principally." Neither the Chicamacomico nor Kinnakeet parties went near the station—evidence corroborated this—but they and others testified that the Roanoke Island group had. This last group made the investigators take note for another reason: its composition. George Daniels, the former Pea Island keeper, and two of his surfmen, Llewellyn Cudworth and Leonidas Tillett, were among them.

George Daniels was, in many ways, the most obvious suspect, as his having been replaced for negligence by a black man must have been painful for him. More recently, he had been among those implicated in the misinformation scandal immediately following the appointment and in the smear campaign against Newcomb. Both Cudworth and Tillett had maintained jobs in the LSS, but both had been among the men who had

---

*African-American Warner Collins held the number three position at the station. He would be out of the service by the fall of 1881. Three other black surfmen had served in District Five stations: two who were gone by 1877, and another who served through the 1877 season.

The Outer Banks of Richard Etheridge's youth: "Negro Water Carriers—Hatteras," from the sketchbook of Edwin Graves Champney. Champney, a student of art, joined the Fifth Massachusetts Volunteers at the outbreak of war and recorded in pictures his stay on the "sandy waste" of the Outer Banks from February through June 1863. (Outer Banks History Center)

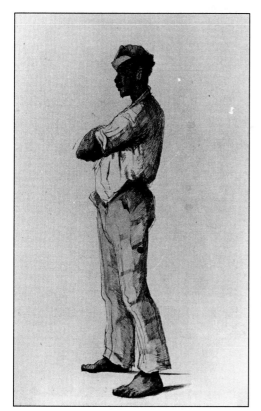

A black Banker, from the Champney sketchbook. (Outer Banks History Center)

Sketch of a U.S. Colored Trooper.
(Outer Banks History Center)

Colonel Alonzo G. Draper.
(Massachusetts Commandery,
Military Order of the Loyal
Legion and the U.S. Army
Military History Institute)

"True Sketches and Sayings of Rebel Characters in the Point Lookout Prison Maryland, by John J. Omenhausser (Prisoner of War), 1865": The bottom rail is on top. (The Maryland Historical Society)

"True Sketches and Sayings of Rebel Characters in the Point Lookout Prison Maryland, by John J. Omenhausser (Prisoner of War), 1865": Guards buying rings from Rebels. (The Maryland Historical Society)

African-American troopers outside of a "bomb-proof" at Dutch Gap. (Massachusetts Commandery, Military Order of the Loyal Legion and the U.S. Army Military History Institute)

Sumner I. Kimball, general superintendent of the U.S. Life-Saving Service. (U.S. Coast Guard)

One of North Carolina's earliest crews (the keeper is standing).
The LSS would not adopt uniforms for crews until 1889.
(Outer Banks History Center)

One of North Carolina's "checkerboard crews."
(Outer Banks History Center)

Unidentified crew practicing the beach drill. (Outer Banks History Center)

"Hauling the Mortar Car," from *Scribner's Monthly,* January 1880.
(Courtesy of Fielding Tyler)

"Drill and Exercise in the Surf-Boat," from *Scribner's Monthly,* January 1880.
(Courtesy of Fielding Tyler)

"Breeches-Buoy Apparatus in Operation,"
from *Scribner's Monthly*, January 1880.
(Courtesy of Fielding Tyler)

"The Breeches Buoy," from *Scribner's Monthly*,
January 1880. (Courtesy of Fielding Tyler)

The U.S.S. *Huron.* (Outer Banks History Center)

The wrecks of the *Huron* and *Metropolis* were top news of the day. Thomas Nast's cartoon of the *Huron* disaster, from *Harper's Weekly,* 1877. (Courtesy of Joe A. Mobley)

"Wreck of the Huron," from *Harper's New Monthly,* February 1882.
(Courtesy of Fielding Tyler)

The "body cart," *Metropolis* disaster, from
Frank Leslie's Illustrated Newspaper, 1878.
(North Carolina Collections)

Assistant inspector Frank Newcomb. (U.S. Coast Guard Academy)

District superintendent Joseph W. Etheridge. (Outer Banks History Center)

The Pea Island crew, 1896. Richard Etheridge stands on the far left. Beside him, from left: Benjamin Bowser, Lewis Wescott, Dormon Pugh, Theodore Meekins, Stanley Wise, and William Irving. (Outer Banks History Center)

Keeper Patrick "Cap'n Pat" Etheridge. (Courtesy of Joe A. Mobley)

Downtown Manteo at the turn of the century.
(Outer Banks History Center)

Wreckage strewn across the beach, 1899.
(North Carolina Collections)

Outer Bankers, salvaging material from a wreck, 1899.
(Outer Banks History Center)

A schooner grounded on the beach, 1899.
(Outer Banks History Center)

The schooner *E. S. Newman.*
(Mystic Seaport, Mystic CT)

Sideboards of ships rescued off the Outer Banks, including the *E. S. Newman,*
displayed at the Chicamacomico Life-Saving Museum. (Michael Halminski)

Portrait of Pea Island surfman William C. Bowser, held by his grandchildren, William C. Bowser III, Pea Island surfman 1935–38, and Izetta Bowser Redmond. (Maurice Duke)

The authors, David Wright and David Zoby, on the beach at Pea Island. (Mimi Zoby)

deserted the station upon Richard Etheridge's arrival and might also have an ax to grind.

Newcomb and Joseph Etheridge gathered as much information as possible before proceeding to Roanoke Island to interview Daniels and the others. Light winds made travel north slow. They landed at Mill Creek, near Daniels's home, two days later. The investigators had evidence about footprints found in the sand leading from the surf to the boat ramp and back to Station 17. They sampled the men's shoes, then took their statements.

Daniels and the others testified that they had indeed been at No. 17 that day. They'd refreshed themselves with water from the station's well upon landing and had recovered a sizable spar that Daniels had found in the surf and left on the beach nearby. The men launched the spar out in the ocean, towed it around through New Inlet, then left the island in their kunner, the spar in tow, arriving back on Roanoke Island between sunset and dark.

Corroborating testimony cleared Daniels and his party. The investigators had determined that the fire must have been set between eight and ten in the evening. The trip from Pea Island, ten miles distance, would have taken three hours, at least. As they'd claimed, Daniels's group had to have left before the torch was lit, removing them from suspicion.

The assistant inspector and the district superintendent returned to Pea Island to take the testimony of the persons in the vicinity of the station. Here, they struck pay dirt.

Three households occupied land on Pea Island: Jesse Etheridge Sr. (John B. Etheridge's brother), about a mile and a half north of the station; his nephew Adam Etheridge, two and a half miles north of that; and Abraham Twine, between the two. Adam was the number one surfman at Station 16, and after interrogating him and his older brother Patrick, who served sporadically as a substitute and was staying with Adam on the night of the fire, the investigators found discrepancies between their testimonies and statements made by others. "Lots of lying has been done by witnesses," they reported to Kimball, convinced they were on the right track.

Adam and Patrick told the investigators that they had noticed the fire between nine and ten at night, but that they had judged it to be a small one. "[A]bout as large as a light house would show on a dark night," Adam said. Patrick said he thought it was probably "someone burning an old wreck to get the iron for his uncle Jesse." They claimed not to have known that the fire was Station 17 burning until the next day at noon when, after a busy morning of piloting boats through Oregon Inlet, they were met by Adam's son and informed of the news.

However, Mrs. Christian Payne, a Banker who was spending time at Adam Etheridge's house helping out his wife, who had been ill, told a different story. She remembered that, on that night, Patrick had come home not too long after sunset from his uncle Jesse's house. She did not tarry upon his arrival, but went up to bed. Patrick, Adam, and Adam's wife stayed downstairs, talking. Through the floorboards, Mrs. Payne heard the brothers mention a fire on the beach.

Payne heard Adam's wife speaking anxiously. Their daughter was spending the night with their uncle Jesse, and Adam's wife was "very uneasy," afraid that the fire might be Jesse's house burning. Payne remembered hearing both Adam and Patrick assure her not to worry, that the fire was not at Uncle Jesse's house.

Mrs. Payne got out of bed and went to the window. In the dark distance, she saw the fire—an aureole pulsing orange on the night sky. It appeared rather large to her, easily large enough to be a house ablaze. And it was definitely in the vicinity of where Jesse Etheridge lived. She, too, became worried. Hearing footsteps on the stairs, Payne left her room and found Patrick in the corridor. "Where is that fire?" she asked.

Patrick assured her not to worry, the fire was not Uncle Jesse's house, and he proceeded to his room.

She only learned the next morning that it was the Life-Saving Service station. Mrs. Payne swore that the fire she had seen by the window looked to be a large one. In fact, she told the investigators, both brothers had, while conversing, commented on its large size and seemed to know its location. This directly contradicted the claims made in their testimony.

Newcomb and Joseph Etheridge pieced together further bits of information that proved to be no less damning to the brothers. They interviewed the captain of the schooner *Pecora*, which had been anchored at Oregon Inlet the night of the fire. The *Pecora*'s captain testified that Adam and

Patrick had been aboard his vessel between 9 and 10 A.M. the morning after—some two hours before they allegedly learned of it—and had told him that the light he'd seen the night before was a burning lifesaving station. Later, Adam also had a conversation with George Riley Midgett, one of the black surfman, claiming to have known at the time of the fire that it was Station 17. He told Midgett he'd watched it grow into a large blaze.

If the brothers did indeed know that the fire was at the Pea Island station, Newcomb and Joseph Etheridge were suspicious of their inaction that night, particularly on the part of Adam, who was in the LSS. Lifesavers who lived in the vicinity of the burned Virginia station reported to have "immediately dressed" and "made all possible speed to reach the station." This was the expected response. Other Outer Banks lifesavers reacted in this way to the Pea Island fire. Although its tremendous size led the keepers of nearby Stations 18 and 20 to think "it to be a large vessel burning with an inflammable cargo on board," they still mounted horses and rode up the beach to investigate when they first spotted it. Separated by New Inlet and unable to find a boat to cross, they could not act further on their suspicions.

Adam, on the other hand, did nothing. He could have traveled down the beach to investigate. He did not. Once he knew for sure that it was the station burning, he could have made a trip to Roanoke Island in six hours or less round-trip to notify the district superintendent. Or alternatively, he might have sent word by vessel to Newcomb at his base in Elizabeth City, "with little trouble to himself."

"Adam Etheridge is surfman No. 1 in Station No. 16, and is an applicant for the position of Keeper," Newcomb reported to Kimball; "it would naturally be expected that he would consider it to be his duty to inform the Officers of the District of a case of this kind."

The investigators learned other troubling information about Adam Etheridge. Some of his fellow surfmen at No. 16 reported that he had been heard commenting "that it would be an easy matter for a surfman who had a falling out with his Keeper, to set a station on fire, or to break into it and . . . injure the property in such a manner as to throw the blame on the Keeper and cause his dismissal from the Service."

★   ★   ★

Evidence pointed strongly toward the Etheridge brothers. A third man, William P. Clark, who also filled in from time to time as a substitute at Station 16 and was a guest at Jesse Etheridge's house the night of the fire, implicated himself along with Adam and Patrick by corroborating in separate testimony their "small fire" lie. Clark's shoes matched, in size and type, the prints found in the sand. Patrick's shoes had also matched. Both had a motive: they only served occasionally in the LSS and wanted positions. The investigators reasoned that they "probably thought that the burning of the station would occasion a change in the Keepership."

Though damning, the case against the Etheridges and Clark was circumstantial and inconclusive. The investigators needed a smoking gun. To turn one up, Newcomb recommended that a reward be offered, as had been done in Virginia. "I find that the people everywhere condemn the burning of Station No. 17," he wrote, "and still incline to the opinion that it was a case of individual spite." The money might induce one to give up the evidence that the investigators still lacked.

Kimball agreed. Posters were printed and put up in prominent places along the coast.

Reward of 300 $ offered for information leading to the apprehension and conviction of party or parties who set fire to life-saving station at Pea Island

Both Newcomb and District Superintendent Etheridge knew that certain individuals could identify the culprits. Newcomb thought it only "a question of time to get at the truth of the matter."

But time played against him. The reward tempted many, but no one came forward. Soon, Newcomb became seriously ill from exposure to the Outer Banks sun. He was laid up for more than a month, incapacitated, and the investigation stalled.

At the end of the scorching summer, the investigators sent their report to Kimball. In it, they accused Adam and Patrick Etheridge and William Clark of, at the very least, suppressing "facts known to them about the fire, which would tend to throw more light upon the subject and perhaps lead to the apprehension of the perpetrators of the deed." As employees of the LSS, this charge was serious. But Newcomb and Joseph Etheridge thought them guilty of a more serious crime still.

Their twenty-one-page report laid out the facts of their inquiry and the information they'd been able to gather, concluding: "The inference is, though merely supposition, that Patrick H. Etheridge set the station on fire after he left his Uncle Jesse's house to go to his brother Adam's, or what is more probable, that Wm. P. Clark was employed by Patrick to set the station on fire, the object being, to secure the removal of the present colored Keeper, thus enabling Patrick to succeed him and giving Clark a situation as surfman in the station." Although convinced of the involvement of William Clark and Adam Etheridge, the investigators were especially suspicious of Patrick. He was known to be volatile, and they thought him capable of violence. He seemed to them to be the ringleader.

For Patrick and William Clark, who had yet to find permanent jobs in the LSS, an all-black Pea Island station threatened their chances of ever being hired at all. Adam Etheridge's motivation is harder to explain. He held a ranking position in a station, but apparently had greater ambitions. In the limited economy of the Outer Banks, having a site of possible employment closed to him—one near his home—and restricted exclusively to blacks might have seemed to limit his chances of rising to a keepership.

The season before, Adam and Richard had served side by side in the Oregon Inlet crew, Adam as number one, Richard as number six. For a period while substituting for Adam, Patrick had also worked beside Richard. A black man, their former slave, skipping ahead of them in rank may also have sparked some resentment in the brothers.

Exacerbating it all may have been some family issues. If John B., the brothers' uncle, was Richard's father, then Richard would have been first cousin to Adam and Patrick. Whether or not the investigators were aware of the possible connection is not known.

Newcomb and Joseph Etheridge closed their report: "Whether the facts are sufficiently strong to warrant the arrest of any or all of the suspected parties, we leave for the Department to decide."

Sumner Kimball decided not to act. He authorized Newcomb and Joseph Etheridge to continue their investigation "as opportunity may offer," but he did not press charges. He did not censure Adam Etheridge, whom the investigators accused of withholding information and who, at the very least, should in some way have responded to the fire when he learned of it. Keeper Marcus Midgett rehired Adam the following season as his number one man at Station 16.

Kimball went on to act in an even more suspect manner. Just two years later, he authorized the hiring of Patrick Etheridge as the number one surfman at Big Kinnakeet station, despite the strong likelihood of Patrick's knowledge of and possible involvement in the Pea Island fire. A mere two years after that, upon the recommendation of none other than Joseph Etheridge himself, Kimball approved Patrick's appointment to the keepership at neighboring Creeds Hill.

While surprising, Kimball's actions made good sense. The *Metropolis* and *Huron* fiascoes were not so long passed that they had faded from memory. The *Henderson* affair, though more limited in scope, showed that grave personnel problems still marred the service—and this, just as the LSS was attempting to expand.

For Kimball, the bottom line was establishing an efficient coastal lifesaving system. To accomplish this, he needed effective keepers to hire and maintain competent crews. In District Six, dangerously unqualified men had to be replaced, but so severe was the need for capable candidates that, in some egregious cases of neglect of duty or improper conduct, Kimball opted to censure rather than discharge the men involved.

Though found guilty, Avery Austin, the fire-lighting keeper who also stole the alcohol from his medicine chest and replaced it with water, and the three surfmen implicated alongside him, were merely reprimanded. Taking stronger action against them would have meant replacing four of the seven men in that crew. B. F. Meekins, the keeper of the Nags Head station whom Shoemaker had described the fall before as "wretchedly imbecile," retained his position. In the case of George Daniels, he resigned from the service—he was not fired. The LSS was prepared to keep him on as a surfman at a neighboring station.

It was this same logic that had led Kimball to appoint Richard Etheridge keeper and put in place the all-black crew. Kimball did not dismiss the Etheridge brothers because, pragmatically, he could not afford to. In a district where too many men of suspect ability were still employed, the general superintendent could afford neither to lose the service of qualified lifesavers such as Patrick and Adam nor to alienate the larger Etheridge clan. Etheridges peppered the rolls of district stations. Also, family members had served in other, influential elected and patronage positions: lighthouse keeper, justice of the peace, magistrate, county commissioner, wrecks master. Alienating the Etheridges could cripple the Outer Banks service.

Kimball understood that, in addition to good keepers and surfmen to people his crews, he also needed local goodwill if he hoped to make the civilian Life-Saving Service work. The fire and the silence that surrounded it were proof that Outer Bankers chafed at the government moves made at Pea Island. To Joseph Etheridge, it had been clear all along that efficiency would not be promoted by having the service appear to be a reincarnation of the postwar occupation against which Southerners, North Carolinians, and Outer Bankers had fiercely fought, and he stated as much to Sumner Kimball in the letter he wrote upon learning of the fire. As much as the arsonists, Joseph Etheridge lay blame for the fire on the myopia of the outside forces from the North: Kimball, Newcomb, and Shoemaker.

Kimball had ignored the early warning, and the Life-Saving Service had toyed with appointments made by Bankers on their own terms. Bankers, in turn, had lashed out against the outsiders who had interfered with local self-rule. The trickery against Case and the rest, the personal attacks against Newcomb, the fire, were as much resistance aimed at "big government"—at the federal building, at the Northern official—as they were a reminder to the blacks themselves to remember their place.

Now, the LSS had to deal with the consequences and make things right in the district.

Fortunately for the black lifesavers, Sumner Kimball still needed their valuable service as much as he did that of the Etheridges. He categorically dismissed Newcomb's recommendation that the station planned for construction at New Inlet also house a black crew, but he did not replace Richard Etheridge.

The investigators made no further reports on the fire, nor did Kimball push for more concrete answers. The service's *Annual Report* tersely described the fire and the failure of the reward to glean the information necessary to definitively ascertain its source. With that, the case came to a quiet close.

For their parts, Richard Etheridge and his crew refused to be victims of the chaos. The season following the fire, Etheridge hired the exact same crew he had had the February before. No one was frightened away by the events of the summer. The stables were made into an "impromptu station," and the men resumed their lifesaving duties. They patrolled the dark beaches, alert for signs of distress. They drilled in a new boat and with the fire-scarred Lyle gun.

The job of erecting the new station was contracted out to a Norfolk man, but the isolation of the location slowed reconstruction as amassing the necessary materials took longer than expected. Keeper Etheridge posted a guard in the dunes to protect the lumber and supplies. The armed black man sent an indelible message to any would-be saboteurs about the unwillingness of the Pea Island surfmen to let themselves be trampled upon.

With Newcomb based on the premises to oversee the operation, laborers finally began work on October 19 and continued through the New Year. On January 26, 1881, the new Pea Island station was ready for occupancy.

As mentioned earlier, although discrimination had deep roots in the Outer Banks service, segregation was the result of directives from Northern administrators, not of local racism. The district had no segregationist tradition before Richard Etheridge's appointment. Not only had blacks and whites served together in checkerboard crews, but in the community as a whole, blacks and whites had worked side by side; some lived in the same households, in a few, rare instances, in legal marriages. Blacks in their "place" was a way of life in the Banks, but that place, while subordinate, was not in a separate sphere from whites.

Things were changing, though. The specter that blacks might rule over whites was anathema in the North Carolina stations, notably among those men who had, quite likely for political reasons, hired blacks to begin with. As elsewhere in the South, segregationist values began to seem increasingly palatable to Outer Bankers.

Richard Etheridge did not misread the message in the tumultuous events of his first year in charge of the crew. He understood that No. 17 would be the only station in which African-Americans would have the opportunity to serve. So he made sure that, on his watch, Pea Island would staff an all-black crew. No. 17 was a place where blacks were in control of their own destinies. Not only were they included in coastal lifesaving, but they received equal pay, had comparable equipment, and were led by one of their own.

Even segregated, though, their future was not guaranteed. Etheridge understood that their allies were few, and that scrutinizing eyes were everywhere. This meant there was no room for error. The continuation of the black station could be compromised by any slipup, no matter how slight. Misjudgment or poor performance could result in his or one of his crewmen's dismissal. Inadequacies, no matter how small, could lead to the reinstatement of a white keeper and crew. They had to excel if they were to maintain their station.

Recognizing this, Etheridge made sure that improper service would no more play a role in undoing his crew than violence and intimidation had. He communicated this message to his men by the demands he put upon them. Etheridge drove them hard. If one did not respond in a manner befitting his expectations, Etheridge knew to let that man go. Inappropriate behavior as much as ineffectual performance could spell the end.

PART THREE

The Life
of a Surfman

NAVIGATIONAL ERROR. THAT WAS WHAT ASSISTANT Inspector Frank Newcomb determined to have been the root cause of the *Lancaster*'s troubles the night she came ashore in October 1881.

The ship's mate, who was at the helm and unfamiliar with the Outer Banks' coastline, mistook the Bodie Island Light for the one at Hatteras, steered south by west after passing the beacon, and sailed right onto the shoals of closed-up Loggerhead Inlet. To add to the mariners' troubles, the *Lancaster* had recently been remodeled, the mainmast moved from centerboard to keel, and the changes had compromised the structural integrity of the vessel. When the pitching schooner began to throw the thousand tons of ice in her hold against the hull, she came undone even more quickly than she otherwise would have. The survivors on board also hurt the rescue efforts. They mishandled the lines fired out, and the strongest among them eventually abandoned ship altogether, leaving only the injured and the weak to manage the shipboard end of the recovery.

The loss of seven lives, though tragic, proved not to be a black eye for the service. "No blame," Newcomb concluded his report, "attaches to the men of the Life-Saving Service for failure to rescue the crew of the *Lancaster* sooner than they did." The surfmen had done all they could to save the mariners. The press did not print stories of bungling lifesavers and pilfered corpses. There were no such stories to tell. The matter of the *Lancaster* was closed.

The mismanagement and incompetence in the ranks that had dogged the service also appeared to have taken a turn. Strict oversight was still necessary to guarantee adherence to duty, but the vigilance, daring, and skill of keepers such as L. B. Midgett and Jesse T. Etheridge, of B. B. Dailey down the coast at Cape Hatteras—and of Richard Etheridge in charge of the Outer Banks' black surfmen—promised to provide proper service.

For Richard Etheridge, enforcing military-style discipline was the key. He hired men for their ability in the surf and their willingness to follow orders. If they slipped in either capacity, their days at Pea Island would be numbered.

When Etheridge's number three surfman, William Daniel, who had discovered the *Lancaster* in the surf, ran afoul of the keeper later in the season following the disaster, Etheridge cut him loose. Etheridge cited as his reason "acts of insubordination." In one instance, Daniel quit the station at midnight, without permission and without providing a substitute, to go searching for his horse. Etheridge stated that, when he reprimanded the man or gave him orders, Daniel tended to be "obstinate with the Keeper." When the crew reported for duty on September 1, 1882, William Daniel was not among them. In his place, Etheridge hired twenty-eight-year-old Benjamin Bowser.

13

The Portrait of a Surfman

The general run of the work of the life savers is not the spectacular kind that sometimes gets into the newspapers. The routine drill, the labor of keeping the station and the boats and outfit bright and clean and ready for business, and the lonely night patrol of the silent beach, constitute the bulk of the men's work.

*—Herbert H. Brimley, noted naturalist and
frequent visitor to the Outer Banks, in the*
Charlotte Daily Observer

Benjamin Bowser had first come to the station the season before. Etheridge had initially hired him to be the "winter man"—the number seven surfman who augmented the crew by one from December through March, the most dangerous months.

As the newest and lowest-ranking member of the crew, Bowser had to prove he deserved his place among the veterans. He was the designated volunteer for all the least desirable duties. When they made mock rescues during the weekly Monday and Thursday drilling with the beach apparatus, Bowser stood in as the "shipwreck victim," waiting out on the wreck pole to be hauled in in the breeches buoy while the others operated the Lyle gun, lines, and crotch. And the keeper thought nothing of waking up a rookie surfman in the middle of the night—any of the crew, for that matter, but especially a rookie—and having him recite on the spot procedures and codes from the "blue jacket" manual. Each man understood that, even in a haze of sleep, he'd better know the material.

When Bowser reenlisted the following September in William Daniel's place, he jumped from winter man to number three, Daniel's former position, skipping ahead of such veterans as William B. Davis and William C. Bowser, both of whom were members of the original crew. Rank did not always reflect just grade and seniority, but also the willingness to take on specific responsibilities. Numbers one and two had to be able to take charge of the boat in the keeper's stead; beyond that, there was a degree of flexibility. With Etheridge's approval, men occasionally exchanged spots according to their needs and desires.

Later, surfmen from coast to coast would wear a common uniform, a dark blue in the navy style with the rank sewn into the sleeve. In the early years, however, keepers had some discretion in how they wanted their crews to dress. Most favored some sort of single-breasted dark coat, the double-breasted model reserved for themselves, to distinguish them from their surfmen. For Bowser, to start at number three put him on his way toward reaching one of his goals: attaining the double-breaster, the sign of keepership.

At twenty-eight, Bowser was the youngest of the crew, and standing five feet eleven inches, he was also the tallest. Lithe and bespectacled, he looked sharp: quick-witted and nimble afoot. Before joining the service, Bowser, like his father before him, had fished. Benjamin J. Bowser Sr. was a former slave from Roanoke Island who had been manumitted sometime around 1842 along with his wife, Director, who was called Polly. They had left the island and moved to Powells Point, on the mainland peninsula just north of Kitty Hawk. Ben Jr., "Benjy," came along April 16, 1854, when his father was already fifty-two years old. The family spent time both on Roanoke Island and at the other place, twenty miles away.

The future surfman learned quickly to work an oar and steer a boat in both sound and sea. He understood the tides, weather, and such of the region, and the Bowsers, father and son, had success fishing. Besides owning the land at Powells Point, Benjamin Sr. was able to save enough to buy a stretch on Colington Island, in the Roanoke Sound behind Kill Devil Hills. In May 1882, the father let the son build his first home on that land.

Still, despite his good fortune as a fisher, the steady income and the status of being a surfman drew the younger Bowser to Pea Island.

Once part of the crew, Bowser quickly learned that serving at Pea Island was hardly the exciting and glamorous stuff that magazines such as *Scribner's Monthly* and *Harper's Weekly* had made out life in the LSS to be. Although the unusual and dramatic nature of the work had long attracted writers to surfmen's exploits, their day-to-day life was, more often than not, tedious and routine. Keeper Etheridge, as a former military man, as a disciplinarian and a disciple of Alonzo Draper, strictly adhered to regulations. When his men weren't walking the beach or standing watch in the lookout, they drilled.

For Etheridge and other keepers of his ilk, readiness was all. Preparedness and stamina were often the difference between success and failure, life and death, so Etheridge demanded much from his men. The service allotted time on specified days each week for drilling with the various instruments of lifesaving, and Etheridge drove his men to proficiency.

Mondays and Thursdays were reserved for drilling with the beach apparatus, including firing the Lyle gun. Tuesdays were for boat drills, Wednesdays for flag and signal drills, Fridays for first aid and practice "restoring the apparently drowned." Saturdays were designated general cleaning days of the station, inside and out. According to regulations, Sundays were to be days of rest, but Etheridge inspected his crew at 9 A.M. on each Sabbath, then read to them from the blue-jacket manual. And every day, Sunday included, the men maintained the regular patrols and lookout duty.

Men went home when they could: to take their weekly twenty-four-hour leave; for sickness or to visit sick family; to get supplies for the station or the mail from the new post office on Roanoke Island; or in November, to vote. They spent most of their time, though, patrolling the beach, drilling, cleaning and repairing the station. Drills and repairs might be subject to the whims of the weather. Patrols were not, except in the most extreme conditions.

Not all keepers ran their stations with prime efficiency. One man, John Allen Midgett Sr., who was appointed just a few months before Etheridge, showed Newcomb that the problem of undisciplined service had yet to be completely resolved.

Midgett moved to fire his surfman Dailey O'Neal for having falsely reported to have met the patrolman from the neighboring station when, Midgett claimed, he had not. With the misdeed falling so closely on the heels of the crises of the 1870s, Sumner Kimball chose to make an example of O'Neal. The general superintendent ordered the man fired, suspecting that the lie was an attempt to hide that he had not properly covered his patrol. Further, though, Kimball prohibited O'Neal from ever being rehired into the service. To top it off, Kimball instructed each Outer Banks keeper to read the details of the case to his crew, with the warning that O'Neal's fate awaited whatever man "fail[ed] to completely perform his patrol duty without a good and sufficient reason."

Within a few months, new information found Assistant Inspector Newcomb's ear, and upon further investigating the incident, he uncovered a completely different story. O'Neal had *not* met the neighboring patrolman, as was reported, but *had* properly covered his beat. His error, in essence, was having crossed Keeper Midgett.

Newcomb found Midgett guilty of several improprieties in the running of his crew, including not keeping the station adequately staffed, inappropriately absenting himself from the premises, and attempting to swindle his surfmen. Lifesavers were responsible for providing their own meals, but Midgett had forced his men, at risk of losing their jobs, to pay him a monthly fee for board of seven dollars and fifty cents, with which he would provide for them. The men submitted, but quickly began to grumble, as they found the food inadequate in quality as well as quantity. O'Neal had been one of the more vocal malcontents, according to Newcomb, "agitating the board question at his station."

"In view of the foregoing facts," Newcomb reported, "it would seem to be my duty to recommend the instant dismissal from the Service of Keeper Midgett, but upon reflection I am of the opinion that it would be for the benefit of the Service to give Keeper Midgett another trial." In this period when the LSS lacked qualified men and could not afford to risk fatal error in judgment, Midgett was indispensable to them. "It is conceded on all sides," Newcomb continued, "that Keeper Midgett is one of the best surfmen on the beach at the southern end of this District, and is eminently fitted for the position he occupies, provided he would attend to his duties properly." Newcomb suggested, and Kimball approved, that Midgett be severely reprimanded and warned that "the first offense willfully committed by him against the Regulations of the Service [would] be followed by his dismissal." But, like Avery Austin, George Daniels, Adam Etheridge, and so many before him, he was not let go.

As for Dailey O'Neal, Kimball ordered him reinstated, but he never served again at Midgett's station nor, apparently, any other.

Applying the lessons he'd learned under Draper, Richard Etheridge kept his station logs in strict, military fashion. He meticulously noted his inventory of supplies; the day-to-day conditions of the wind and surf; the number of ships sighted and the type; the patrols—who walked which beat, at what time, whom they met, and when they returned.

Although the entries accurately inform contemporary readers about the conditions of the wind and surf on any given day over a hundred years ago, they offer little insight into the personality of the man who religiously wrote them day in and day out. His Pea Island lifesavers, like Etheridge himself, remain enigmatic. What can be gleaned of Etheridge's character, from his personal history as well as from the way he ran his station, probably also reflects to some degree the character of the men he chose for his crew. Those who endured under him were men of the same mettle as the keeper.

Under Etheridge's tutelage, Bowser quickly showed himself to be an exemplary surfman as he worked toward his goal of eventually becoming a keeper. His initial stint as a surfman was cut short, though. Bowser fell gravely ill in late September, not long after replacing William Daniel, and became so incapacitated that the keeper had to send him home to Colington Island.

For six weeks, he was laid up. On October 28, 1882, Bowser had still not recovered. He sent in his resignation. The nature of the illness was never reported.

THE LIFE OF A SURFMAN

By the time he realized that conditions were unmanageable for boating, it was too late. Just south of Oregon Inlet, a waterspout rose wickedly from the Pamlico, too close to avoid, and William Davis's canoe capsized, toppling him out of the stern, where he'd sat rowing. The canoe crashed over him. The blow dazed him, and he swallowed water and became disoriented, unsure which way was up, which way to fight toward to clear his head and get precious air. He flailed his arms, took big gulps—some air, some spray. The mail he'd been carrying to Manteo whipped round and round above him, and bigger things that he thought he should dodge, but to dive down was to breathe water, to drown.

Davis suddenly understood he might die here.

Fifty-one years old. Four years in the service, four years away from home during the holidays, four Christmases gone. He'd just wanted to celebrate the New Year with his family. Not too much to ask.

December 30: the eve of New Year's Eve and his day to do the mail run. The surf had been rough, the winds whistling, when he pushed off from the marshland creek behind the station where he and the others moored their skiffs and canoes. But the conditions hadn't concerned him. In fact, he'd imagined the head winds might keep him grounded at home—just one day, long enough to be with family during part of the holidays. That wasn't too much to ask.

The thought of crossing Oregon Inlet in that tide worried him. Even on a clear day, the current was so strong a person looking down could see it cut through the sand below. He hadn't made it as far as that, and here he was, drowning, too far away for his crewmates and not yet far enough for those from Station 16 to spot him.

But not dead yet. Davis found breath, enough to sustain him for a moment, and located his canoe—overturned in the water just yards away. He fought the winds and whipping water to right it. It was the capsize drill on a smaller scale: he spun her on her axis, grabbing the gunwales to keep her right side up, and he pulled himself over them and in. An oar nearby—he reached for it, paddled toward shore, toward the salt marsh where the thickets would shelter him.

He waited out the storm.

As suddenly as it had erupted, the whirlwind collapsed back into the sound. *The Pamlico tossed and rocked in its wake, spilt mail littering the water. Davis took stock of himself. He was soaked, but essentially unhurt.*

Oregon Inlet would be impossible to cross. And besides, the mail gone, he now had no reason to attempt it and continue his trip. He turned his canoe back toward the station, toward his new home, resigned: another New Year away from his family.

14

Life at the Station

All along my back, the creeping
Soon gave place to rustling, leaping
As if countless demons,
Had concluded to explore
All the cavities—the varmints!—
'Twixt me and my nether garments,
Through my boots on the floor;
Then I found myself shaking,
Every moment more and more.

—*"The Ague," cited in the* Elizabeth City Economist,
November 24, 1875

The newspapers from the communities around the sounds made it a point to often comment on the vigor of surfmen. According to reports, Outer Banks lifesavers represented "the Ideal of Manhood." The population of Roanoke Island was generally said to be "remarkable for robust and healthy development." The *Elizabeth City Economist* boasted in the summer of 1880 that the island's "men are larger, more athletic, and bigger boned, than the same number of men on the same area in any part of the State." One year later, a columnist from the paper, reporting the findings of an unidentified "eastern physician," explained: "This is probably attributable to their proximity to the ocean, to the abundance and superior quality of their food, and to the hardy and strennuous [*sic*] labors that they are often compelled to perform in the perils of their adventurous life."

Despite this, the danger of contracting some sort of disease was great in a semitropical, isolated, and underdeveloped region such as the Outer Banks. One of the criteria for employment as a surfman was that the candidate yearly pass a physical exam before an LSS-certified doctor. Benjamin Bowser must have done so in August 1882. Still, within a few weeks, he fell victim to some affliction.

Malaria—the ague, Bankers called it—plagued residents of the marsh and swamplands around the sounds. The number of ads for tonics to defend against it that regularly appeared in the *Economist, Fisherman and Farmer*, and other area newspapers suggests that the disease struck hard and struck often. Though less prevalent on the windswept barrier islands, it was a common ailment nevertheless, particularly during the humid autumn months, and Outer Bankers suffered mightily.

Swamps stretched along the inland side of Pea Island, and as a result, Stations 16 and 17 were said to be "the worst . . . in the [district]" as "hordes of mosquitoes . . . breed in the marshes closeby and in the marsh grass washed up on the sound side." The journalist who made this report claimed that a "surfman on beach patrol on bad mosquito nights, no matter how warm, [was] compelled to wrap his head in towels [and] don his oil-skins" for protection. Medical technology of the era had yet to make the direct connection between mosquitoes and malaria, but the insects' prevalence helps identify one of the illnesses that afflicted the black surfmen.

But bouts of malaria did not last six weeks. Bowser suffered from something much more severe.

Lifesavers were susceptible to a wide range of disease. Typhoid occasionally posed problems to Outer Bankers. In July 1880, an outbreak struck Dare County and spread into neighboring Tyrrell. "Mosquitos and chills and fevers abound," the *Economist* reported. "Nothing like it known by the oldest inhabitant." Other diseases that periodically infected Outer

Bankers included dysentery, yellow fever, and smallpox. Cholera, another menace, would, in the 1890s, ravage the inhabitants of Pea Island.

Surfmen, who regularly exposed themselves to the elements while on patrols or assisting shipwreck victims, were especially liable to become ill. At one time or another, most Pea Island surfmen did. In one instance, five crewmen were laid up, sick and incapacitated, all stricken at the same time (probably by the same contagious disease, passed from one to the next).

Outer Bankers have always had to be self-sustaining folk, given their isolation from the mainland, and most among the surfmen had some knowledge and experience with first aid. During the 1870s and most of the 1880s, there were no physicians in Dare County. The first set up practice only in 1889. Seven medical practitioners were registered in Currituck County, well to the north, but it was too far and too expensive to travel to consult these men, except on rare occasions. When accidents occurred, Bankers doctored the injured. They set bones, closed wounds. When their loved ones or neighbors fell ill, they pooled their stores of information and folk wisdom, diagnosing and treating them as best they could. This knowledge, accumulated over a lifetime, served the surfmen well.

Station 17 was some thirty miles from the county line and the nearest doctors, and most often, the infirm lifesavers were kept on at the station until they could regain their posts. Etheridge and his men cared for their own. The LSS manuals furnished to the stations added to the Pea Island crewmen's understanding, but the Friday drilling was just fine-tuning. When the boom of the keeper's voice stole a man from peaceful slumber and demanded he recite the procedure for reviving the apparently drowned, it was as much an exercise in discipline as it was proof of the man's medical preparedness.

Yaupon, a plant that grew wild on the Banks, was said to have curative properties when brewed into a tea. Its processing was long and tedious, but a black Banker, "Old Man Scarborough," kept a "factory" farther down the coast, north of Hatteras, and his children sold his product, twenty-five cents a bushel, to families in the region, as well as to lifesaving crews. The general store in Manteo, Griffin, Sample and Co., also kept plenty in stock, which crewmen would purchase when they went after supplies for the station. Sick Pea Islanders spent many a long night drinking the purgative in an effort to vomit poisons from their systems.

Etheridge also kept on hand plenty of linseed oil. Commonly used in paint and varnish, it could be rubbed into aching or injured limbs. Of all the remedies, the brandy in the medicine chest probably most appealed to the bunk-ridden surfmen looking for relief.

In some cases, Keeper Etheridge recognized the afflictions that felled his crewman as being too serious or, possibly, contagious, and those men were relieved of duty. In September 1881, Etheridge himself got so sick he had to be carried home to Roanoke Island by Bill Charles Bowser. He only returned to duty after several days' absence. The illness that struck him then and the grievous one that forced Benjamin Bowser to resign a year later remain unknown.

Disease, overwhelmingly more than any other cause—including drowning or injuries suffered while going to the aid of vessels in distress—was the agent of death for the majority of the Outer Banks lifesavers who lost their lives in the line of duty. In the LSS's first four decades, forty-six North Carolina surfmen died from illness. During one particularly bad two-year stretch, eight perished from what may have been an outbreak of smallpox that *Fisherman and Farmer* reported to be plaguing the region.

For every surfman killed by disease, countless others merely suffered the agonies caused by their illnesses and continued on. In the fall of 1880, Assistant Inspector Newcomb commented on the "great deal of sickness" he encountered while touring the stations—"principally chills and fevers," he noted. The conditions of the men prevented "the drills from being as thorough and effective as [he] would have wished," Newcomb informed Superintendent Kimball. Though not as "thorough," the drilling and patrolling went on as usual.

Sick or spry, daily life at Pea Island was drilling, and though it exposed the men to the elements and put them at constant risk of injury, it became as natural to them as it was tedious. Launching and rowing a surfboat (Tuesdays) was, to each one, what driving a horse and plow was to corn-belt farmers. These men had grown up on the waters of the Outer Banks, had handled boats in all kinds of weather since they were children. Some, such as Bill Charles Bowser, so knew watercraft that they became renowned as expert boatbuilders. For them, the surfboat—a thirty-foot-long craft, double-ended for maneuverability and bearing cork fenders for buoyancy—was no different from the ones they'd launched and rowed and sailed and landed their whole lives.

Still, the men took the drill seriously because they knew to take the sea seriously. Surfmen often injured themselves and were sometimes killed during attempts to rescue mariners by surfboat, as had been the case in 1876, when the keeper and entire crew of the Jones Hill station had drowned while coming to the aid of the wrecked *Nuova Ottavia*.

Before setting out, Keeper Etheridge made sure that each man donned a cork life vest—something the men from Jones Hill had not done—then the Pea Islanders hauled the boat cart to the water's edge. To launch their boat from the beach in rough surf was a game of timing between crashing waves. Once out, the surfmen might have to endure hours of exhausting rowing to reach the side of a stranded ship. The weekly training kept them fit.

While out in the boat, Etheridge would purposely capsize her, tumbling the crew into the sea while he, himself, would scramble over the upturned hull, barely getting wet at all. The surfmen had to right the boat and regain their positions at the oars. Before long, this was no challenge. It was just swimming in the sea.

But each man was made to understand the significance of the exercise. In time of crisis, when maneuvering over rough surf, past pitching wreckage and the tumbling spars of a broken ship, mastering the surfboat meant mastering the situation at hand and, as a result, saving lives—their own included. The only weeks when Etheridge called off boat drills were those when the weather made the exercise too dangerous to needlessly risk the lives of his crew.

Flag and signal drills (Wednesdays) were new knowledge to most, but quickly learned, particularly with the threat of Etheridge's late-night quizzes. Also new was the practice with the beach apparatus. Despite the complex nature of the equipment, the crew all understood that proficiency with it was sine qua non.

Vessels that grounded off the Outer Banks often did so relatively close to the beach. Ship captains, hoping to take advantage of the currents, hugged the coast for speed as well as to seek out beacons and other landmarks by which to fix their location. As a result, many ran afoul of the shifting shoals. For the surfmen, firing a line out from shore was the preferred way to save lives. Though generally slower than use of the surfboat, where shipwrecked crews could often be taken off in one pass, the beach apparatus allowed the lifesavers to rescue mariners without having to jeopardize their own safety—and therefore, the lives of those shipwrecked—by having to enter the turbulent waters.

Twice weekly, the Pea Islanders, like other crews, drilled with the beach apparatus—on Mondays to kick off their week and again on Thursdays. So regularly did the boom of Lyle guns drumroll up and down the coast that Banker fishers complained that it disrupted the runs of blues.

This exercise more than the rest was a true test of a surfman's qualification to serve. Each person had a specific task to do quickly and efficiently, and the whole did not function if anyone failed in his assignment. Inspecting officers Newcomb and J. W. Etheridge, who regularly tested the crew, expected that they could perform the operation in five minutes or less, firing a line out sixty to eighty yards. This was the measure the men had to maintain. Anything longer than five minutes Sumner Kimball considered proof that the crew had been "remiss in drilling."

The drill began with the surfmen wheeling the half-ton cart out of the boatroom onto the beach. Once in place within proper range of the wreck pole (a fifteen-foot-tall beam planted in the ground that simulated the spar of a ship), the lifesavers stood at attention beside the cart, each man in position according to his rank. Etheridge began. He recited verbatim his specific tasks to be done. Afterward, the surfmen, one by one in descending order of rank, followed suit. When they were done, Etheridge called, "Action!" and with military precision, the men went to work.

Each man knew his task by heart. It never changed unless his rank did. When the keeper set them in motion, the surfmen dashed to their assigned positions, each activity scripted. One teamed with the keeper to unload the Lyle gun from the cart. The keeper loaded the barrel, during drills with three ounces of black powder, while the other man prepared the shot, an eighteen-inch projectile that weighed twenty pounds and had the whip line attached. Another surfman removed the wooden faking box—in which rope was "faked" around pegs to keep it from tangling—and dumped the line on the ground, while a third retrieved the breeches buoy and a fourth the X-shaped wooden supports. Two more attacked the beach with pick and spade, digging a two-and-a-half-foot pit in which to bury the stabilizing sand anchor.

When all was in place, Etheridge elevated the barrel to the appropriate height to reach the target, then two of the senior surfmen sighted the gun to his commands: "Right!" "Left!" and when the aim was true, "Well!" Kneeling beside the gun, Etheridge prepared the ignition device, then stepped back, verified that all was in order, and called, "Ready!" Each man covered his ears. The booming of the shot shook them to their core. Even if one was ready for it, the thunderous detonation had the power to startle.

The line burned through the air and landed across the wreck pole. The men worked in unison to send out the block—a pulley device that worked like an old-fashioned clothesline—then the hawser with breeches buoy attached. The keeper raised it onto the wooden supports. Once it was secure, number six climbed in, and the crew, running a sort of relay from front to rear with the line over a shoulder, manually hauled in the "stranded victim." Etheridge recorded in his station logbook the distance to the pole, the elevation of the barrel, and the amount of powder used to fire the shot.

Half their workweek was taken up with training with the beach apparatus and surfboat. During good weather, practice sometimes drew crowds of nearby residents, and before long, the surfmen made a pageant of demon-strating their ability with the equipment.

A surfman might woo his sweetheart, promising her the role of victim to be hauled down the hawser in the breeches buoy; or crowds of children would line up at the wreck pole, each hoping for a ride, if the keeper would let them turn the day into a carnival event. The black lifesavers came to be known up and down the coast for their ability to launch and maneuver their boat in heavy seas, a reputation that later Pea Island crews strove to maintain. A Nags Head fisherman who grew up after the turn of the cen-tury remembered, "On days when it was too rough to see the surfboat drill, the inspectors would say, 'Let's go to Pea Island.' Those fellows could launch the boat in anything."

Ben Bowser's resignation in 1882 was not the end of his career as a surf-man. Once he'd recovered, he applied for another opportunity to serve at the station. As he'd already proven his worth, Keeper Etheridge rehired him on September 1, 1884, as the station's number three surfman, the rank he'd held when he resigned. Bowser was thirty.

In September 1886, at the start of Bowser's third full season as a life-saver, Etheridge promoted him to the number one rank after the former second-in-command, Lewis Wescott, failed his physical exam—from a grave illness, like so many before him. Ben Bowser was now only one place away from the keepership.

THE LIFE OF A SURFMAN

The night of December 11, 1887, was the kind all surfmen dreaded. It was unseasonably warm, nearly sixty degrees at sunset, but Pea Island was draped in a blanket of fog, had been all day, and the air was wet with mist. A rough surf sounded up the beach, tossing spindrift onto the shore. Conditions such as these were especially dangerous for mariners. With the light from the Bodie Island beacon obscured by fog, the surf and poor visibility might draw sailors toward land.

Ben Bowser set out into the darkness to fetch a horse from the stable. Charged with covering the south patrol from midnight to 3 A.M., he took the horse by the reins—surfmen were not supposed to ride their beat—and began his slow walk toward New Inlet. It was familiar terrain. He had covered every inch of it, every other day, each week of the past three seasons. The roughness of the surf had not yet abated this night, and the taste of salt was heavy in the air.

Bowser peered over his left shoulder out to sea. The waves only came into view as they tumbled up the beach in heaps of spume. Out there was milky gray obscurity. Bowser's ears had to fill in where his eyes could not serve him. He could hear large breakers crashing on the outer bar, nothing more. He scanned the foam for debris or wood, signs that a ship had come ashore, but he found none. Still, the beach was somehow ominous, the tension almost palpable.

The horse sensed it, too. Planting its hooves in the wet sand and seashells, it pulled up, refusing to go one step farther. Bowser held his lantern forward, looking to see just what was causing the horse to shy. The horse began to snort, its wet nostrils flared, and it reared its head. Bowser pulled the reins to calm the animal, but it bucked, turned toward the roaring surf, and suddenly and without warning, dashed headlong down the incline of the beach toward the sea. Bowser was just barely able to hold on.

The splash of seawater extinguished the lantern's flame, and it was suddenly pitch-black. Waves crashed upon man and animal, the frightened horse kicking wildly. Bowser clutched the reins, trying to pull the horse out of the sea. The surf fought against him, pounding man and beast with unrelenting power and, in its retreat, pulling both toward the dark shapes of breakers. He could hardly keep his own footing. It seemed the only way to save himself would be to let loose the horse and scramble for dry land. Still,

Bowser tugged, pleading with the panicky horse, clicking his tongue, cooing, and finally, he was able to tow the goggle-eyed creature back onto land.

The surfman staggered on the sand, soaked with frigid seawater. His Coston lights were wet, and the time detector, which let the keeper know the beat had properly been covered, had stopped. He led the horse away from the waves and calmed it. When it seemed sufficiently pacified, Bowser was able to leave it long enough to recover the lantern from the sea.

Whoever or whatever had spooked the animal was now gone. He waited a few minutes more before completing his patrol.

Later, his patrol done, the wet and exhausted surfman would head back to the station where he would sit by the stove, sipping a cup of coffee. He would have to report his "encounter" and the damaged time detector to the keeper—all deviations from routine had to be accounted for. Etheridge reported it in the spare language of a military man:

(Form 1808)
WEEKLY JOURNAL

Pea Island Station   *Sunday, Dec. 11th, 1887*

GENERAL REMARKS
It will be seen that there are 2 impressions on the dial for the 11 inst and no dial for the 12 inst   the reasons for it: B. J. Bowser while on his patrol his horse become frighten and went into the Surf and the time Detector accidentally got some water into her and Stopped but she appears to be all right since

[signed] Richard Etheridge

15

Patrolling the Beach

The beach guardians are no idle promenaders. A march of four or five miles through the soft sea-sand is a task at any time; what is it in the fury of a winter storm?

—"*The United States Life-Saving Service,*"
Scribner's Monthly, *January 1880*

Unusual events such as the one that spooked Benjamin Bowser's horse were a constant threat to patrolling lifesavers. The desolate beaches of the Outer Banks lent themselves to the eerie and unpredictable. Surfman Ed Gaskins of the station at Hatteras, while patrolling one night in raging winds that whipped blinding sand into his eyes, had his horse suddenly pull up, much as Bowser's had.

Gaskins, as he reported it, was walking down the beach toward some wreckage that had washed ashore from a recent disaster. He described the night as "black dark," with the white sand glowing luminescent. Picking his way "between slippery wet timbers and piles of seaweed," the aura of some presence—the memory of lives lost from the shipwreck—seemed all around when, without warning, a dark mass rose with a grunt underfoot. He stumbled, trying to jump away, but it jolted him, knocking him over as it dashed between his legs.

"I knew it was a hog," he later said, "but that didn't make no matter; I was too scared to holler!

"Man!" he continued. "I was all of a sweat. I just lay there. At last I got up, and as I did, I let a yell and I kept on yelling for a mile."

During his long career in the service, Ben Bowser trekked about 24,500 miles of beach, patrolling between Station 17 and New Inlet, two and a half miles to the south, or between the station and the halfway point to Oregon Inlet, three miles to the north. Before sophisticated ship-to-shore technology, patrolling was the best way for lifesavers to be sure that no vessel was in danger or had encountered difficulty off the coast. Beach patrols were made from sunset to sunrise and on days when visibility from the observation deck atop the station was poor.

A surfman walked, watching the sea for signs of passing shipping: the distant outline of a vessel against the night sky; a flurry of sails; or perhaps just the glittering of light from lanterns on a deck. He counted their number and, if he could tell, the type. He kept alert for the sounds of tattered sails beating the wind. He was also careful to pay attention to what washed ashore around him: pieces of rent planking, a wooden pail, baggage—any sign that might herald news of a ship in distress.

Most nights, there was nothing. He pushed on, watching for other things—changes in the shoals, waves cresting on the outer bar—until he met the patrolman from the neighboring station. The two men swapped whatever information needed to be shared from the recent patrol—the vessels they'd spotted and the direction they were headed—as well as news from their stations: gossip they had heard; well wishes for sick crewmates or family; and when the occasion warranted, condolences for those who'd passed. The men also exchanged proofs to show to their keepers that the beats had properly been covered. In the early years, it was letters or lanterns, then eventually, a stamped badge that each man carried with his station number and rank inscribed on it.

Along lengths of coast separated by inlets, the lifesavers carried with them a time detector, which operated on the same principle as a modern punch-clock. A key, attached to a post at the far end of the beat, would stop the clock. By inspecting the time the key was turned, the keeper could monitor the diligence of his crewmen.

Though not as treacherous as the infamous Diamond Shoals off Cape Hatteras, the coast at New Inlet was, according to Assistant Inspector Newcomb, "one of the most dangerous points on the beach, as the number of wrecks seen there, will testify." Patrolling there from Station 17, he added, "taxes the endurance of surfmen." Keeper Etheridge identified six places along this stretch where, during rough surf, the water washed over the beach face from sea to sound. It was here that Leonidas Tillett, from the first Pea Island crew, had neglected his patrol and missed the signs that the *M&E Henderson* had come ashore. Despite the challenges of this beat, Etheridge made sure to impress upon his surfmen the importance of remaining watchful and reminded them of the consequences.

Instructions for patrolling were explicit and ordered copied into the station's log; negligence of any sort was not tolerated. The penalty was dismissal and prohibition from ever rejoining the service. As mandated by regulations, Keeper Etheridge had to account for irregular or missed patrols in his daily reports, as he did when Ben Bowser's horse damaged the time detector.

Sumner Kimball only officially allowed crews to keep horses at stations beginning in 1880, with the understanding that the horses would just be used to drag the heavy carts to the sites of wrecks. He resisted their use for patrolling, although it had been a common practice along the Outer Banks. Speedier and less attentive patrols, he feared, would be the result. Richard Etheridge had his men train with their mount, but despite this, in late April 1888, Jeremiah Wescott was thrown from the station horse and dislocated his shoulder. He was incapacitated for several weeks. For Kimball, this risk of injury, to man or property, as in the case of the broken time detector, was but another unnecessary problem that horses posed to the efficiency of crews. More often than not, Pea Islanders walked their beats.

Most patrols were not as exciting as on the night Bowser's horse had spooked. Usually patrols were quiet and uneventful. A patrolman carried with him a lantern and a satchel of bright red flares, called Coston lights. Unless visibility was impaired by the weather or a marked obscurity, he wasn't allowed to light the lantern. Headquarters had received complaints from shipmasters who, from sea, had confused the lights with beacons. The lifesavers let the moon light their path.

With shipping lanes so close to shore, passing vessels frequently strayed too far inland, and the surfman on his beat had to be alert and ready to act.

WEEKLY JOURNAL

Pea Island Station   *Sunday, March 30th, 1884*

1 Coston Light Expended by Surfman Robert Toler [Tolar] *for the purpose of Warning a Vessel to keep off the Beach about one 1/2 mile north of New Inlet. Surfman Robert Toler discoverd a vessel on the morning of March 30 a bout 1/2 passed 4 o clock almost on the beach   he immediately burned his Coston Light and she immediately Keept off from the beach it is almost likely she would have struck on New Inlet Shoals had she not been warned.*

WEEKLY JOURNAL

Pea Island Station   *Sunday, Nov. 16th, 1884*

the Patrolman B. J. Bowser no. 3 from Sunset to 9 p.m. discovered a Steamship in great danger heading on the beach.   a North West gale was raging and he immediately burned a Coston Signal and the vessel at once changed her course.

Under the worst conditions, beach patrol was hell on earth. Ripping winds whipped sand that cut like glass. At a moment when a patrolman's vision was most important to him, he often found himself blinded. His hearing was hardly of any more use, for little was audible over the ocean's roar and the whistling winds. Grit collected in his ears, his nostrils, his mouth. He'd try to keep his lips shut tight, to breathe only through his nose, but this, along with the pounding wind, made breathing difficult. His clothes beat mercilessly against his skin. When the wind blew in his face, he had to lean precipitously forward to keep upright; when at his back, it pushed him to a run that he had to fight to properly cover his beat.

Under normal conditions, walking a beat, though no promenade, could be a marvel. Here were the Outer Banks at their most splendid. Breakers cresting one hundred yards out were white foam on a dark background, and the beach a wide plain that glistened. Even in light surf, the sound of crashing waves dominated. Alone on the beach at night, the patrolman listened for the sighs of porpoises as they sculled along hunting gray trout just outside the breakers. In spring, odd pieces of menhaden washed up at his feet like so many silver coins. He could hear the ravenous jaws of hungry bluefish—*Chop! Chop! Chop!*—as they devoured the menhaden out in the dark wave troughs.

Closer, onshore, he might also hear the chirping argument of sandpipers as they raced other shorebirds behind the receding waves to the best spot to probe for a meal of tiny crustaceans. With each step, phosphorescent organisms burst into a shimmer of illumination underfoot. His became the foot of a god walking through a field of stars. He passed the fragmented carcasses of former wrecks, sometimes spaced no more than a few hundred yards apart, protruding from the breakers at low tide and occasionally washed completely up on the beach. Some were decades old. Each was a point of reference by which to orient himself, and also a companion he was happy to come upon, like an old man left too long alone, with stories to conjure and tell.

As patrolling lifesavers scanned the beach for signs of trouble at sea, what they came upon as often as not, particularly in rough or freezing weather, were the corpses of the drowned.

WEEKLY JOURNAL

Pea Island Station   *Wednesday, April 24, 1889*

the South patrolman of the Station from 3 am to Sunrise [Henry Daniel] *found the body of a drowned man which he hauled upon the beach and a later Examination by the Keeper + crew.   papers was found on his person which identified that he was Robert Nolan age 17 years old he had twenty five dollars in his pocket paper currency and two certificates showing the employment + discharge as Cabin Boy on the English ship Canute (official no. 47560) and the American ship David Crocket. He also had on a cork jacket the name of the ship could not be distinguished. the man was given a decent Burial. the Certificates and money was turned over to David F. Jones of the Department at Washington D. C.*

Surfmen had to try to identify the bodies that washed up on the beaches, so that next of kin could be notified. They also built coffins and buried them behind the dunes.

As Outer Bankers spent so much time in boats and around the water, in many cases the drowned who came ashore were neighbors, folks the lifesavers knew—or thought they might.

WEEKLY JOURNAL

Pea Island Station   *Monday, Nov. 18, 1889*

the Patrolman north from 3 a.m. to Sunrise this morning found a drowned man (Col[ored]) there was no papers or mark to identify the man the head and face was badly mutilated   he was 5 foot 9 inches in Length. he had on a pair of pants 2 shirts and a pair of Low quartered shoes no. 9. the man was given a Decent Burial.

And, in the worst cases, the drowned were fellow surfmen, crewmates. Despite their knowledge of the seas and sounds and their proficiency as swimmers, two Pea Island surfmen would lose their lives when the mercurial Outer Banks weather forced them to quit their boats and attempt to swim for shore.

Though patrolmen kept their eyes fixed on the sea, sometimes the menace for which they needed to be prepared originated on land. The April 24, 1883, issue of the *Elizabeth City Economist* reported: "A few days ago M. D. Etheridge and E. T. Owens while on their patrol from Life Saving Station No. 10 were attacked by [a great many muskrats] and after a desperate fight Owens was compelled to retreat after receiving a slight wound on the leg." M. D. Etheridge killed several before having to flee himself. "M. D. Etheridge says he don't like to hear of muskrats," the newspaper followed up a month later, "for they once came near whipping him."

The rodents, also called "Russian rats" by Bankers, became a problem up and down the coast, for they grew as big as two feet and were fearless. Several surfmen encountered them and, more often than not, were forced to defend themselves against them. One swarm unhorsed a mounted patrolman and attacked him. "There was a desperate fight," the *Economist* reported, but the surfman saved himself.

Because of the vast marshlands behind their stations, the crews at Pea Island and Oregon Inlet had much to fear in the Russian rat attack. Both crews began keeping cats. The proprietor of the nearby hunt club immediately complained that the cats were killing or chasing away the wildfowl that prominent visitors traveled great distances to shoot. The protests worked their way to the top, reaching Sumner Kimball's desk. The general superintendent did not bend to the pressure. He let the lifesavers keep the cats.

More than combative muskrats onshore, storm systems posed the greatest threat to lifesavers. While they were there to assure the safety of people caught in dangerous conditions, patrolmen themselves were as vulnerable to the ravages of the weather as anyone. The LSS's published *Annual Report* tells of the risks surfmen ran when caught out on the beach during a gale. "The extraordinary fury of this tempest [blew] one of the crew out on duty in the Sixth District . . . off his feet . . . and tossed [him] over a sand-bank several feet high, his lantern being whiffled out of his hand and carried entirely away. Another of the patrolmen was pitched over three times, and finally had to crawl off and seek shelter behind the sand-hills." Though the dangers of patrolling in inclement weather were great, keepers rarely canceled patrols, except in the most extreme conditions. It was when the weather was bad that ships came ashore.

Not only surfmen but their buildings ran the risk of destruction in bad weather. In the spring of 1878, a storm blew up the Atlantic seaboard with such fury that several stations were damaged by the winds and surf assaulting the beach. One crew found three feet of water in the boatroom "and rapidly rising." They rushed to store the valuable lifesaving equipment upstairs just as the station was "lifted from it [*sic*] foundation, the earth around it was being washed away. . . . The floor was bulged up by the power of the sea, and the walls vibrated and groaned as the surf and tempest beat against them. The joints of the building, as it rocked backward and forward, opened and closed with menacing creakings."

The lifesavers saved themselves by climbing into the surfboat and allowing it to be sucked out to sea. Once clear, they were able to row to shelter at a nearby lighthouse. The station on Cobb Island, Virginia (in the neighboring Fifth District), was moved seventeen feet from its foundation by the very same storm.

During the October hurricane of 1896, the Pea Island surfmen found themselves in a similar spot. As the tide and current rose, washing over the island from sea to sound, completely inundating it, Etheridge and his crew, hearing the increasingly pitched moaning of the wood, rushed outdoors fearing that the structure might surrender to the pressure from the sweeping surf. With axes and crowbars, whatever tools were available, they knocked off the boards surrounding the base, allowing the ocean to run freely underneath. Etheridge's quick thinking saved the building.

The same storm wreaked havoc on Station 16, destroying the boat ramp and the bulkhead, taking away the key post, knocking over the flagpole, and blowing off much of the wooden siding. Jesse Etheridge and his crew, like the lifesavers in 1878, escaped in their surfboat, rowing to safety some five hundred yards away to a rise of sand hill that still remained above water.

Pea Island surfman George Riley Midgett found himself out on the south, 3 A.M. to sunrise beat in conditions that he wished had compelled Keeper Etheridge to call off the patrols. The weather was stormy, the tide high and sweeping across the beach, so much so that Etheridge had canceled the scheduled drilling with the signal flags. But not patrols.

Midgett, though he might have been cursing the keeper under his breath, did not begrudge him the decision. He had known Richard Etheridge most of his life—they were slaves together, had gone off to war with General Wild. Midgett understood the responsibility placed on Etheridge's shoulders. During Reconstruction, when Etheridge was just starting in the LSS, Midgett himself had served as a justice of the peace, the only black one in the county, and was eventually elected to the Board of County Commissioners. Later, when the Northern inspector made the all-black crew, Etheridge chose Midgett to be his number one man because he knew that, in his stead, under conditions such as these, Midgett would carry out the duty as regulations required. So he didn't begrudge Etheridge his decision.

Portly, Midgett had a distinctive waddling walk that folks recognized from a distance. But on a morning such as this, no one would be out to recognize his walk or to trade halloos with him. Gale-force winds blew across his body and in his face. Spray whipped about, soaking and chilling him to the core. The walk down to New Inlet was a chore. Beach tide washed over his feet and into his boots, and the wind fought his progress with every stride. He leaned sideways against it until suddenly it changed, and he had to fall forward or be blown off his feet. Midgett lit his lantern to better keep on his path. He made the key post in adequate time, saw sign of no one across the inlet, turned the key in the time detector, and turned back. This was not a night to wait for the nicety of acknowledging the light of the New Inlet patrolman across the way with a wave of his own lantern.

On his way back to the station, the wind now persistently at his back, he was struck and suddenly felled by a piece of wood, hurled up the beach in the sweeping surf. He dropped the lantern, clutching at his leg, seawater rushing over him. Sprained, he deduced, when the searing pain eased enough to allow him to regain his senses. But his mind raced back to the plank of wood.

Was there a wreck out on the shoals?

He rose up, resting his weight as much as he could on the good leg and using the other to keep his balance in the washing tide and ripping gale. He scanned the sea. Listened for rending beams, the clanking of metal, the cry of voices. Nothing. He looked for other debris. Again, nothing. Then Midgett noticed that the wood that had struck him was not new, but time-worn and polished smooth by the wear of water. There was no ship.

He recovered the lantern, now extinguished, and, in great pain, hobbled up the beach. He made it back to the station, where Etheridge attended to his wound. In the log, the keeper noted the event, but added that Surfman Midgett would be able to stay on duty. The crew could not properly function undermanned or ill-staffed, and Midgett would have to tow his line, injured or not, or be replaced.

THE LIFE OF A SURFMAN

Life as a surfman meant that you were always on duty.

Ben Bowser set sail in his kunner from his home at Powells Point for Elizabeth City. He had business to attend to, and it was already July 23, little more than a month before the start of the season when he had to report to Pea Island for duty. He still had to prepare his uniform and personal affairs, to take his yearly physical exam—perhaps, while in town, he'd stop by the physician's office and make an appointment.

It was a beautiful day, with a nice breeze, the kind that was better spent with lines and nets rather than sweating in the crowded streets of Elizabeth City. As his sails caught the wind, Bowser noticed something strange in the distance, a mass on the still surface of the Albemarle. It was a capsized vessel. He immediately set sail for it.

As he neared, Bowser could see a figure—a man—struggling to keep a hold on the hull of the upturned boat. Bowser called to him, Halloo there!— to let him know he was coming. When he reached the boat, Bowser saw it was William Perry, a man he recognized from Colington Island. A gladder face the surfman had not seen in some while.

Bowser pulled Perry into his skiff as Perry's strength gave out. The man was exhausted but relieved. He told Bowser he did not know how much longer he could have held on, and Bowser knew he was not exaggerating: all color had gone from Perry's face, he panted and could not catch his breath.

The lifesaver let the man recover in the skiff and surveyed the scene and tried to figure how best to save the boat, if she was salvageable at all. Alone in the middle of the sound, he could not right it—the boat was too big—nor could he tow it. And he feared that, before a tug or help could be sought after, she might sink. Besides, Perry insisted on not leaving it. Then, Bowser heard a cry in the distance. A ways off, another kunner approached.

When the skiff pulled up alongside, it proved to be the keeper of the lighthouse at Wade Point. He told Bowser he'd noticed the accident from his tower. Perry still lay stretched out in the bow of Bowser's kunner.

Two skiffs were hardly more useful than one, but the two government men figured they had little recourse. Bowser dove in the sound and under the boat and fastened lines to her stays to secure her to the two kunners. The two men rowed as best they could while the enfeebled boater managed the sails and lines. The light summer wind helped only slightly, and several times they had to stop to rest. Finally, they managed to tow the capsized vessel to shore. There, they righted it and freed it of water. Perry could not thank them enough. Elated, though still exhausted, he went on his way.

Bowser was now exhausted, too. And his day was shot. He headed back home. When he next saw Keeper Etheridge, he would report the incident to him. Etheridge reported it in the log. For his efforts, Bowser received three dollars, standard per-rescue recompense for off-duty service.

16

No. 17

The Coast Guardsmen of our community were always looked up to. They were community leaders, and citizens who reflected credit on their families as well as their Service.

—*D. Victor Meekins, sheriff of Dare County in the 1930s, of his youth on Roanoke Island*

Life-Saving Service stations were a wonder, different from the typical Outer Banks house. Kimball had commissioned Francis Chandler, who had joined the office of the Supervising Architect of the Treasury Department, to design and build them. A Gothic Revivalist, Chandler had been moved by the stylings that typified the centuries-old edifices of France, Belgium, and England, where he had studied his art, and he drew from his heart. By these influences, a little bit of Chartres found its way onto the beaches of the Outer Banks.*

Painted olive drab with chocolate trim, the buildings were, first and foremost, built to be functional. The first stations were two-storied buildings with steep, gabled roofs, constructed of weathered pine boards and

---

*After leaving the government service, Chandler became the head of the Department of Architecture at the prestigious Massachusetts Institute of Technology and adviser on city planning to the mayor of Boston.

cedar shingles. The keeper and crew slept upstairs, the keeper in his own quarters and the lifesavers in bunks in an adjoining space, while downstairs was devoted to the boatroom, which housed the boat and the beach apparatus, and a dining area, for meals. The observation deck, or "crow's nest"—an open platform built on the roof—could be accessed from a second-floor ladder and by crossing a narrow "widow's walk." In a small outbuilding next to the station was the kitchen.

To this basic design, Chandler had intricate wooden gargoyles sculpted into the gables to oversee the station. In the ornate eaves, images of porpoises, modeled after ones Chandler had studied on a French château at Cannes, could be seen breaching toward the sky. His set pieces were hardly just cosmetic. A Gothic arch supported the A-frame of the steep-pitched roof. Chandler incorporated into his design the system of X-bracing of a building he'd seen in the Rhône region of France. Board-and-batten siding—vertical strips of planking, with hewn points at their bottom end—adorned the upper house, but it also strengthened the structure against dangerous winds, as did the side buttresses. Wisely, he also fastened the houses only with wooden pegs and joints. No nails were used, a measure that Chandler felt (and rightly so, as the number of stations still standing today attests) would help the houses resist rust from salty sea spray.

No. 17 was a variation of Chandler's basic design. J. Lake Parkinson, Chandler's successor in 1875, replaced the vertical boards covering the lower half with cedar shingles, a row of decorative fish-scale shingles separating it from the upper siding. Parkinson designed a more ornate crow's nest and installed dormers, the better to light the second floor. The Pea Islanders added their own touches. With the assistance of Richard's lifelong friend Jesse T. Etheridge and his men from Station 16, the Pea Island crewmen built a stable in which to shelter their horse.

For the black surfmen, this was home.

Ben Bowser's "second" home remained the stretch of land at Colington that he worked with his father and his new wife, whom he'd married in June 1885, on the island. She died unexpectedly not long after, and Bowser married her younger sister, Mary Wroughton. In 1891, he and his family bought a piece of farmland in Currituck County, near Powells

Point. They grew potatoes and corn, and on his weekly leave, Bowser brought home fresh fish, whatever was running and the lifesavers had had time to catch. In the fall, it was fowl, mostly Canada geese, which fed on the wild peas that grew all over the island behind the station. Still, he was gone more than not, and the job of raising the crops and the budding family fell on Mary Bowser.

Before constructing the stations, LSS officials had consulted locals for assistance in picking sites that would least suffer from the variable nature of the barrier islands, whose physical characteristics could change in any violent storm or merely with the passage of time. Inlets opened and closed regularly. New Inlet, which, during Richard Etheridge's time as keeper, was the southern border of Pea Island, no longer exists today. In a bizarre instance at the southern reach of the Banks, the station at Beaufort nearly collapsed into the sound when the land upon which it was built suddenly sank. Without warning, a subterranean water vein running between the sound and the sea had widened by 150 feet. A pier and breakwater near the station actually dropped below the waterline.

The instability of the land and the gradual encroachment of the sea, as well as the wear and tear caused by weather systems, took their toll on the facilities. The Pea Islanders had to remain vigilant to structural changes in their station, and Etheridge kept them busy maintaining the place in tip-top shape. Upkeep was part of a surfman's daily routine. If shingles needed to be replaced or a boatroom door was broken, crews made the repairs.

WEEKLY JOURNAL

Pea Island Station   *Wednesday, April 18, 1883*

Crew Engaged White Washing the Building on the inside . . .

WEEKLY JOURNAL

Pea Island Station   *Friday, Sept. 21, 1883*

Crew Engaged stoking out the channel for the Benefit of Navigation at Pea Island . . .

WEEKLY JOURNAL

Pea Island Station   *Wednesday, March 18, 1885*

Crew Engaged working on the telegraph Line the heavy Snow Storm on March 18 instant broke ...

WEEKLY JOURNAL

Pea Island Station   *Tuesday, Sept. 26, 1893*

Crew Engaged shoveling sand from a round the station ...

Shoveling sand was a regular activity. Winds were a daily feature of life on the Outer Banks, causing dunes to migrate and raising others where the week before there had been flat beach. The lifesavers had to keep their station from being buried, particularly after storms.

At Pea Island, modernizing the facilities ranged from digging a well in 1881, to building their stable in 1885, to establishing a telephone line in 1887. In April 1886, Assistant Inspector E. C. Clayton, Frank Newcomb's replacement, sent Richard Etheridge the materials and detailed instructions for making mesh screens to cover the windows and doors at Pea Island. "Close all cracks that will admit of a mosquito," his orders read. The connection between malaria and the mosquito's bite would not be made for another ten years; that which was probably intended primarily for comfort also inadvertently helped promote better health at the station.

Libraries of books, donated by various organizations, were kept in the stations. Literacy was new for Ben Bowser, who did not learn to read as a child, and he spent hours honing his skill—required of all keepers—and broadening his knowledge. However, during time free from duties, Bowser and other lifesavers mostly tried to profit from the sea and sounds.

The Banks' best watermen made their money as fishers, and from the start, the fishing industry and the LSS had vied for their services. Early on, the LSS had difficulty retaining these men in the service when the fish were running. To keep them, Sumner Kimball allowed them to fish, fowl, or hunt, as long as these activities did not interfere with their duties as surfmen. Most of the Pea Island surfmen owned boats and nets.

The local newspapers are full of accounts of lifesavers harvesting fish, processing beached whales, and otherwise banking off of the profitable resources of the Outer Banks. One October, Keeper Jesse T. Etheridge of Station 16 and two of his surfmen caught five hundred mullet by wading out with their nets. On another occasion, District Superintendent Joseph W. Etheridge, it was claimed, "took nearly all day" and landed a haul of "300,000 herring" off Hog Island. In one instance, Keeper Daniel Austin of Station 10 almost drowned while fishing off the coast near his station. Luckily, his surfmen noticed his calls of distress and were able to launch the surfboat in time to rescue him.

"When they reached him," reported the *Economist*, "he was entirely unconscious. They hastened to the shore with him and [*sic*] at once and proceeded to recuperate him his crew being well skilled in the method of restoring the apparently drowned, and were successful in bringing him to life in a very short time after reaching the shore."

At other times, lifesavers, in their zeal to profit from the sea, ran afoul of the law, as in 1890, when Patrick Etheridge, the suspected Pea Island arsonist, was charged with, pled guilty to, and was fined for "dredging oysters unlawfully." By most accounts, though, the Life-Saving Service and the fishing industry maintained a mutually beneficial relationship.

The Life-Saving Service became the center of life in the Outer Banks. It had brought income to the region by hiring men onto crews, but also by employing others to work on and supply the stations. Small communities began to form around some, such as the village of Corolla near the Currituck Beach station in the northern Banks. Locals looked to the nearest stations for all sorts of aid.

When severe weather struck in the winter of 1889, fourteen locals caught out in the storm sought shelter at No. 17. They were housed until the gale blew itself out, forty-eight hours later. Including the eight lifesavers, the premises, despite Jim Crow, were integrated and particularly overcrowded during those two days. Sick Bankers came to the station for relief, as when the wife of a local wood contractor fell ill while aboard his schooner and was brought to Keeper Etheridge. The Pea Islanders treated her for two days before sending her home. Etheridge and his surfmen even played the role of paramedic on occasion.

WEEKLY JOURNAL

Pea Island Station   *Thursday, March 10, 1881*

[Dispensed] *1 small piece of wading and adheasive plaster on Capt. Jesse Etheridge an old citizen living on Bodys Island who Dangerously wounded himself by shooting and sent for me to come to his relief   the blood was soon stopped and I left him doing well.*

The injured man, the uncle of Patrick and Adam Etheridge, had, the year before, housed the third suspect the night before the fire.

Although, ten years before, Charles Shoemaker had recommended that the LSS uniform its lifesavers—as a way to create an esprit de corps and instill a sense of pride in the bungling groups of surfmen he'd found during his 1879 tour of the district—Kimball did not adopt the measure until 1889. The garb, based on a navy model, distinguished surfmen from others in the Outer Banks communities. Locals came to look upon the lifesavers as figures of authority to whom they could turn for guidance.

When, in 1885, residents of the unnamed "eastern end" community of the southern Banks could not agree on a name for their newly consolidated township, they appealed to an LSS figure to intervene. District Superintendent Joseph Etheridge resolved the issue, suggesting they adopt the name Diamond City, after the black-and-white pattern painted on the nearby Cape Lookout Lighthouse. The visible symbol of the government service came to signify the town's identity.

As much as was possible, surfmen made themselves available to the various needs of the communities near their stations. One *Annual Report* lists the miscellaneous acts performed over a season by the various LSS crews as including cornering thieves; capturing two runaway boys; apprehending "lunatics" who had escaped from an asylum; as well as assisting other branches of the federal government, from the Corps of Engineers and the navy, to the Immigration and Public Health Services and the Post Office. Most famously, at the turn of the century, the keeper of the station at Kill Devil Hills reported that his crew had put themselves at the disposition of "Mr. Wilbur Wright, while conducting experiments with [his] flying machine near the station."

In one bizarre request, the chief of the Weather Bureau wrote Richard Etheridge asking that he send as complete a list as possible of "Weather Proverbs of the United States" for a new collection the Weather Bureau man was compiling. He wanted Etheridge to distinguish "between those which are of American origin and those which [had] been imported, giving, when possible, the origin of each." Though his response is unrecorded, Etheridge surely complied.

Uniforms arrived at No. 17 just after the New Year, 1890. Ben Bowser donned the tunic, a number 1 stitched on the sleeve, with pride and didn't mind that he didn't have matching pants to complete the ensemble. Only jackets had been received in the shipment to Pea Island. Keeper Etheridge maintained a vigorous correspondence with C. E. Corey, the manager of the Uniforming Department in Philadelphia, but the trousers were held up for three years. As was the case up and down the coast, the Pea Islanders themselves had to pay for the uniforms.

Though they were absent for nine months of the year, the Pea Island surfmen occupied a revered place in the eyes of black Outer Bankers, what an assistant inspector described as a "unique and enviable position among their own people." The black lifesavers recognized this, and despite making only infrequent visits home, they strove to play an active role in the development of their families and in the sustenance of community.

The surfmen made it a point to cultivate ties to the young men of the island. They were like fathers to them, teaching them to clam, to swim, to row a boat. They understood that they were doing the groundwork of preparing future surfmen and future community leaders, so they drove home lessons about responsibility, discipline, and hard work. The Pea Islanders would trust a boy with a skiff, even at a young age, and send him off on errands. The boys ate it up.

Bill Charles Bowser's grandson and namesake recalled of his youth: "The first thing we learned to do, we used to swim there, dive off a boat and go to Pea Island. While at the station we'd recite the duties. That's all we had on our minds, finding out the duties and all—to be just like them."*

---

*Mr. Bowser III went on to serve at Pea Island in the 1930s.

★   ★   ★

Most Pea Island surfmen also stayed active in the life of the larger community. In November, men would absent themselves from the station to go to Manteo to vote in elections. They took leaves to serve on juries or as witnesses in court or to fulfill other civic duties. Just as the black lifesavers strove to contribute to the vitality of the Outer Banks communities, so, too, did their wives in the ways that women of that era did such things, primarily by being active in the churches and volunteering for service with a variety of benevolent organizations.

Like their husbands, the wives of black surfmen held a certain status in the community. Trips to Elizabeth City did not go unnoticed. They were the class of people who would be reported upon in the "Our Colored People" section of the *Economist*, the *North Carolinian*, and *Fisherman and Farmer*. Segregation kept them separated socially from the wives of white surfmen—otherwise there would have been no need for a section devoted especially to "Our Colored People." When danger was at hand, though, Jim Crow let down his guard. Racial distinctions meant nothing when a storm blew through and the women, congregating at the post office, wanted news of their husbands.

The world of coastal lifesaving was, and still is today, considered male, one in which men sacrificed and endured hardships to ensure the safety of others. However, women—the wives of surfmen, their mothers and sisters, daughters, cousins—also played significant roles. Lifesaving stations and the crews who operated them were not autonomous units, but members of families and communities. Those families and communities contributed to the lives of the surfmen just as they were bolstered by them.

Women had impacted upon the world of the LSS from the start. Martha J. Coston, the widow of nineteenth-century inventor B. F. Coston, took her dead husband's flawed idea and perfected the flares that would prove indispensable to surfmen to warn off or otherwise signal ships from shore. The Women's National Relief Association, a benevolent society, provided the clothing and other items that lifesavers dispensed to the survivors of wrecks. And in the earliest years, some women served as cooks in stations, including an unidentified black woman at Pea Island in the late 1870s. More important, though, women, in the absence of the lifesavers, sustained the families and communities that produced these men who would fill the ranks of, first, the Life-Saving Service and, later, the Coast Guard.

Unlike some North Carolina stations that had been built near villages or clusters of homesteads, No. 17 was in a desolate spot. Bordering dense marshland on the sound side and with only a few houses to its north, Pea Island stood isolated, separated from adequate medical care, stores, or other amenities by miles of beach and inland sounds. The surfmen's families rarely resided out on the beach, as was the case with other crews. They would visit for day trips, though, for group outings or organized Sunday picnics. Gangs of children explored the station. Sometimes, one, riding alongside on horseback, might accompany a patrolman as he walked his beat.

Once the crew had left after the season, Frances Etheridge, Oneida, and Richard's youngest daughter, Maggie, spent summers with him at Pea Island. Sumner Kimball was prepared to accommodate the presence of families at or near the stations, as long as their presence did not interfere with lifesaving duties.* Etheridge's wife and kids assisted him in the day-to-day upkeep of the facilities. In February 1900, Etheridge secured use of the "dwelling house" of substitute surfman J. W. Wroten so that Frances might be closer during the active season.

Contrary to Sumner Kimball's fears, women were a welcomed presence, particularly in times of crisis. They helped by cooking, making coffee, and otherwise ministering to the exhausted and injured shipwreck survivors as well as providing for the lifesavers who had spent hours on the beach landing the sailors. At the tragic *Lancaster* disaster, L. B. Midgett's wife was largely responsible for sustaining the life of Mrs. Hunter, the wife of the ship's captain.†

★   ★   ★

---

*During the summer of 1893, Kimball authorized an Outer Banks keeper to "erect a dwelling house for the use of his family on the station premises." The general superintendent insisted, though, that family residences be built at least 200 feet from the station, that the LSS not incur any expense in its building or maintenance, and that the keeper be prepared to remove the house upon fifteen days' notice.

†Edith Morgan, the daughter of the keeper of the Grand Point au Sable station (Michigan), was awarded a Silver Life-Saving Medal for assisting her father on two separate occasions to land stranded mariners.

In April 1892, surfman I. M. Ward left Pea Island on his weekly leave. He was just a substitute at the station, though he, like most black fishers, aspired to eventually make the regular crew. When he arrived at his home on Roanoke Island, he found his wife gravely ill, near death. Nearby, their child already lay dead.

How could so dire a tragedy befall him after such a brief absence?

Keeper Etheridge, accounting for his shorthanded crew, wrote in his log: "[Ward] could not find a Substitute to fill his place so he was absent for one day and two nights Without leave. but I think the man did the best he could under the Circumstances." Ward served out his term of enlistment as a substitute. Afterward, he removed himself from the roster of eligible candidates.

When Benjamin Bowser began his life as a surfman, he earned forty dollars a month during the active season. This was raised to fifty in the mid-1880s. During the last two months of duty, Kimball granted North Carolina lifesavers a five-dollar supplement, enticement to keep them from quitting the stations to take advantage of the fishing season. As keeper, Etheridge made four hundred dollars annually.

Etheridge, Bowser, and the rest spent Christmases away from their families. They worked six-day weeks, each week characterized by night patrols and daytime drilling. Despite this devotion to duty, by 1915, when the LSS merged with the Revenue Cutter Service to form the U.S. Coast Guard, wages had increased to only sixty-five dollars per month, inadequate compensation for the rigors and risks of service. And until the merger, there were no pensions for lifesavers. If a man died on duty, his family was paid the sum owed him for his service until the date of his death. Nothing more. Such were the hazards of the life of a surfman.

The Life of a Surfman

Army Signal Service Station, Hatteras, December 22, 1884:

> *Unknown barkentine struck on Hatteras Shoals at four P.M. yester-*
> *day during a southeast gale. Crew remained in the rigging during*
> *the night the sea washing everything movable from off her decks.*
> *This morning the vessel was discovered abreast Big Kinnakeet Life*
> *Saving station flying signals of distress she having floated during*
> *the night. Vessel full of water to her decks. Cape Hatteras Life Sav-*
> *ing crew have just launched their surf boat and are now on their*
> *way to the vessel. Wind, Southwest—Sea very heavy.*
> *—Private Crawford, Chief Signal Officer*

Crawford's concern was not exaggerated. The sea was, in fact, running
"mountains high," according to those gathered on the beach, among them
lifesavers from the Durants, Creeds Hill, and Big Kinnakeet stations. The
Cape Hatteras crew, on their way out in the boat, had among them Patrick
Etheridge, the Creeds Hill keeper, in place of their own number one man.

Each of the four crews had spotted the bark the night before—a complete
wreck: her deck awash and broken in two, drifting northward. She lay well
out, perhaps as far as seven miles northeast of Cape Hatteras. There had
been no sign of life aboard, and the surf—the heaviest and most dangerous
in years, according to old-timers—made the LSS keepers cautious. Crew-
men had watched the ship through the night for a sudden change in her con-
dition or a signal that would indicate survivors were aboard. Nothing.

At daybreak, the men saw that the ship had beaten over Diamond
Shoals and still inched northward. Successfully making the trip out seemed
as unlikely as it had the day before, but as the lifesavers stood watching, they
saw a flag run up the masthead: a distress signal and a sign of life on the
wreck. High surf be damned, it was time to act.

The Cape Hatteras crew, whose boat they'd hauled to the site, began
stripping away any clothes that might impede their movements in case they
capsized, and they strapped on their cork life belts. Not all among them
agreed the undertaking possible. The number one man, in fact, called it a
suicide run and refused to go.

Just then, someone on the beach heard Patrick Etheridge utter words that would echo up and down the Banks and, though they could not know it then, would ring in the lore of lifesaving and become the service's motto: "The book says we've got to go out—it doesn't say a damn thing about coming back!" With Keeper B. B. Dailey at the rudder and Patrick Etheridge at number one's oar, they launched into the surf. It was half past ten.

From the beach, the rest tracked their treacherous route. The breakers on the inner bar stood as high as a barn roof and detonated at regular, quick intervals. The more dangerous ones on the outer bar, a half mile out, seemed as tall as a lighthouse. Dailey steered over the inner bar, and with quick strokes, the boat cleared her. "The whole scene was awfully grand," one of the observers onshore recalled, "and enough to make the stoutest hearts quail."

And quail they did, as the surfboat lay rolling between the sets of breaking waves, the lifesavers struggling to maintain their position and looking for an opportunity to pass over the outer bar.

Back on the beach, the Big Kinnakeet crew brought their boat and attempted to launch in support of the Hatteras men or in case they did not make it. So rough was the sea, they could not even get their craft out from shore. Again and again they tried until finally they had to give up.

The observers watched as Dailey perceived some favorable change in the rolling breakers, called an inaudible order, and quickly, the surfboat was again under way. The waves were so pitched that, at times, the men on the beach could see the entire interior of the boat as it climbed the seas. They stood, muscles tensed, not even breathing, expecting to see the boat tumble over backward. As if ordained by God, she cleared the breakers. On she went.

Two hours after launching, the Hatteras boat came abreast of the bark. Dailey had to carefully maneuver his craft close enough to the ship to throw a line by which to carry off survivors, however many there were, but stay far enough away to keep from getting swamped or pitched into the wreck by the surf. He accomplished this while, one by one, his men took off the exhausted sailors. Many of them were unable to carry themselves and had to be lifted bodily by surfmen who crossed over to get them. They were nine: too many to safely carry in the boat with the seven surfmen. But Dailey and Etheridge knew there would be only one trip, so they packed them in.

Dailey took a seat at an oar, Patrick Etheridge relieved him at the rudder, and the boat, laden gunwale deep in the sea, turned for shore. The ocean still raged, but Etheridge managed the overburdened boat with precision and skill. An observer boasted that she "rode the still tremendous seas like a duck, and, after safely passing the outer line of breakers, reached the shore in good shape."

Those on land gave a loud Hurrah! They met the boat and ran her high up on the beach. The bark's survivors were drenched to the core, freezing and hungry after being lashed for ninety-two hours in the rigging of the bark, but they were all alive. She was the Ephraim Williams, the lifesavers learned, bound for Providence, Rhode Island, from Savannah with a cargo of pine lumber. The Kinnakeet crew whisked the survivors off to their station, to revitalize them, while the rest marveled at the feat they'd just witnessed.

Private Crawford, among those who had watched the entire operation, felt compelled to report the lifesavers' bravery over the telegraph wires: "I . . . beg leave to state that the heroic conduct of Keeper Daily and crew, also Keeper Etheridge, should not be passed unnoticed." It was not. Each man received a medal of the first class—the Gold Life-Saving Medal—for conspicuous bravery.

17

Pressures
Particular to
Pea Island Surfmen

Between me and the world there is ever an unasked question:
. . . How does it feel to be a problem?

—*W. E. B. DuBois,*
The Souls of Black Folk, *1903*

By the mid-1880s, Congress and the country had acknowledged the value of maintaining a well-kept, publicly funded Life-Saving Service. Modern equipment made it possible for them to respond swiftly to disasters, and disciplined keepers led surfmen to rescues of shipwrecked crews and cargoes. The LSS officer who investigated the *Ephraim Williams* rescue, awed by the facts he uncovered, reported in the *Annual Report:* "These poor, plain men, dwellers upon the lonely sands of Hatteras, took their lives in their hands . . . and all for what? That others might live to see home and friends."

Patrick Etheridge's take on the events of the day were much plainer.

WEEKLY JOURNAL

Creeds Hill Station   *Monday, Dec. 22, 1884*

at day light I was to Cape Hattras station on discovering the bkne. Ephrian
Williams   I went to Kennekeet there by the request of no. 1 man and
Keeper of Cape Hattras station   I went to sea in no. 1 mans plas.

He offered no more detail. He sought no praise or glory.

The investigating officer, in his report on the *Ephraim Williams,* concluded: "As long as the Life-Saving Service has the good fortune to number among its keepers and crews such men as these, no fear need ever be entertained for its good name or purposes." In a few short years, Patrick Etheridge had gone from suspected arsonist to exemplar of what a lifesaver should be.

Patrick Etheridge's rise from outcast to keeper was steady and quick. Soon after the Pea Island fire, in November 1882, he was one of four men hired by Keeper John Scarborough to replace members of the Big Kinnakeet crew that the LSS's passing Board of Examiners rejected as unqualified. Patrick was married to Easter Scarborough; the Kinnakeet Scarboroughs were his in-laws. He joined the crew as the number one surfman.

Hiring a man like Patrick Etheridge into one's crew could readily be justified: he was fearless. He was also rowdy, headstrong, and prone to articulate his opinions by violence. During this same period, the state Superior Court brought him up on charges of assault and battery and of unlawfully dredging oysters. A hung jury delivered him of the first charge, but he pled guilty to the second and was fined ten dollars and court costs. Surfmen could be dismissed for such things. Still, despite his checkered past and recent troubles with the law, in the fall of 1884 Joseph Etheridge proposed, and Sumner Kimball approved, Patrick's appointment to the keepership of the Creeds Hill station, just south of Cape Hatteras. His career as a lifesaver was thriving. He took over on September 4, four months before the *Ephraim Williams* ran afoul of Diamond Shoals.

Kimball's reasoning remained the same as before. Operations in the district stations, while improving, did not run without hitch; the "demoralization" of the 1870s and early 1880s was not so far from memory as to be without impact. The issue of annexation into the navy resurfaced from time to time, and Kimball knew that the service was still just one disaster away from renewed debate and, perhaps, disbandment.

The year before Patrick's appointment at Big Kinnakeet, in late April 1881, John B. Etheridge, the patriarch of the family, died at seventy-five, afflicted with a cancer of the face. Patrick's own father had been dead since 1868. With these passings, "Cap'n Pat," as he came to be known, became an elder statesmen of one of the Outer Banks' premier families. District Superintendent Joseph Etheridge and Superintendent Kimball, understanding this, were prepared to overlook any misgivings and circumnavigate their own guidelines to advance efficiency in the still-fragile district.

On March 30, 1885, three months after the *Ephraim Williams* rescue, the Cape Hatteras crewman G. L. Williams commented of Pat Etheridge's Creeds Hill surfmen that they "did not know there drill." Cap'n Pat himself, according to Williams, "did not Know the no. 5 drill." Despite his ability at an oar, Patrick still lacked the qualities that made a good keeper. He was not quick to improve. Joseph Etheridge's successor, District Superintendent E. C. Clayton, made a special trip to Creeds Hill in March 1888 to follow up on troubling reports made about Patrick and his number one man.

Clayton's investigation uncovered several damning facts against Patrick. Worst among them, Patrick, on several occasions, had left the station without leave during threatening weather. In one instance, he took his entire crew except the patrolmen to attend a "frolic" where the men drank and partied. On April 17, before the end of the active season, Clayton discharged Patrick from the service.

"I have repeatedly warned Keeper Etheridge of his carelessness and lack of system," Clayton wrote Kimball, "and as often has he promised to do better. . . . Keeper Etheridge is a daring surfman. . . . While he will make a good surfman under a Keeper who is a disciplinarian, as a Keeper himself he is a failure. Keeper Etheridge in his present position is a detriment to the service." This did not block Patrick's appointment to one position after another, however.

The following December 1, B. B. Dailey, with whom Patrick had orchestrated the *Ephraim Williams* rescue, hired him, not as the winter man but as his number one surfman, demoting all the other crewmen one stripe to accommodate the new arrival. Within the year, the keeper and his number one man had fallen out with one another. Dailey found Patrick to be negligent in his lookout duties, but when the keeper confronted him, Patrick denied it. A few days later, Dailey upbraided Etheridge for his poor record-keeping. Soon, his belligerent attitude became too much for Dailey to bear.

"In getting the beach apparatus cart in the Station this afternoon," Dailey recorded in the log, "P. H. Etheridge surfman no. 1 had a great deal to say in what way to put it in and I Keeper told him to Keep his mouth shut. and had to use rough Language to him." Dailey concluded: "his mode of doing business does not suit me in the way I have always had it done and to save further trouble, I propose to make other arrangements after this month is out." Patrick had not even been in the crew a full year.

Patrick, knowing trouble was near, was not one to let himself be pushed around. The very day following this last run-in, he wrote Sumner Kimball to request his discharge, turning the tables on Dailey and charging that he would no longer "stand the Keeper abuse." The general superintendent abided by both men's wishes, approving the midseason discharge, but he admonished Dailey to act only if he thought "it for the good of the Service." Dailey did, and Patrick was gone.

Not long thereafter, Patrick again fell afoul of the law. He was charged with assault and battery in November 1890 and, a few months later, with assault with a deadly weapon. In the first case, he was found guilty. Yet despite his questionable personal and professional record, by the fall of 1891, Cap'n Pat had found his way back into the service, this time in charge of Cape Hatteras station, of all places, as the successor to B. B. Dailey, who'd resigned because his "health [was] impaired." Before the LSS would bring Patrick back on, a petition had to be raised and sent to Washington. It was signed by, among others, B. B. Dailey, E. C. Clayton, *and* Richard Etheridge. Kimball approved.

Patrick went on to run the New Inlet and eventually the Bodie Island stations and led his crews on many rescues. He died in 1920, leaving a white son and an illegitimate biracial one, both of whom would go on to run coastal lifesaving stations. Cap'n Pat is remembered today as the model of an "old salt" Banker and hero of the surf.

★   ★   ★

In December 1883, Richard Etheridge's number two surfman, Robert F. Tolar, just cracked. Tolar had gone to Manteo for the mail two days before, but when he returned, he was stumbling drunk. Drinking on duty was strictly forbidden, and when Etheridge confronted Tolar, a man with whom he had served since his first years in the LSS, the surfman turned belligerent. He began ransacking the place, kicking and tossing over furniture. Etheridge reported: "it took two or 3 men to hold him."

Incidents like this one, while not everyday occurrences, were not uncommon in stations either. The tone of Patrick Etheridge's correspondence with Sumner Kimball suggested that he verged on violence with B. B. Dailey. At the Kitty Hawk station in 1884, tensions reached an extreme and ended in a Wild West–style shoot-out.

Assistant Inspector Clayton arrived at the station to investigate charges against Keeper James R. Hobbs, who was accused by different parties of a variety of infractions: of plundering a wreck, political patronage, and other abuses of his position. Hobbs was also said to use the service of his men and the property of the station for his personal ends. While Clayton interviewed the keeper, one of his surfmen and accusers, T. L. Daniels, entered, furious, and confronted Hobbs directly. Clayton tried to calm him, but as the dispute escalated, Clayton soon found himself caught between Hobbs and Daniels. A scuffle ensued. Daniels reached for a pistol in his hip pocket; seeing this, Hobbs grabbed up a double-barreled shotgun that lay nearby. Using Clayton as a shield and the inspector's shoulder to prop the barrel, Hobbs fired. Daniels collapsed, dead. Hobbs was indicted for felony murder, but found not guilty.

The Kitty Hawk incident was an extreme example, but the life of a surfman was difficult. The tedium and pressures of service were tremendous and taxed the fortitude of crewmen. In Tolar's case, alcohol contributed to his "crazed" outburst. For him, though, as well as for other Pea Island surfmen, different sources added to and fueled the rage that these usually reliable lifesavers exhibited when the pressures got to be too much.

Richard Etheridge was neither a tyrant nor an exploiter of his men. He was strict, but fair. Still, tensions existed within the station. Tolar was not the sole Pea Island crewman to erupt. Henry Daniel shot the side of the building with a shotgun and a month later swore at Etheridge. While Benjamin Bowser was serving as acting keeper in Etheridge's absence,

Theodore Meekins struck him. These men, whatever else they might be expressing, were venting a common resentment and anger that built up within the black surfmen. Its source: pressures, on top of the ordinary ones, that Pea Islanders suffered, pressures created by the poisonous racial climate that they lived in daily.

The last two decades of the nineteenth century and the first of the twentieth have been called the "nadir" of the African-American presence in the United States. With the Compromise of 1877 that signaled the beginning of Southern Redemption, the national attitude toward blacks took a dramatic shift for the worse, and relations between the races became increasingly strained. As black voters refused to fall in line with old-guard political machines, the seething tensions gave way to ugly racism.

Behind the banner of "white supremacy," a more or less unified effort got under way to marginalize blacks from mainstream Southern society. For the conservative-minded Democratic Party, newspapers—the television of the nineteenth century—were the weapon with which to spearhead the assault on African-American inclusion in the state's social fabric. Readily accessible and blatantly partisan, newspapers kept people informed about and involved in the issues of the day, appealing to group unity, identity, and collective action. The Democratic strategy was to use the print media to unify whites across party lines against blacks by fomenting fear of a coming "Negro Domination."

As polling time approached, columnists voiced increasingly racist ideas, according no "place" to blacks in the "New South." Articles of various lengths and on a variety of events centered on the notion of the black as "beast" in language that Josephus Daniels, the editor of the white-supremacist *Raleigh News and Observer,* would, in retrospect, call "lurid . . . sometimes too lurid." "Negro rapists" ran riot through the columns of Southern papers, "ravaging," "despoiling," and otherwise "ruining" defenseless white women. The message the radical racists exhorted was clear: although docile when enslaved, the black race, which had been unloosed by emancipation, was retrogressing to the ferocious, murderous, and licentious impulses of its African origins and, at the risk of race war, had to be subjugated. White unity and supremacy was the only answer, with the legal disfranchisement of blacks the primary goal.

Many whites bought the rhetoric. A fever caused by an editorial by African-American Alex Manly in his *Daily Record* led to violence in Wilmington, a city just two hundred miles down the coast from Pea Island. Manly's paper castigated lynching in the name of white Southern womanhood, but white supremacists denounced the article as an attack *on* white womanhood. Mobs thronged around Manly's office, looking for him, and when they could not find him, they prowled the city, randomly attacking innocent blacks. As many as thirty were murdered.

And Wilmington was just one example. The lynchings that Manly decried had become common occurrences, with white-on-black violence reaching its highest proportions ever in the history of the country during the 1890s. Race riots erupted all over the South—in Lake City, South Carolina, in Memphis, in New Orleans, in Atlanta—and also in places in the North, such as Springfield, Illinois. Segregationists running on the platform of "white supremacy" and promising to legislate Jim Crow in the state law books rose to power. By the turn of the century, they had staged political takeovers in every Southern state, including North Carolina in 1898.

The federal government, blasé after three decades of sectional strife over race, validated the white supremacists with the Supreme Court's 1896 *Plessy v. Ferguson* decision. In *Plessy,* the court ruled that "separate but equal" was constitutional, barring blacks from having any recourse against the rising wall of Jim Crow laws quickly and completely engulfing them.

As season followed season and year followed year, the Pea Islanders read the papers and watched as the Outer Banks changed. White supremacy was not just the war cry from distant Raleigh but prevailed closer to home, as newspapers such as Elizabeth City's *Economist* and *Fisherman and Farmer* fell right in step with other race-baiting rags. On Roanoke Island, R. Bruce Etheridge, a recent graduate of Trinity College in Durham whose father was keeper at the Nags Head station, founded and chaired the Manteo White Supremacy Club.* The club's membership included important local officials, such as T. S. Meekins, the commissioner of wrecks, who later would be elected Superior Court clerk. Working with

---

*R. Bruce was also Patrick Etheridge's cousin.

the Dare Democratic County Convention, the club raised enough support to endorse the proposed state constitutional amendment to disfranchise blacks.

At election time, Dare, a county previously balanced between Democratic and Republican constituencies, voted overwhelmingly for Jim Crow, supporting Charles B. Aycock, the outspoken white-supremacist candidate for governor, and electing segregationist J. H. Small to the U.S. Congress. In the referendum on disfranchisement, Dare supported the measure to deny black North Carolinians the ballot, easily defeating their opponents by a margin of 151 votes. Just a few years later, in 1903, the county would send the same R. Bruce Etheridge to Raleigh to represent the coastal region in the state's General Assembly.

These were trying, dangerous times.

Jim Crow weighed heavily on the Pea Islanders. These men had known racial strife, even before the fire, as keepers quit hiring them because of the malaise their presence caused within crews. The old allies couldn't be counted on anymore. Edward Drinkwater, Malachi Corbell, even Joseph Etheridge, who was a longtime friend to the black community and with whom Richard still debated politics—all had deserted them. The district superintendent, Richard's immediate superior, publicly supported African-American Henry P. Cheatham in his bid for a seat in the House of Representatives, but he'd declared himself "against colored Keepers and colored crews entirely."

It became hard to know who was friend and who was foe and how to interact with them, whatever the case. Other lifesavers, keepers as well as surfmen, and store owners in Manteo referred to Keeper Etheridge as "Capt. Richard"—as they should have. The title reflected the respect and the authority due him in the community. George Riley Midgett, however, was "Uncle George"—not "Mr.," not "Surfman," certainly not "Sir," the title due the man who had been a county official. "Uncle" was intended as a term of affection. His wife was "Old Aunt Nancy."

The *Economist* spoke of "Captain Dick Etheridge, (colored) our old friend," and when he made a trip to Elizabeth City, the white-supremacist mouthpiece reported it, saluting "the worthy Keeper of Pea Island Life Saving Station" who was in town on business. The newspaper praised

Etheridge as "a representative of the old time colored man—polite, respectful, considerate and self respecting," casting him for its readership as the rare "good" black man who was acceptable in the new order that the paper espoused. To the white supremacists, he, and also Benjamin Bowser—who, the paper stated, "was well spoken of"—knew their "place."

The African-American lifesavers could not know how to read these mixed messages. If the *Economist* and its like-minded readers were to have their way, they would be relegated to the shadows of society. Yet the segregationists praised Pea Island.

There was no Jim Crow at the scene of trouble. Ships did not come ashore neatly near a single lifesaving station; two or more crews worked most wrecks. Within the reaches of Pea Island, black and white worked side by side.

When the *George C. Wainright* shoaled on a bar in the Pamlico Sound during the summer of 1893, the group of volunteers who assembled to form a makeshift crew did not sass Etheridge, the only African-American present, nor resist his authority. The white surfmen had grown up around Captain Richard, they respected the position he held and his capacity to fill it, and they obeyed his orders. He instructed them on how to bring the impossibly stuck schooner off the old-timer's way: by "kedging" her free. Etheridge had the men run an anchor off the *Wainright*'s bow and seat it; when the sound rose with the tide, they hauled on the chain with the schooner's capstan, "warping" the ship forward until she slipped off the reef.

Together, white and black celebrated the satisfaction of successful saves, and when they were unsuccessful—when life was lost—they shared the lingering doubts and burdens of their failure. Even if it meant ignoring deep-seated prejudices, they fought as one, at least during those hours when shipwrecked sailors relied upon their ability to work together.

But what about at other times? When they sat around the dinner table with their children and told stories? Or when they went to the polls? Were these men who called him Captain Richard also virulent advocates of white supremacy? In fact, a great many were. As the issues of pensions and workers' comp came to a head, the Pea Islanders' white counterparts showed their stripes.

★   ★   ★

Repeatedly over his lengthy career as head of the LSS, Sumner Kimball urged Congress to institute a pension system for surfmen. More than any other reasons, poor pay and the lack of a pension drove men to quit the service. After twenty years of failure, a group of North Carolina lifesavers decided to take matters into their own hands. They planned the formation of the Surfmen's Mutual Benefit Association. Members would pay dues, and in the absence of pensions, the association would provide benefits and support to the families of those who died in the service. The association's first annual meeting was held in Elizabeth City in June 1900, with Malachi Corbell, among other prominent lifesavers, in attendance. The organization intended to expand to include the lifesavers of all districts, and membership quickly reached fourteen hundred.

All lifesavers were included—all except those from Pea Island. The *Economist,* which advocated for the organization, declared: "Each station in the United States and in the world should be of the family of the Life Savers . . . a compact and solid body, bound together, as by 'hooks of steel' . . . united for the benefit of all and each individual member." Yet the founding surfmen felt that black participation would in some way compromise or weaken the compact. The association's bylaws stated, "Any commissioned or appointed officer, or any surfman in the thirteen districts of the United States Life-Saving Service, and no others will be eligible to membership: provided, however, that no gentleman of color will be admitted as a member." The only "gentlemen of color" in the LSS served at Station 17.

The Pea Islanders protested and pled for admission. They made it clear that they had no aspirations of seeking out positions of governance, the fear that had driven white keepers to stop hiring blacks in the first place. They only wanted to assure a measure of security for their loved ones should tragedy befall them. "There are no desire on our part to participate in any way with the management of the affairs of the association other than share its benefits," Lewis Wescott wrote. Their repeated petitions met with silence. Pea Island surfmen were never allowed access to the association and the benefits that it offered.

In the LSS, blacks received the same wage as whites, their station was equipped similarly, but "separate" was rarely also "equal," and the Pea

Islanders, unable to know definitely who was a friend and who a foe, had constantly to fear for their place in the service, regardless of the quality of their performance. With the changing times, would their white-supremacist neighbors allow Pea Island to continue?

W. E. B. DuBois summed up the dilemma perfectly when he wrote: "[The American Negro] simply wishes to make it possible for a man to be both a Negro and an American, without being cursed and spit upon by his fellows."

The Pea Islanders resisted the pressures as best they could. No. 17 did not remain all-black by decree, but because Richard Etheridge assured it would be so. As keeper, only he had the authority to select his crews. Each year, he made it a point to choose black Outer Bankers. As long as he was keeper, African-Americans *would* have a chance to serve. He and his men nurtured the interest of the black boys of the region, creating a legacy so that black service at the station would be perpetuated.

But the blade of self-segregation was double-edged. There was no such thing as a transfer from Pea Island. If a black man could not serve there or did not want to, he didn't serve at all. Ben Bowser, like Lewis Wescott before him, lived more than forty miles away. On his leaves, he spent as much time in transit as with his family. In case of emergency, illness, or injury among his loved ones, what could he do?

The reality about promotion was also clear to them. Here was a place where each *could* be keeper, yes, but advancement would only come if higher-ranked bunkmates resigned, were dismissed, or died. Ben Bowser did not wish Richard Etheridge ill in order to wear the embroidered *K* on his jacket. He understood, though, that only the keeper's removal would enable him to ask his wife, Mary, to do the stitching on his sleeve.

For Bowser, the rewards of service were worth these costs. Not so for all the black surfmen. For some, service at Pea Island began to feel particularly claustrophobic. Bill Charles Bowser, who had been a surfman since 1875, left the service after more than a decade as the number five man. Rather than persist in the dead-end career of lifesaving, he began building and repairing boats full-time, a potentially lucrative but far more speculative enterprise.

Most stayed on, working until old age or deteriorated health drove

them out. William Davis and George Riley Midgett quit the service when
they could no longer pass the physical exam. Each had worked dutifully
for more than a dozen seasons; Midgett did sixteen, most of which he was
ranked as either the number one or two man. Though both were qualified,
neither ever served as keeper.

Theodore Meekins, who joined the crew in 1890, would serve twenty-
seven years, sixteen as the number one surfman, and never get an opportunity to run a station.

Lewis Wescott, a surfman since 1874 and one of the original crew
members, would serve twenty years at Pea Island and only reach the keepership when the keeper before him died.

So, too, with Benjamin Bowser. He would serve seventeen years, fourteen as the number one man, before attaining his goal of becoming a
keeper. But he would only gain it because of Richard Etheridge's death.

For white surfmen, too, the chance to be appointed keeper could be long
and promotions slow in coming. But, more often than not, this was not the
case. There was no lack of employment opportunities for whites in the service. Circumstances permitting, they could move from station to station (as
Patrick Etheridge had done), even from district to district, either to advance
their careers, get closer to home, or merely change their environment.

In a racial climate such as this, the station might, at times, seem like a
prison behind whose walls the necessity of success had bearing not only
on the individual, not even only on the crew, but rather on the whole community. For each black surfman knew that failure at Pea Island would be
seen as the failure of the entire race, further proof of African-American
cowardice and inferiority, evidence to justify and support the arsonists'
act. William Simmons, who served at the station later in the Jim Crow era,
explained baldly: "We knew we were colored and, if you know what I
mean, felt we had to do better whether anybody said so or not."

Richard Etheridge understood that sometimes these pressure could over-
whelm. More than a sign of bad character, insubordinate conduct might,
in fact, be an expression of frustration turned inward, on the facilities or
on colleagues who were also trapped within the confines of Station 17.
Etheridge, torn between his effort to enforce discipline and his need to
maintain the morale of his crew, seemed willing to make allowances.

Robert Tolar was a ten-year veteran and Etheridge's number two man. During the off-season, Etheridge had no qualms about leaving the station in Tolar's charge, alone to manage its affairs. Etheridge had done so one summer for three weeks. After Tolar's alcohol-induced rage, Etheridge pled in his favor: "this is the first offense of this kind that has been commited by the Said R. F. Tolar since he has been in the Service with me." Etheridge reinstated the surfman onto the duty roster.

District Superintendent Joseph Etheridge, on the other hand, would not tolerate Tolar's breach of discipline. His drunkenness had caused him to miss his patrol, and although another crewman had taken up the slack for him, Tolar had, according to regulations, overstepped the bounds. When the district superintendent visited Pea Island two weeks after the incident, he ordered Keeper Etheridge to get rid of Tolar.

The LSS was sensitive to the public image of its lifesavers and looked unfavorably upon intemperance. Still, many surfmen were known to take a drink and sometimes to abuse alcohol. Joseph Etheridge did not have them fired. And in the cases of men like Malachi Corbell, the district superintendent lobbied to see them reinstated after they had been dismissed.

Perhaps in Tolar's case, Joseph Etheridge was being pragmatic. Though the district still suffered from a lack of good keepers, Tolar could never be one. He would never run one of the Outer Banks stations besides Pea Island, and other good black surfmen also stood in line for that singular job. Joseph Etheridge could afford to take a hard line with Tolar, to set an example.

Whatever his reasoning, for the Pea Islanders, the district superintendent's actions must have seemed inconsistent, a double standard: dropping the hammer on one of theirs after showing preferential treatment for white lifesavers. Still, Richard Etheridge had no choice. He did as instructed and discharged Tolar.

Tolar was the descendant of slaves, none influential in the Banks. Unlike Patrick Etheridge or Malachi Corbell, he had neither the family connections nor the political clout to bail him out of his trouble. He appealed to the one person he could, the Northern official Assistant Inspector Clayton, both in person and in writing.

Sir

  asst. inspector of the Life Saving Survis Sir as i was talking With
you a bout goin back in the life saving survis Sir i Would bee glad if you
will see Capt Richard Ethridge and fix for me to get back With him as i
am informed that ther Wil bee a vacunce in his station and he told me
When i Left ther if the Superintendent ancerd [answered] my Letter but
that he Would give me my place back Sir i Would bee glad if you Would
see him a bout it as ya know just What shape to intur seed [intercede] mor
better then i can tell ya so PLeais Do all you can for me i know if you
Will talk With him you can get him to Do it

  sir Pleais Do all for me you can i am not bragin on my self but sir i
Will inshure you that ther cant bee found Eney colord man that can go
ther and Do Eney more in the regards of the survis then i can Do that i
Will inshure you.

So Nothin mor
your Humbul survant
R. F. tolar

Tolar never worked in the Life-Saving Service again.

For all the black surfmen's lives were changing for the worse outside the
station, their duties as lifesavers had been uneventful. Several gales but no
severe storms. Too many ships warned off to count, but none run
aground, in need of succor. The odd incidents of locals seeking out first
aid, but few lives truly threatened. The 1880s closed with a taste of the
seaborne challenges that the black surfmen would soon face.

THE LIFE OF A SURFMAN

At just past eight-thirty on the morning of October 24, 1889, the bell on the wooden telephone box began to ring. Typically, the daily phone check came later. The crewman nearest removed the earpiece from its hook, expecting the broken-up voice from Station 18, saying all was well and to relay the message north. But it was not Station 18. It was Keeper Payne of Oregon Inlet, and he demanded to speak with Captain Richard. The crewman hustled upstairs to the keeper's quarters and brought back Etheridge. The others all stood at the ready. They knew what this call foretold.

Etheridge went ahead of his surfmen, leaving them to haul the beach cart and No. 7 line that Keeper Payne had requested. The Pea Islanders would provide support for Payne as his crew assisted a schooner he had spotted in distress off the coast. Etheridge could see the vessel from shore: a three-master, not yet grounded but dead-drifting southward toward him, her crew tied in the rigging. It was rainy and cold, the sky deep gray, and a wind raged, sometimes blowing seventy miles per hour and more. The heavy surf swept far up the beach. Just before ten, Etheridge arrived abreast of her, about three miles north of his station.

As he did, the schooner finally struck ground, and when she did, it was catastrophic. All three masts toppled over, the snapping of the beams violent like a detonation. They collapsed onto the sailors who were tangled in the rigging, taking one into the ocean, injuring God knew how many of the others. Scores of lengths of lumber, suddenly released from the cargo hold, burst out onto the water, pitching about in the turbulent seas. Etheridge could only watch as the one man drowned, entangled in lines and battered by rent planking.

Payne, who, with his crew, had been following the vessel down the coast, arrived in time to witness the horror. The Station 16 surfmen immediately set about preparing the beach apparatus as Payne apprised Etheridge of what little he knew. He'd spotted her that morning, about half past eight. The mariners had apparently lost control of the vessel and, thinking she'd run aground, lashed themselves down for the impact. Not grounded, the vessel went helplessly with the tide. Payne followed with both the boat and the beach apparatus—the one cart tethered to the surfmen, the other to the government team of horses—waiting for her to shoal so they could go to her aid.

Payne prepared to call "Action!" just as the Pea Islanders arrived. The black surfmen stood at the ready. Payne landed the first shot successfully across the wreck. As the two crews worked in unison to haul out the whip, wreckage pitching in the surf fouled the line, snapping it in two. The crew fired another successful shot, but again, the debris fouled the line before they could secure the hawser.

Meanwhile, they watched as lumber mercilessly pounded the sailors with each crashing wave. Some appeared to just surrender to the sea.

With the third successful shot, the surfmen were able to secure the line and send off the hawser with the breeches buoy and a cork life vest attached. They watched as two of the mariners tried to force the limp body of a third into the buoy, but could not wrestle him in. Finally, one of them sat in the breeches.

The seas still ran high, higher than the raised hawser, dangerously tossing about debris. The lifesavers had to wait for a lull before trying to carry him ashore. When they finally hauled him in, he was blue with cold and so weak he could hardly speak. He identified himself as William Sawyer, the ship's master. His schooner, the Lizzie S. Haynes, had been bound from Pensacola to Baltimore carrying a cargo of lumber that had suddenly turned deadly.

The lifesavers sent the breeches buoy back out with another cork vest. The seas worsened, and this time the wait was even longer before they could bring in the other man, the ship's steward. His condition was no better than the captain's. It was nearly sunset.

Sawyer and his steward told the lifesavers that the only other one left alive was the ship's mate, and that he was just barely so, unable to pick himself up. When they looked out to sea, neither keeper saw any sign of him aboard the remains of the Haynes. But neither Payne nor Etheridge hesitated. They sent the breeches buoy back out. Who knew but that seeing the first two safely landed might revive hope in the man. Perhaps he might be able to pull himself into the breeches.

While being sent out, the line again fouled in the wreckage. Communicating by line with the ship, in the dark, with no one to secure it, was now impossible. The surfboat still stood at the ready, the men fresh enough to row, but both keepers knew that, in such high, cluttered seas, at night, they could not use her. Not only would they needlessly risk the lives of their men, but they would not be able to land her beside the Haynes.

They built a fire and waited anxiously onshore for the seas to calm so they could launch. The opportunity did not come until midnight, and when they reached the Haynes, they found only two bodies, a sailor stiff with death and the mate. The mate was still limber. Etheridge and Payne knew he'd been alive at sunset when they'd landed the steward, so they figured that perhaps he'd only just succumbed and might be resuscitated. They rushed back to shore.

Rather than try to carry him the three or so miles to either station, they had their lifesavers load him onto a board and hurry him, along with Sawyer and his steward, to a nearby house. While their surfmen scoured the shore for the last three sailors, Etheridge and Payne nursed the motionless body of the mate, hoping to restore life. They placed hot bricks on his chest, wrapped him in blankets, and rubbed and rubbed pungent linseed oil into his arms and legs. For two hours, they worked. But the man was dead.

The lifesavers never recovered the other corpses. Two days later, with Sawyer and the steward safely housed at the station and out of danger, the crews of Nos. 16 and 17 reunited on the beach. They wrapped the mate and the sailor in blankets, said a word for the disappeared, and buried the dead over the dunes. They had never learned either of the men's names.

18

The Right Men
in the Right Place

Legislation is powerless to eradicate social instincts or to abolish distinctions based upon physical differences. . . . If one race be inferior to the other socially, the Constitution of the United States cannot put them upon the same plane.

—*Justice Henry Brown, majority opinion,*
Plessy v. Ferguson, *1896*

The October gale that devastated the *Lizzie Haynes* wrecked six other vessels off the Banks as well, from Wash Woods to New Inlet, and took a total of twenty-four lives. A more dangerous, deadly storm had not hit the coast since 1878, when the *Metropolis* came ashore. The black surfmen had been vigilant, at the ready, and, once beside the *Haynes,* had done all they could. Yet they had suffered five deaths. Richard Etheridge and his men could only pray this wasn't an augury of things to come.

Their prayers were in vain. Severe weather systems increasingly struck the Outer Banks over the next few years and, with them, hurricanes unlike any Outer Bankers had seen before. At the same time, trade steadily increased over the decade, with the shipping lanes off the Outer Banks becoming a waterborne highway. Shipping off the coast suffered.

Almost half as many ships were lost off the Outer Banks in 1889, when the *Haynes* came ashore, as had been during the decade up till then. Nineteen vessels fell victim to shoals and foul weather that year, whereas the year before there had only been four losses and in 1887, one. In 1890, there were ten; in 1891, seven, including the *J. W. Gaskill* off Pea Island; 1892, six; 1893, fourteen; in 1894, seven. All the while, numerous others grounded but were saved and salvaged. In August 1895, Richard Etheridge and his men were summoned to the wreck of the *Rosa Cora,* which had capsized in the Pamlico Sound. The combined Chicamacomico, New Inlet, and Pea Island crews raised and righted her and sent her on her way. But more dangerous weather and the resultant disasters were still to come.

Vigilant service and good fortune had helped keep ships off the shoals at Pea Island for the better part of the 1880s. With the new decade, Richard Etheridge and his crew suddenly found themselves confronted with disaster after disaster. The ten months between Christmas, 1895, and November 1896 were particularly nasty at Pea Island. Ships came ashore like never before, their hapless crews leaving their fate in the hands of the lifesavers.

The first warnings came in mid-December, with the temperature near freezing and a gale blowing through. The surf ran high, sweeping across the beach on Pea Island. The winds tore some 150 shingles from the roof of the station, and the storm was sufficiently strong that Keeper Etheridge canceled the general cleaning for the day. But the men still patrolled. Etheridge himself took the station's horse and rode his regular route to the key post, as was his duty, to check the impression and assure that the south beat was properly covered.

Etheridge informed District Superintendent P. H. Morgan and Assistant Inspector J. C. Cantwell that his crew could restore the damage to their station if replacement shingles could be had. His superiors forwarded Etheridge's request to Washington. All the men liked to take leave around Christmas, but Dorman Pugh had a unique motive: he was getting married. Etheridge granted Pugh's request for a twenty-four-hour absence on the twenty-seventh. Pugh sent L. W. Tillett out in his place. That night, while Tillett was on patrol, disaster struck.

Tillett came upon a three-masted schooner, just two hundred yards offshore and grounded. He ran the mile and a quarter back to the station and sounded the alarm: Ship ashore! It was two-thirty; by ten past three, Etheridge and his men were at the site. Readying the Lyle for firing, the men heard a call from sea: the ship's captain was hailing them. Etheridge and his counterpart from Oregon Inlet, whom he'd telephoned for assistance, made out the sailor's request. He wanted them to await light before throwing the line.

Though the surf was rough, it wasn't particularly high. Etheridge and the Station 16 keeper judged the ship wouldn't come apart before daybreak, no more than three hours hence. They would wait. In the meantime, Etheridge had a group from his and No. 16's crew return to their station for the surfboat.

Day broke at six-thirty, and in the light, Etheridge saw that they wouldn't need the beach apparatus at all. The surf had calmed sufficiently for them to stroke out to the schooner. They made two trips to the ship— the *Emma C. Cotton,* bound for Savannah from Philadelphia with a load of coal—and within an hour had landed the crew of seven, as well as all their baggage. The Pea Islanders housed them for three days, then transported them to Oregon Inlet station, from where they boarded a steamer, bound for home.

The schooner and her cargo of coal proved a total loss, but the day after the New Year, Etheridge's men joined those from Station 16 to salvage what they could off her. They recovered the topsails and other sundry equipment that washed ashore. On January 3, the commissioner of wrecks—the "vendue master," Bankers called him—sold the remains at auction, as the *Cotton*'s master, Thomas Ayres, who'd stayed behind for the occasion, looked on. The vessel, of which he was co-owner, had been valued at nearly $8,000 and the coal at $2,000. Her insurance picked up $1,500 of the cost, and the vendue brought in $102.96. Five days later, Ayres left Pea Island a broken man.

The day he left, word came over the wire from the Signal Service that a storm that was centered off the Florida coast was now heading northeast up the Atlantic seaboard. Etheridge wanted to beat its arrival, so two days later he set his men to work replacing the shingles that had been blown off the month before. The temperature never topped the mid-forties, and in the brisk winds it felt even colder. They got the job done.

Ben Bowser, on watch in the crow's nest, was saved from the onerous chore, though not from the biting cold.

Two days later, Sunday, January 12, the storm blew through and the steamer *James Woodall* ran aground three hundred yards off New Inlet. Josiah Wescott, the keeper of Station 18, called Etheridge to bring his men, and the Pea Islanders spent their off day on duty, helping the other crew land the shipwrecked sailors. The checkerboard contingent saved all ten men aboard, but the steamer was a total loss.

Trouble again called the black surfmen to action just three days later. Lewis Wescott, who had the day's watch, spotted a boat midmorning, about five miles out in a rough Pamlico Sound and flying a distress signal. He couldn't tell, but from that distance she appeared to be the government sloop *Alert*, the assistant inspector's boat. Keeper Etheridge recognized her right away, as he knew that Cantwell along with District Superintendent Morgan were due for their official visit, part of the regular inspection throughout the district.

Etheridge mustered his crew, and they sailed the supply boat into the sound. Should they need to kedge her, he wanted to have the proper equipment. The *Alert* proved not to be grounded, but damaged: she'd lost her rudder. Cantwell had tried to sail for shore after it came unshipped, but the sloop became unmanageable and they'd had to anchor her where she stood.

Cantwell was sure they could repair the rudder enough to return the boat to Elizabeth City. He asked Keeper Etheridge to go to shore and bring back nails, bolts of iron, and other tools to do the work. The Pea Islanders did. They repaired the piece and, once done, carried Cantwell and Morgan ashore and dropped them at New Inlet, from where they continued their tour. For all intents and purposes, the black surfmen had passed inspection—this time around. The *Alert*, with the remainder of her crew, set sail for Elizabeth City for more permanent repairs.

Later that evening, newlywed Dorman Pugh, on the nine-to-midnight patrol south, mistakenly turned the key the wrong direction in the post, leaving no impression on the dial. The keeper dressed him down and recorded the mishap in the station log.

January 18 portended more trouble from the sea. The day began like many that time of year, overcast and gray, but by midday the clouds had dropped low and the sky became a thick fog. The surf remained rough.

Etheridge called off the general cleaning, but he had Ben Bowser and substitute W. H. Wescott patrol throughout the afternoon in case of some crisis. Bowser also had the beat from midnight to 3 A.M., so he spent twice his normal workday walking the beach.

No trouble came from the sea, but Etheridge got news of trouble down the coast. Cantwell and Morgan discovered that members of the Durants station crew had taken to using the government telephone for unofficial dealings. The inspectors sent word to all the stations along the Banks that keepers should inscribe in their log: "any further violation of [the telephones] will not be tolerated." Etheridge had not had this problem among his men, but he made it clear to them that he did not expect to either.

By the time the *Maggie Lawrence* came ashore three weeks later, on February 10, 1896, the Pea Islanders had already experienced several seasons' worth of disasters.

Ben Bowser was on leave on urgent family business, but George Riley Midgett, the number two surfman, could amply back up Etheridge, should the need arise. Since William Davis's disability and retirement, Midgett had become the old-timer on the crew. He was three years the keeper's senior and, like Etheridge, had seen a world of living that the younger crewmen—Dorman Pugh, Theodore Meekins, Bill Irving, and Stanley Wise—could only imagine. Bowser and Wescott had as much experience in the service, but neither had seen war and the North and far-off Texas. When times had been better for blacks, old man Midgett, while a justice of the peace, had once even married a white couple.

Midgett had the midnight to 3 A.M. beat south, and when he and the north patrolman, Dorman Pugh, returned, Theodore Meekins and Stanley Wise headed out. The surf crashed upon the beach with unusual power and deafening thunder, and the northwest squall stung Wise's eyes with sprays of sand and salt water. He worked his way north, scanning the surge for debris or other signs of a shipwreck. Just a half hour later and only a quarter mile from the station, he caught sight of the black shape of a vessel—a large one—foundered in the breakers, maybe 250 yards out.

Wise lit a Coston light to let the mariners know they had been spotted. Then, as fast as he could, the surfman raced back to the station and sounded the alarm.

Another ship ashore, their fifth that season. Keeper Etheridge notified the Oregon Inlet station by telephone, then he mustered his crew and set out to the scene with both the surfboat, dragged by the government team of mules, and the beach apparatus, dragged by the men. With the ship so close to the station, he knew to haul both in case one method should prove to be more efficient than the other.

Midgett, as stout as Etheridge had ever known him to be, lashed himself to the half-ton cart. He and the rest heaved and hoed her wide wheels through the wet, sinking sand. Within an hour, the Pea Islanders had arrived in view of the wreck. Etheridge could clearly see the outline of the schooner: a three-master, over on her side and gradually working her way toward shore. She was not firmly grounded—it might be risky to communicate by line—but she did not appear to be at risk of coming apart either. Etheridge remembered the *Lizzie Haynes;* he'd seen the damage that could be done when a drifting ship suddenly shoaled. But he knew also that a pitching spar could snap a line and the breeches buoy become an instrument of death. The surfboat would be no more practicable: he could not land her aside the rocking, drifting ship.

Etheridge decided to wait for daylight, no more than an hour or so away and, he imagined, bound to give him a clearer view of his options. Sixteen years as keeper had made Etheridge a cautious man, not one lacking in daring, but one who was deliberate and thorough. Too much was at stake to act otherwise. In the meantime, he and Midgett led the crew in setting up the beach apparatus and preparing the surfboat for launching.

Etheridge's caution paid off. At sunrise, the surf diminished. Etheridge did not know how long it would last, but he seized the opportunity. He ordered the surfboat launched. The crew ran the boat into the waves during a lull in the pounding and took up position at the oars. Etheridge steered from the stern. Through troughs and over the crests of waves, the lifesavers fought their way toward the wreck. When they came abreast of her, Etheridge was careful to land seaside of her, in case she suddenly shifted again toward shore. He also knew that, with these winds, the seas might pick up, making a second trip impossible. He shouted to the sailors to all come, one by one, and to bring any baggage they could salvage.

A much-laden surfboat pushed off for land. She ran low in the sea, and the Pea Islanders had to work hard to clear the wreck. With the skill of an expert waterman, Etheridge picked his way through the surf. Once clear, they rode the tide back toward the beach. The Oregon Inlet crew, who'd arrived as the Pea Island surfmen were taking the mariners off the wreck, assisted in landing the boat.

Etheridge had his men help the sailors salvage the sails, rigging, and whatever stores they could. The remains only brought the ship's captain, E. M. Holloway, $160.20 at auction. The schooner had been carrying coal to Charleston and, including her cargo, was valued at over $4,000. She had no insurance.

For the lifesavers, the *Maggie Lawrence* and her crew were just more sad victims of the sea, but they were fortunate ones, too. They were alive and uninjured. The Pea Islanders had seen to that. They'd responded to the emergency with dispatch, but also with care. Etheridge had used his lifetime knowledge of that stretch of coast to save the stranded mariners without needlessly jeopardizing their lives or the lives of his men. The rescue was textbook. It was also the third of 1896. It would not be the year's last.

It would, however, be the last for George Riley Midgett. In the middle of the night on May 18, he fell gravely ill—so sick, in fact, that Etheridge ordered Theodore Meekins to carry him home. Midgett recovered, but never sufficiently to serve again at Pea Island. He was fifty-seven years old. First Etheridge's longtime friend Fields Midgett, then William Davis. Now, Etheridge aside, the last of the old-timers was gone.

The same day that sickness struck Midgett, the U.S. Supreme Court legitimized the growing, national illness. By a majority of seven to one, the justices decided in favor of "separate but equal" in the benchmark *Plessy v. Ferguson* case. The most dangerous storm—the dark cloud of white supremacy—had rolled over the land.

Yet, as the conditions of black life were taking a turn for the worst in the state, in the South, and throughout the nation as a whole, the Pea Island lifesavers were doing their best work. And their very best was yet to come.

19

Their Finest Hour

The Wreck of the E. S. Newman,
October 11, 1896

The people cried mercy in the storm,
The people cried mercy in the storm,
The colored and the white stayed awake all the night,
Crying Lord have mercy in the storm.

—*"Florida Storm," sung by*
African-American Shape Note Singers

Etheridge drove the men as hard as he did the mules.

He called out cadence over the shrill winds: "Heave to, men, heave, heave!" And the men called back, "HOO-AH, HOO-AH," more grunt than chant.

The stretch of beach between Pea Island and New Inlet, the same one all had spent their entire careers patrolling, was like no place they had ever before been. It looked unearthly.

Heave it, heave it!
HOO-AH, HOO-AH.

Meekins and Irving were harnessed to the front of the beach cart. Wescott and the Preacher—Stanley Wise, who'd just as soon save a soul as a life—pushed the cart from the rear. Bowser was at one wheel, Etheridge at the other, each man helping the wooden spokes around, keeping the cart from getting bogged down. Dorman Pugh sat atop the creaking driving cart, reining the wild-eyed mules. They traveled in a tight group, with their collective wills focused on keeping the carts in motion. With the beach inundated, the tempest raging, and in the blackness of night, this was no mean feat.

Keep the wheels rolling!
HOO-AH, HOO-AH.

Waves rushed up the slope of the beach, the spindrift racing up their legs to their waists, at times bogging them down. By looking back at the lights of the station, still dimly visible to the north, Etheridge tried to estimate the spot where he and Meekins had seen the signal flare. As they pushed south, the station lights faded from view, leaving the crew with only a single oil lantern to illuminate the way.

There were only two directions to walk on Pea Island, north and south. The Atlantic was on the doorstep and the Pamlico Sound, the back porch. The October storm had squeezed the corridor of sand even tighter, and as the evening descended that night, Etheridge had witnessed the ocean spilling into the sound. Sweeping tides and roaring winds rushed across what was left, and only a few dunes of terra firma peeked above the waterline.

Might they get disoriented, lose their bearings? Nothing was where it had been. Dunes that had marked the way for years had now been cleaved away by the sea. Fishing shacks were demolished and swept from the beachface. Old wrecks were resurrected from the sand and sent back to the Graveyard of Ships. The keeper used what few telephone poles remained aloft to guide the crew over that which, under normal circumstances, would have been dunes and sea oats.

The men trusted his direction. They listened to the cadence, each man bending his body against the weight of the cart, focusing his energy at his feet and the rhythm of the beat that Etheridge called out. Soon debris—broken boards, a piece of railing, a stray oar—washed up against the cart and into the men's legs. No one needed to be informed that the grounded ship was coming apart.

> Roll the wheels, roll them!
> HOO-AH, HOO-AH.

How many miles gone? Not one yet. Maybe only a half. Probably just over a quarter. How many more to go? Two, three at the outside. A half mile felt like ten days of backbreaking dock labor under a July sun.

> HOO-AH, HOO-AH.

It was a wonder that Meekins had even seen the signal flare. Assigned watch duty, he could stand on the observation deck for only a few minutes at a time, spending most of his energy trying to keep from being blown off as he scanned the turbulent sea for signs of distress. Even his bulky frame was hardly anchor enough in these conditions. Alone atop the unenclosed platform, with only the roar of crashing waves and the *brang-brang-brang-brang* of the metal tackle striking the flagpole, he had fought the winds beating at him, blinding him, and had kept his attention focused out toward the darkness. Meekins praised the keeper's having called off patrols—something Etheridge never did. But he cursed that Etheridge insisted the men spend equal time on dogwatches from the crow's nest. With the wind and whipping rain, there was nothing to see—not two feet in front of you at times, much less a mile out to the outer bar.

The first hour passed, each man maintaining a fifteen-minute shift. Strange breaks in the rain occurred from time to time with no rhyme or reason. One minute it would be pouring, then it would shut off as if someone had got tired at the pump handle. Walls of wind-driven rain would come up the beach—Meekins could see their approach—and like spirits, their force would pass over the station and continue toward Oregon Inlet. Between deluges, the lifesaver saw the surf: not towering now as he had expected, but pushed over by the wind, flattened and broken in all directions.

When Meekins had first seen the signal—a faint, plum-colored glow to the south—he didn't think he'd seen anything at all. Meekins imagined that his eyes, irritated and stinging, were playing tricks on him. Or was it real? He knew Etheridge would want to know about it, so he lit a Coston flare and had Pugh go after the keeper. The surfman waved the flare over his head.

Etheridge arrived just seconds later, and both men scrutinized the darkness to the south. Etheridge ordered Meekins to bring up a red rocket. Meekins hurried over the widow's walk, down the narrow crawl space, and past the rest of the crew, who were gathered around the portal that led to the deck. He sprung to the equipment locker and rummaged for a flare. Returning to the crow's nest, he handed the cylindrical rocket to Etheridge, who fired it in the direction Meekins had pointed out.

The rocket's Fourth of July burst was startling, even in the deafening wind, and its flash illuminated the entire roof before arcing a bloodred tail across the turbulent sky. Just then, it was answered by a barely visible red light—a definite sign that a ship was out there, and in distress.

Etheridge darted away, his voice booming throughout the station, Meekins and the others following.

Captain Sylvester Gardiner kept telling his wife that things were not as bad as they seemed. Winds blasted from the northeast and shrieked in the stays. Gardiner's ship, the *E. S. Newman,* pitched and rolled among the waves as if she were a rowboat, not a 393-ton schooner. High seas flooded her decks. She shed them as best she could, each time slowly righting herself, her structure creaking and moaning pitiably.

Reckoning position in conditions such as these was part science, part guesswork. With several successive days of clouds and rain, the captain had not been able to use his sextant to take a sight. Now, it was too rough even to take soundings; he'd probably lose men overboard in the attempt. By the reddish hue of the sea, Gardiner knew they must be over some shoal or close to shore, although land was nowhere visible. The storm intensified, and Gardiner feared the seas would devour his ship.

The day before, on the morning of October 10, the sea had been almost smooth, only cat's-paws wrinkling the surface. The *Newman* stretched under a crowd of sails. As the day progressed, so did the breeze. *Haul main sail, haul!* cried the captain. The *Newman* leaned with the wind and her canvas filled. *Haul all, let go and haul!* The crew worked the ropes hand over hand, sailing the schooner beautifully.

Late that afternoon, Captain Gardiner had noticed the ocher-colored clouds above, long, thick bands of them, each punctuated by intermittent windows of blue sky. He checked the barometer, an instrument he valued more than any other on board. The readings were all over the place. First the glass rose, then dropped, then plummeted. The graceful swells that normally coursed past, eight per minute, now stretched long—thick, deep-troughed waves rolling at half that rate. The sea seems to slow before a gale. Gardiner recognized the signs. A giant tropical depression was poised somewhere just beyond the horizon. Still, even as the waves pitched and the winds began to howl, Gardiner figured he could reach the safety of the Chesapeake Bay before the leading wall of the storm seized his ship.

Captains, then as now, used the Beaufort system to rate the strength of storms. The scale ranged from zero—glassy, calm waters—to twelve—mountainous, hurricane-driven seas that endangered even the largest vessels. As the day progressed, Gardiner judged the seas reached a legitimate nine on the scale. He sent his crew high into the rigging to reef the uppermost sails. The high winds made working aloft difficult and deadly dangerous. The crew flattened themselves along the yards on foot ropes, and when they looked windward, their eyes teared. Below, the *Newman*'s decks were awash with green water.

It took hours for them to reef a single sail. As the gale grew impatient, sails were blown out, ripped from their stays in explosive bursts like cannon fire. Gardiner ordered his men down, and they scurried out of the rigging, thankful to be back on the deck. The winds increased, and more sails gave way until the *Newman* went from goose wings to bare poles—no sails at all.

Captain Gardiner ordered the crew to batten down the hatches. Everything movable was lashed down: barrels, chains, anchors, gaffs, tackle blocks. First mate J. B. Crandall stayed with the captain at the helm. The rest, including Gardiner's wife and three-year-old son, Thomas, went below.

Once they had secured the hatches, they grimly awaited their fate. Mrs. Gardiner attended to her son. Baptist and Henry Bravo played cards in the flickering illumination of a single whale-oil lamp, as though this were nothing out of the ordinary. The old shellback Arthur Tehuy spun three-braided sinnets. Others silently prayed. Seawater began to gather and slosh about on the deck, but they all worked at ignoring it.

Topside, Gardiner and his first mate fought to hold the wheel, the shipmaster reproaching himself. What had he done? He'd played a dangerous game, trying to outrun an Atlantic storm, racing for Hampton Roads before the seas became unnavigable.

Perhaps the entire voyage had been ill-fated. It had all begun for Gardiner on a stroke of bad luck. The *Newman* had set sail from Providence, Rhode Island, several days earlier en route for the Chesapeake Bay. It was a routine commercial jaunt along a familiar Atlantic trade route: in Norfolk, she would take on a cargo of coal and sail back to Providence. But the weather was thick at Point Judith, Rhode Island, and an unknown schooner, heading north, had appeared out of the fog and glanced off the bow of the *Newman*.

The collision shook the schooner, her jib and headgear stripped away by the dark vessel. Gardiner could hear the other ship's bell tolling and her crew scrambling as it pressed farther into the night. He ran forward to inspect the damage. Though not severe, the damage would have to be repaired before they could continue. Gardiner set course for their home port at Narragansett Pier. The repairs took longer than expected, delaying their departure five more days.

As the hours passed, the storm looked more and more like a hurricane. Struggling to keep his ship afloat, Gardiner estimated—hoped—that they were somewhere off the Eastern Shore of Virginia, near the safety of the Chesapeake Bay. Through the gloom, he searched for the beacon of the Cape Charles Light, which would guide him in behind the capes. In the meantime, Gardiner decided it best to keep plenty of sea room, holding the schooner well offshore until the storm passed. The vessel rode up the faces of enormous swells and surfed wildly down their backs. He and Crandall battled to hold on to the wheel—the force on the rudder would often wrench it from their hands and spin it at whim.

As evening approached, the atmosphere seemed the color of fish flesh and was thick enough to choke on. The sea around the ship was latticed with frothy combs of white seawater. The crowns of these thirty-foot giants would crest above the *Newman*, then the winds would shear off their tops. Discordant blasts of wind passing through the rigging were a shrill otherworldly chorus.

Gardiner had known the *E. S. Newman* longer than he'd known any of the crewmen aboard her, longer even than he'd known his wife. He had commanded the trim three-master for twenty-four years, virtually an entire career. He had sailed her through many tight spots and several storms, and she had shown pluck each time. But he had encountered nothing like this one. The wind blew with an intensity he'd never before witnessed, the sea gone white with spray and foam filling the air, making it impossible to breathe, let alone see. Gardiner had to confess, to himself at least, that he was no longer in control of his ship. He merely tried to steer her clear of the breakers that bucked and pitched all around him.

The *Newman* fought the swells, clawing off as best she could, but still, the northeast gale pushed her south, probably far past the entrance of Chesapeake Bay. No lighthouse beacon shown.

Night came on, and Gardiner, exhausted at the helm, wondered if they were off the Eastern Shore of Virginia or off the coast of North Carolina. In the darkness, he could not tell: Were they ten miles from shore, or one hundred yards?

It seemed clear they'd missed the Bay. If they kept pushing south, they'd hit the Diamond Shoals and Cape Hatteras. All sailors knew the stories of the Graveyard of the Atlantic, swapped freely in the taverns of Providence, swapped freely along the wharves Gardiner had known all of his life. Even the most seasoned captains feared Cape Hatteras. Many would just as soon beach their vessels as attempt to clear the Cape in foul weather.

Gardiner could not but think of his wife and son below, bracing themselves as the schooner rode up a swell, then nose-dived into the unimaginable trough.

The storm had been working on the *Newman* for nearly ten hours, and each wave took its toll. With each wash, she shipped seas, shedding them as best she could, righting herself as the seawater gushed from the scuppers. But she rolled as though waterlogged. Gardiner stood in a foot of water at the helm. His charts gone, his sails blown away—another huge sea and her spreaders might be in the water. Another sea and she might not come back.

Gardiner was forced to a decision. She had fought bravely, but the *Newman* was whipped. His only chance to save his crew, his wife, and young Thomas was to drive her ashore, hoping help would come from land.

★   ★   ★

Every shipwreck seems to have a similar story—a set of variables leading to disaster, a mistake, a miscalculation, something so obvious it is overlooked. In the story of the *E. S. Newman,* the collision off Point Judith looms large. As the crew awaited repairs at Narrangansett Pier, a giant tropical depression formed into a hurricane out in the vast Atlantic, then began to drift west toward the Caribbean. Though the Weather Bureau warned of a large system approaching, Gardiner, perhaps preoccupied with the bizarre accident, perhaps overconfident with his many years at sea, thought he could make Norfolk before the full force of the storm struck.

The 1896 hurricane was not just any storm. It was one in a series of storms that ravaged the Atlantic coast unlike anything that had passed before. Between 1893 and 1899, this coast, particularly along the dangerous shoals off North Carolina, bore witness to sister hurricanes that would each leave as many as thirty vessels crushed in its path. Maritime historians have identified these years as among the worst on record, with an average of one wreck per week during that span.

One storm, with winds that reached an astonishing 140 miles per hour, broke the anemometer at Cape Hatteras. Nearly every building there was leveled. Inhabitants huddled in the few remaining dwellings, and when they emerged, they were shocked by the devastation. The fishing industry, upon which most residents depended, was completely destroyed, fleet and all. Schooners and barkentines came ashore battered and unrecognizable. On Ocracoke, thirty miles to the south, every single horse, hog, and cow was drowned and swept out to sea. And farther south, Portsmouth Island took similar punishment, its churches and homes either blown over or picked up by the sweeping tides and moved from their foundations.

When hurricanes of this magnitude struck the Tar Heel coast, virtually every house, lifesaving station, hotel, and weather outpost felt the impact. Storm surges inundated the beach, making the Pamlico Sound and the sea one body of moving water. After the hurricanes passed, surviving residents would find themselves cut off from their neighbors by new inlets that had been carved into the barrier islands virtually overnight.

These weather systems were fantastic displays of natural forces, and the 1896 storm had all of these characteristics and more. Keepers from Beaufort to Cobb Island canceled patrols—an indication of the magnitude of the hurricane. The *Norfolk Virginian* reported the hurricane to be "decidedly the most severe since 1847," which had blown open two new inlets along the Banks. The 1896 storm produced the highest Atlantic tide in a half century, flattened telephone lines, and damaged a dozen lifesaving stations between North Carolina and New Jersey.

Communiqués from Nags Head reported that every dwelling on the beach had been leveled and swept away, the stately hotel suffering terrible damage. At Kinnakeet, just south of Pea Island, the house of U. G. O'Neal was whisked from its foundation and carried half a mile into the sound. Then, the wind changed suddenly, and the sound brought it back and dropped it at almost its original spot. Elsewhere, the topography of the Outer Banks was radically transformed. A Signal Service observer watched as "the terrific surf cut a new inlet from the ocean to the sound."

In all, scores of fishing boats were smashed in their slips, and four seagoing ships were totally destroyed off the coast on October 11, 1896. Six others were damaged but freed from tight situations by the vigilant work of Life-Saving Service crews. During the ensuing two days, the hurricane continued to destroy everything in its path as it spun north, punishing shipping all the way to Massachusetts.

October had begun as a normal month at Station 17, with fields of menhaden splotching the surf and porpoises appearing each morning just outside the breakers. The skies stayed overcast. At night the only celestial bodies to appear were the dim North Star and the moon, dull as if under gauze. Temperatures reached into the seventies, not unusually warm for the time of year. Nothing let on that a tremendous storm was a few days from striking the Outer Banks.

On October 9, it became "airish," and a strong southwest wind kicked up to forty-two miles an hour. The surf churned, and clouds, in low, unbroken banks, settled over the island. The atmosphere had a greenish hue, the sea was dark as blood, and a mood of anxious anticipation spread among the inhabitants. Lifesavers stationed along the Banks felt the winds increase steadily all evening long. Fishermen hauled in their nets, stowed their boats, and left the beaches for refuge on Roanoke Island.

On the tenth, Etheridge received a bulletin from the Weather Bureau. The news was not good: forecasters predicted a tropical storm, possibly a hurricane. At sunrise that day, the barometer at the Pea Island station had read thirty inches and dropping. The keeper called the wind "Fresh" and the weather "Stormy" and noted in his logbook that the wind had swung around and was now a true gale blowing from the northeast. By mid-morning, Etheridge saw the barometer plummeting, and a hard, stinging rain soon obscured the beach. Waves rushed past the high-water mark, flooding the dunes, combing over the ribs of old wrecks. Pea Island Creek, a bight where the men kept their skiffs, was blown empty, the black mud exposed from bank to bank.

By noon, Etheridge was calling the storm a hurricane, and he wrote the baleful word in the station log. The telephone lines buzzed with keepers' voices, north and south, checking in with each other, grousing over the flood tides and the winds, which tore shingles from rooftops.

To the north, Keeper Malachi Corbell called the storm the worst in fifty years. With "Seatides Sweeping Every Moving [object] off the Beach," he and his surfmen at Wash Woods spent the evening transporting their children and wives via boat to the protected woods on the sound side of the island. To the south, the schooner *John W. Bell* grounded on Rebecca Higher Shoal, and the crew of the Portsmouth Island station went to succor her. At Cape Hatteras, Keeper Patrick Etheridge plucked several fishermen from the surf, then worked with the lighthouse keeper to latch down the lens so the storm would not snatch it away.

Storm surge was "crotch deep" in all directions at Chicamacomico, prompting journeyman keeper L. B. Midgett to call it "the worst storm [he'd] ever experienced." Sportsmen from the hunting clubs and area fishermen came to the station in dreary groups, terrified by the storm. The New Inlet crew arrived later with tales of freak tides and winds that made them fear for their lives.

On Pea Island, the crew from Oregon Inlet quit their station for safety inland, as the storm surge nearly lifted the building from its foundation.

Everyone along the coast, surfmen, residents, and fishermen alike, hunkered down and prayed the storm would abate. Meanwhile, the Pea Island crew went out into it.

The storm drove the *Newman* toward land. The unknown beach and surf, churning somewhere to the west, would be the schooner's final destination. Gardiner and his first mate Crandall wrestled the helm to control the rudder as the ship was tossed with the swells.

The best way to beach a vessel was with a full head of steam. If they could ground the schooner firmly on the beach, their chances of survival would be much greater. If the *Newman* did not ground, she would run with the currents and drift with the shifting tides, pounding against unseen shoals and glancing off sandbars. There would be no way to light a distress flare, no way to get the others out of the hold. She would spin, topple, and be reduced to kindling wood in a short time. So they wanted to put her aground with force.

Gardiner and Crandall watched intently, both knowing that the jolt traveling from the rudder to the wheel when a ship struck ground could snap a man's arm. Breakers hollowed and boomed beside the schooner. The Beaufort scale be damned, these seas were off the scale! All around the *Newman* was white, broken sea and rips rushing across shoals. The schooner was close to shore, but the *Newman,* with an empty hold, rode high and did not strike the outer sandbars.

Suddenly, the keel struck. The schooner buckled, her timber rending and snapping. The masts flexed, and the sea ripped the tiny yawl away from the starboard rail. But she grounded hard in the pounding surf.

Immediately, Crandall and Gardiner wrenched open the hatches and rushed the others out. In the fury of wind and rain, Gardiner ordered his six crewmen and his family to secure a hold topside. *Climb into the rigging,* he instructed, *climb as high as you can.*

Men scurried here and there, lashing themselves down with lines or whatever was handy, one—Eugene Colho, his hat now lost to the sea— merely entwining his limbs around the forecastle railing. The Bravo brothers handed out cork life belts and helped others secure themselves as waves poured over the ship. Mrs. Gardiner, shaken, her calico dress soaking wet, embraced her husband. Tommy also clung to his father and would not let go, his openmouthed weeping inaudible in the din of the men's hustling and the roar of the storm. Gardiner moved his wife and son aft, bracing them against the mizzenmast, a thick rope clove hitched around his wife's waist and Tommy in her arms—as safe as they could be under these circumstances.

A breaker rose up and crashed down on the cabin, staving it in and dumping water into the hold.

Crandall found the red distress torch and lit it. Gardiner fought his way forward and looked toward the beach, but could hardly distinguish land from sea. Everywhere was moving water, and he knew that shoals sometimes reached five miles out. Just how far from shore they had grounded was unknowable. But he also knew that, in October, the lifesaving stations should be manned, so he did all that he could do: he moved aft beside his wife and child and waited.

The sea's relentless pounding immediately began to take the ship apart. The remainder of the sails were carried off. The rails collapsed and washed away. A wave snatched the jib from its mooring, its tackle waving in the wind.

Since the yawl had already been lost, the crew would have to swim for shore if help did not arrive soon. Reaching the beach in such conditions would be nearly impossible, even for the best of swimmers. The chances that he and his wife would safely reach land, with three-year-old Tommy in tow, were considerably worse. Gardiner ordered a second distress signal lit.

To the north, through the drizzle and fog, there was a tiny red light, but it fizzled, then faded.

Had they been spotted?

Before Gardiner could order it, Crandall was lighting another flare.

Then a single red rocket was fired from shore. A lifesaving crew had seen their distress call! Henry Bravo cheered, and Gardiner instructed Crandall to keep a red torch lit to help the rescuers locate their position.

At last, salvation. If only the *Newman* would stay together long enough for the lifesavers to arrive.

The beach cart weighed a half ton, literally. Projectiles and shot. The hawser and lines. The breeches buoy. The sand anchor. The brass Lyle gun alone weighed more than 250 pounds, and Benjamin Bowser could feel every ounce of it resisting the revolution of the beach cart's wheels, the wide, metal rims sinking into the sand.

"Hoo-ah! Hoo-ah!" he growled, angry, expressing his rage in time with the keeper's cadence. It was a directionless rage, aimed at nothing in particular but pointed nevertheless—at the wind slapping sand and spray against his uncovered face; at the hang of his drenched rain slicker pulling against his legs, already knee-deep in rising and receding water; at the barely turning wheels that he dared not let stop lest he have to dig deep inside for some burst of energy to get it going again.

Keeper Etheridge sloshed ahead, scanning the darkness. In his absence, the men maintained the chorus.

HOO-AH, HOO-AH
HOO-AH, HOO-AH.

Unless some other crew had also spotted the distress call, the Pea Islanders were on their own. Before leaving the station, Etheridge had furiously cranked the arm of the wooden telephone box. Empty clicking. No signal. The wind and surf had downed the lines, preventing the keeper from alerting other stations.

As the number one surfman, Bowser had made sure the cart was properly equipped while two men harnessed themselves to it and two others slid open the boatroom doors. Ropes, line, powder flask, spare powder, medicine chest, flares, shovels, blankets, mortar, heaving sticks, sand anchor.

The keeper knew that the surfboat would be impracticable in this wind and heavy surf, so they had left it. But he had ordered Pugh to hitch the team to the driving cart in case survivors needed to be carried.

From the moment the keeper had begun shouting his orders, with water up to their knees and wet sand swallowing each step, not one of the men had uttered what they all knew was true: rendering any assistance under such unfavorable conditions would probably be impossible. Maybe they could help land those who, still capable of braving the surf, tried to swim to shore—those few who successfully completed the dangerous voyage. Or maybe they'd be forced to sit and watch as the shipwrecked sailors were washed out to sea, one by one, from the deck of their doomed vessel. Maybe by the time they arrived, it would already have been done. Maybe the driving cart would merely serve as a hearse to carry the dead. But no one said as much.

They pushed ahead, step by slow step.

More burdened their forward progress than merely the weight of the cart and the grim prospects of their mission. Ben Bowser was forty years old. The keeper himself was fifty-four. They knew the score. All the men did. Etheridge had always been one who adhered to regulations and insisted on vigilant, dutiful service. Sixteen years as keeper, and not once could he breathe easy, not once could he feel that they had earned their station.

HOO-AH, HOO-AH.

Keeper Etheridge disappeared over a rise just as the mules stopped in their tracks. Bowser knew to keep the team moving. He reacted instantly, dropping back and striking the mules' rumps with his wet cap, calling, "Haw! Haw!" to spark them into motion before the whole operation stalled. One mule brayed, both sprang forward, and the cart continued to roll, haltingly at first, but soon steady again. Bowser regained his spot at the wheel and, in Etheridge's absence, took to calling out the cadence. "Heave to, men, heave to!"

HOO-AH, HOO-AH.

But before he could call out a second cadence, the Preacher broke in: "Well, Capt'n, Capt'n . . . ," and the men, recognizing the ditty, laughed and called back:

WELL, CAPT'N, CAPT'N
You must be blind . . .
YOU MUST BE BLIND
Look at your watch . . .
LOOK AT YOUR WATCH
It's quitting time . . .
IT'S QUITTING TIME.

Even Bowser had to smile. The song energized the men's strides. Bowser called out a second verse:

Well, Capt'n, Capt'n . . .
WELL, CAPT'N, CAPT'N
How can it be? . . .
HOW CAN IT BE
Whistle keep a-blowing . . .

WHISTLE KEEP A-BLOWING
You keep a-working me ...
YOU KEEP A-WORKING ME.

Step by step, they progressed up the beach.

Sand and water poured into the *Newman's* hold, weighting her down, mooring her to the bar as the ocean hammered away. Piece by piece, she was coming apart, and with each pounding wave, the mariners got battered, too. The water struck like fists, knocking breath from lungs, tearing clothing and ripping it from bodies, pitching debris at the stunned, hapless people.

Every crew member had a whistle, which, if he went overboard, he was instructed to blow as loudly as he could so he could be located. Gardiner watched his wife place hers around little Tommy's neck.

How long till the lifesavers arrived? It had already been an hour. Longer. Could they last two if they had to?

How long till a wave crashed over the rail and someone vanished with its passing, the frantic screech of a whistle fading out at sea?

Then, there was movement, barely visible, a few hundred yards distant. Seven hazy figures. In the dim light of a lantern, they saw two carts, one pulled by mules, one by men. The sea rushed over the entire beach, bogging the lifesavers down, knocking some to their knees. They pushed forward. Gardiner and his crew began to cheer.

Cries of joy emanating from the grounded schooner—"The voices of gladdened hearts," as Etheridge later remembered it—greeted their arrival. It had taken them two hours to cover two miles. The wind—blowing hard enough to damage the anemometer at the Kitty Hawk Signal Service station: ninety, maybe one hundred miles per hour—had dogged them the whole way. Several times the Pea Island crew and their team of mules had been brought to a standstill by the wind-driven tides sweeping across the beach, the lumber in the surf crashing against the cart, striking the men across their legs. But they had arrived. Hearing the cries from the ship reenergized the lifesavers.

The dark shape of the schooner sat perched on the inner sandbar, close enough to shout to, but she was in a frightful shape. The keeper quickly reconnoitered the scene: a three-master, maybe four hundred tons, judging by the length of the deck; keeled over on her starboard side, the deck facing landward; the masts still in place but the headsails coming unfurled and whipping in the wind; and the ship's effects—jibboom, cabin, yardarm, forecastle—greatly damaged. Including passengers and crew, there were ten, maybe twelve, people aboard. The schooner was close to shore, no more than fifty yards out—close enough that the life-savers could see what must have been the majority of the crew, cheering and waving from their holds in the rigging.

Although the distance to the ship was short, the sea was running very high and violently tossing debris in its roiling surf. At times, the Atlantic surrounded the surfmen, washed up over their waists, forced them to grab for the beach cart and each other to keep from being swept away. The dark schooner rocked and tossed, and with the pounding of each succeeding wave, the mariners scrambled to hold fast and keep from being thrown overboard to a sure death.

Before Etheridge had uttered a single order, the surfmen, by rote, began readying the beach apparatus. Like any practiced crew, they would have the operation up and running, the Lyle gun ready to fire, in less than five minutes. Pugh and Meekins unloaded the X-braces and the breeches buoy, but there was nowhere to put them without the threat of losing them to the Atlantic. Wise and Irving were supposed to dig a hole in the beach for the sand anchor. Each time they tried, sweeping tides filled the hole with sand.

Etheridge ordered Wise and Irving to build a mound of sand upon which to place the Lyle gun. But there was water up to their knees. They turned their backs to the wind and scooped sand, patting it down with the flat sides of the spades. The mound eroded before their eyes, disappearing in a wash of water. There was no beach.

Etheridge didn't have to explain the problem. He ordered the men to fan out, to search for a rise, a dune, a hummock, or any bit of ground that felt steady beneath their feet. Each man combed the area, stomping his feet into the water, feeling the ground for what was not there.

Etheridge called the men back together. Painful though the realization was, there was nothing they could do.

★   ★   ★

Gardiner expected that the lifesavers would fire a line to the ship, so he instructed his first mate and steward to spread out and be ready to bring it in. Crandall and M. J. Vierra moved cautiously over the slippery deck, sliding from one handhold to the next.

Though help had arrived, the mariners understood that they were not yet saved. Each person waited expectantly for the boom of the cannon that would announce the launching of a line. They waited, but it did not come. Gardiner scrutinized the darkness in the direction of the beach for some signal from land.

The cries of joy from the ship had died, but the presence of the mariners was ominously there with the lifesavers on the beach. They could feel their expectant eyes watching their every move, their anxious ears anticipating the sound of the shot that would carry the line that would bring them to safety onshore. The surfmen stood in silence, helpless.

No one was ready to admit defeat. Someone suggested they send four men with the government team after their surfboat—or better yet, after the New Inlet station boat. They were no more than a mile and half from that station; they could get there and back in two hours, two and a half at the outside. But even if the Pea Islanders could get a boat to the scene, launching it in this surf would be impossible, which had been clear all along, which was why they hadn't brought their own in the first place.

The younger men looked to the older ones—Bowser, Wescott, Keeper Etheridge. These men were the coastal heroes they had watched in awe their whole lives. Here they stood, helpless in the worst silence any had ever heard, the wind whistling past their ears and slapping wet oilskins against their backs and necks, the sound of surf crashing up the beach, taunting them, jostling them as it shoved past their legs.

Then the keeper spoke up. He told the men that he had a plan, if they were willing.

Gardiner couldn't account for why a line hadn't yet been thrown. Certainly, the *Newman* was well within range; he knew tales of rescue lines being fired four hundred yards or more. Were the lifesavers waiting for another crew to arrive at the scene? Or maybe for a lull in the storm? Gardiner prayed not, for that was a miserable prospect.

It was his wife who first noticed the movement on the beach. Between the ship and the shore, two figures were pushing out into the surf. She pointed in that direction, and Gardiner gasped. To attempt to swim to the ship was suicide!

The first wave caught the Preacher full frontside, knocked the air out of him, and almost carried him away into the darkness. The slack between him and Meekins snapped tight, and the line, tied fast around each one's torso, dug painfully into Meekins's ribs. Meekins looked back toward Wise—Wise's face a fist, fighting to keep his head above the water that climbed past his neck—and tried to encourage him with a look. To panic might spell the end for both of them. Wise's eyes told him he didn't need encouraging, just a breath of air and the goodwill of God—keep pushing forward, keep pushing forward.

Men, we must try to swim out to the schooner. Keeper Etheridge had said this. That was no order. Keeper gave orders—*Meekins, man the aft oar! Son, pull that line taut! Take Bowser's night patrol!* "Trying" to swim out to the vessel was something else, but it wasn't an order, especially not from Etheridge.

No one questioned Etheridge's mettle. Yet here he was, asking for volunteers. Was this some sign of weariness in the keeper or a testament to the foolhardiness of the undertaking? Whatever it was, it had been clear to Meekins that, of the men who made up the crew, he was the one to go. Not a surfman among them, hardly another along the coast, could keep up with him swimming.

The keeper's plan was to lash two men between eight feet of No. 7 braided line and, with another section, connect them to the lifesavers on shore. The swimmers would carry a heaving stick, tied to a separate line, which they would toss aboard the ship once they got close enough. The volunteers, Meekins and Wise, stripped themselves of rain gear—what good did it do them in the water?—and wore their cork life belts over their tunics. They struck out.

Most of the trip was part wading, part swimming. By anticipating the breaking waves, Wise worked his way back to within a foot of Meekins.

The life belts proved more hindrance than help, floating each man toward the surface when he went to dive under rolling planking and other debris. Protruding nails, rivets, and jagged lengths of wood ripped past like razors.

When they had covered half the distance to the ship, they felt the sandy bottom drop out from beneath their feet so that they were suddenly bobbing in the rocking ocean. Each man swam—the crawl, hand over hand, kicking as best he could, careful to keep his legs from getting caught up in the lines. When the waves fell upon them, they duck-dove, held their breath, then surfaced to see that they had just lost much of the progress they had made.

Meekins knew that they had reached the trough between the beach and the inner bar on which the schooner was foundered, that a sort of river raged beneath the surface here, particularly on a night like this, and that the undertow it formed could pull them out to sea. Not a boy in the Outer Banks had not at one time or another tossed a bottle into the surf to watch it whisk away in the currents. For hundreds of yards the bottle might flow parallel to the beach, then it would suddenly break for the open sea, never to be seen again. Now, Meekins and Wise felt the pull of these same forces. The Preacher, like Meekins, knew to pump his arms double-time and kick his legs harder. The current tugged at them, the schooner seeming to veer to the right and away.

With the next wave came a higher-pitched moan than before, then another thunderous *crack,* and the two men quickly fought downward, duck-diving, dodging below the surface to avoid the incoming wave and the dangerous debris that tore through the surf. If the line were to foul with some wreckage, they would likely be dragged away before they could fish out their marlinespikes and free themselves.

The line dug tight again into Meekins's ribs. He looked back but could not see the Preacher. Flotsam crashed together around him, a barrel with *E. S. Newman* stenciled above its iron ring, and he feared the worst for Wise, the tight pulling still seizing his rib cage. Meekins, born an orphan and a slave, recognized his crewmates as family. Etheridge, Wise, the others—they were fathers and uncles and brothers. Had the Preacher been knocked over the head? All Meekins felt of Wise was the immediate pull of dead weight.

As the next breaker rolled past, Meekins saw the Preacher, still there, still fighting. Meekins surged forward, swimming only a few strokes before again feeling sand under his feet—the inner bar—and waist-deep water. The next wave almost forced them back into the trough, but Meekins dove down and dug his free hand into the bar. When the wave had passed, he stumbled, stood, and helped the other man stand. Running in knee-high water and paddling forward with his hands, he first pulled the Preacher, then felt him running alongside. Lumber struck their bodies, pitched up at their faces.

The ship—the *Newman*—was now not ten yards away. Meekins dragged Wise forward, one last good burst. Above them, leaning spars pitched ominously and dangerous pieces of iron tackle whipped in the gale. Meekins swung the heaving stick over his head and tossed it to the waiting crew. The crew had lowered a rope ladder down the lee side of the ship. Meekins beelined for the ladder: he and the Preacher had to make it before the next wave. The risk of being killed by planking or other debris was greatest here, so close to the ship.

As the roar of surf rose, the two men reached the schooner. Wise thrust his arms in the ladder's lattice, securing himself to the hull. Both surfmen covered their heads with their arms as another wave crashed over the top of them.

This close, Meekins understood the nature of the ship's groaning. It was a collective moan: the wooden deck and masts bending, sometimes buckling, beneath the weight of a wave; the mariners holding on as best they could, screaming, praying, crying; a child's near inaudible wail.

They had arrived, the lifesavers had arrived.

Gardiner and the others, perched upon the foundered schooner, had watched the surfmen battle the waves. Billows washed over the two swimmers, and they often disappeared under mountains of water. Several times Gardiner thought they had been swept away. Yet the lifesavers, alternately wading then swimming, pushed forward, fighting their way through the surf to cheers from the *Newman*.

As they reached the disintegrating hulk of the ship, their tunics tangled and life belts all but torn from their torsos, the cheering on board faltered an instant. Gardiner focused on the faces of salvation. These men were Negroes.

Negroes? Were also those onshore?

Wasting no time, Gardiner loosed his mooring to the mizzenmast, slid down the deck with Tommy in his arms. He handed the child to the larger of the two men, who wiggled out of his life vest and, shushing the crying boy, slipped it around him. The bigger man carried the boy in one arm and clung to the free line with his other hand. The smaller man picked a path through the rent lumber, pausing to toss boards and debris from their path. And they were off.

On the beach, Etheridge tied the line from the heaving stick to the beach cart, his hands casting a perfect steamboat hitch in the light rope. Now, with a guideline to travel upon, the surfmen could make trips back and forth to the wreck. They were, in effect, the breeches buoy.

The return trip was nothing compared to the outbound voyage. Meekins, again tied to the Preacher, the boy strapped in his life belt, pushed away from the schooner. It was a swim at first, pulling themselves along the line, the boy clutching Meekins's neck, and Meekins kicking his legs and being carried along in the wake of a wave and the others' pulling from shore. A few stroke-pull-lunges and they were over the trough.

From shore, Etheridge noticed the bowed arc of the line. It was the pull of the powerful undertow. He barked for the men to keep the line taut.

The surf, receding, rolled over the swimmers. They had to stop and just hold fast as it rushed past, water with the power to blow open new inlets buffeting their bodies. Next would be another breaker, debris crashing through the surf from behind them, their blind side: tumbling pieces of spars and jagged metal and the crying boy in their arms.

It was a mad rush from there. Etheridge cried for the men to haul. Meekins and Wise, high-kneed sprinting, worked hard but moved forward little. Etheridge, just twenty yards away, rushed toward them, the hiss of a rising wave behind them. A roar and crashing and water pushing them along. Meekins, fighting forward, shielded the boy's head with his arms.

Etheridge took the boy from Meekins's grasp. The voices from the schooner raised a raucous cheer.

It could be done! Each person, on land and ship, knew now that it could be done.

Meekins and Wise, bent at the waist and struggling to regain their breath, relayed the information to the keeper: the number aboard; the apparent state of the schooner; the conditions of the shipwreck victims. Etheridge took it all in, then turned to the others and asked for the next pair of volunteers. Before anyone could step forward, Meekins said he was ready to go again.

He *was* ready. Meekins was charged with a rush such as he had not felt since boyhood, seeing blue-clad soldiers all over on Roanoke Island to free them. Here was something special, extraordinary. He would not miss it.

Etheridge must have seen it in his face. He told them, Go, and Meekins and Bowser dashed into the surf behind a receding wave.

The Pea Island lifesavers, in teams of two, made nine trips in all. Next, they brought off Mrs. Gardiner, hindered by the ragged remains of her dress entwined in her legs, but driven to be reunited with her son. Then the cook, Arthur Tehuy, an old salt who'd spent a lifetime at sea. M. J. Vierra. Eugene Colho. Henry Bravo, the senior brother by five years, insisted Baptist go next, the *Newman* coming undone around them. First mate Crandall made the penultimate voyage. Then Gardiner quit what remained of his battered ship.

Once the mariners were all safely ashore, the Pea Islanders stripped Tommy and wrapped him in dry blankets. They checked all the survivors for signs of hypothermia, tended to significant cuts and scrapes, and loaded the most heavily burdened—Mrs. Gardiner, Tommy, and old man Tehuy—into the driving cart for the trek back to the station.

It was just past 11 P.M. The rescue had taken less than an hour.

Sea tides still rushed over the beach, flooding the island as far as the mile-distant Pamlico Sound. But the most dangerous part of the night was behind them.

The silence of the return trip bespoke the conflicted emotions that flowed between the rescuers and the rescued, feelings of both loss and relief, of terror that was supplanted by great joy, the joy become anxiety that had now gone to despair. Accomplishment. Seven silently exultant black surfmen, sympathetic to the others' pain but proud, led the way up the beach. They knew the magnitude of what they had done that night.

Back at the station, just after 1 A.M., the lifesavers made the mariners as comfortable as they possibly could. There was plenty of doctoring to be done. Etheridge spent the night with the medicine chest wide open, tending wounds, bandaging bruises, and treating cuts with alcohol. The surfmen prepared cots. Someone made coffee. Another brought down the trunk of supplies donated by the Women's National Relief Association. They gave Mrs. Gardiner a proper dress to replace her torn, wet one. Dignified, she had carried herself as though appropriately dressed before fourteen men; nevertheless, she was relieved to receive the new one.

There were shirts and trousers, whatever else was needed by the men. There was also reading material—books, magazines, and newspapers—to occupy the mariners during their stay at the station, which was sure to last several days.

While the others took care of the crew, Irving manned the watch. Who knew but that another vessel was out there in distress?

Keeper Etheridge surrendered his quarters to Gardiner and his family. While his men went about their tasks, he wrote up the report in the official log, concluding: "Although it seemed impossible to render assistance in such Conditions, the ship wreck crew was all safely landed." There were no flourishes added, no embellishment. It was all in a day's work.

EPILOGUE

During the days that followed, the wind abated and the sea tides slipped back into the ocean. On the fifteenth, the weather cleared. The *Newman's* crew, with the aid of the surfmen, scoured the beaches for anything that might be salvageable from their ship. They recovered little. They found lumber, ruined charts, tangled rope, a few bundles of clothes. Nothing of worth. The *Newman,* valued at four thousand dollars, was a total loss.

While searching the beaches, Captain Gardiner happened upon the ship's nameplate, still nailed to some wreckage. He pulled it free and dragged it up the beach through fields of standing water and flattened yaupon trees that still marked the fury of the passing storm. At the station, the captain awarded the signboard to Etheridge and his crew. For one hundred years, this was the only recognition the Pea Islanders would receive.

Unanimously, the crewmen voted to give the memento to Theodore Meekins, the surfman who had spotted the *Newman's* distress flare and who, according to folklore, made all nine trips out to the wreck. He took the board back to Manteo in his skiff. News of the rescue had reached the town by then, so when he nailed the *E. S. Newman* nameplate to his barn for all to see, passersby knew the significance. On the sandy lane that passed Meekins's house, the story of the *Newman* was remembered in hushed conversations with insects ringing in the marsh.

Meekins served at No. 17 for twenty-one more years, until 1917, when, while he was boating home on leave, a storm came up suddenly at Oregon Inlet and blew his skiff out to sea. He drowned trying to swim to shore.

Not four years after the famous rescue, Richard Etheridge fell ill at the station he had struggled to maintain as a site of African-American service and a source of community pride. Too weak to walk, he had to be carried home for medical treatment. He returned four days later, but suffered a relapse.

With Etheridge lying incapacitated in his cot upstairs, Benjamin Bowser stepped in as acting keeper. Applying the knowledge he had learned under Etheridge, Bowser kept the log and otherwise ran the station without missing a beat. But for Etheridge's stricken presence, life went on as normal.

Winter brought ominous storms, and with them, shipwrecks.

WEEKLY JOURNAL

Pea Island Station   *Monday, January 29, 1900*

Watch for the day, W. D. Pugh no. 3
B. J. Bowser, no. 1 with 5 others. Members of the crew, as follows—L. S. Wescott, Theo. Meekins, W. S. Wise, W. H. Irving + R. G. Pigsford left the Station at one o.c. a.m. to assist New Inlet's Crew at the Wreck of the Steam Ship Master Moore. Keeper very sick at the Station to day.   unable to Perform Duty.   Used the Boat and 1 no. 7 Shot line Braded apart of which wase expended.   The Condition of the Telephone at this Station is good.

WEEKLY JOURNAL

Pea Island Station   *Sunday, February 25, 1900*

The Crew of this Station assisted the Crew of Oregon Inlet at the Wreck Schooner Jane C. Harris to day.   Carried one no. 7 Shotline, [word illegible] and the Blankets.   Shotline was used at the Wreck and had to Be expended by Hard Hazardous Work.   The Crew Was Saved.   the old Team on the way up to the Wreck give out to day. and like not have pulled the emty cart.   My self, B. J. Bowser got a very serious lick on the top of head at the Wreck wich felled me to the Bottom of the Boat.

Keeper very sick at the Station to day, unable to Perform Duty. The Condition of the Telephone at this Station is good.

"Keeper very sick at the Station to day, unable to Perform Duty" became a daily refrain with only a few breaks, when the crew tried to carry him to Manteo or to get help for him from there. Neither course was successful. As the active season was coming to a close, Bowser reported:

WEEKLY JOURNAL

Pea Island Station   *Tuesday, May 8, 1900*

Keeper Richard Etheridge Dide at this station at 20 minutes to 7 o.c. a.m. to day. the Condition of the Telephone at this Station is good.

[signed] B. J. Bowser, Acting Keeper

Benjamin Bowser took the oath of office on June 27 before the Dare County court clerk. He had reached his goal: he'd become keeper. His success was as short-lived as it was bittersweet. Just two months later, Lewis Wescott, Bowser's number one man, reported:

WEEKLY JOURNAL

Pea Island Station   *Sunday, September 2, 1900*

Watch for the day Theo Meekins no. 3
Keeper B. J. Bowser Died to day at 3 oclock AM
S.Wise absent to visit his family from 6 am to 6 pm and returned the same day
the condition of the Telephone at this station is good

L. S.Wescott acting Keeper

Benjamin Bowser, like Etheridge before him, had contracted some disease while serving. He was just forty-six years old.

Frank Newcomb, the man responsible for recognizing in Richard Etheridge a model surfman and leader, went on to captain an interracial crew aboard the cutter *Hudson* during the Spanish-American War and, for his valor, was decorated with the Congressional Medal of Honor, the only one awarded. After the war's close, he rose to the rank of Inspector of the Life-Saving Service, the number three man behind Kimball. His cohort Charles Shoemaker is remembered today by Coast Guard historians as one of four early officers who "earned reputations as spearheads of a drive for service betterment." After his stint in the Outer Banks, he went on to hold many posts in the service and its sister organ, the Revenue Cutter Service, before being appointed captain commandant, the RCS's highest position, in 1895. He oversaw operations of the nation's entire Coast Guard cutter fleet. As for Sumner Kimball, he oversaw operations of the LSS for forty-three years. His dogged efforts to establish a civilian corps of lifesavers had paid off.

The Life-Saving Service had become the pride of the American civil service and a model organization worldwide, and its North Carolina branch boasted some of its best crews. These were not the men who had bungled the *Metropolis* rescue or political appointees afraid to launch a boat into a medium surf; they were Outer Bankers who took pride in service and who would risk their lives at nominal pay and without benefit of pension or job security. By the turn of the century, North Carolina life-saving had come to represent the federal service at its finest and embodied what would become the Coast Guard's motto: *Semper Paratus,* always ready. Richard Etheridge, his crew, and their successors were a leading and steadfast part of that proud tradition.

Many estimates have been made about the number of sailors who were rescued by the African-American crews of Pea Island. Most are grossly inaccurate, citing as many as six hundred. Etheridge, Bowser, the old-timers, would probably not understand today's obsession with tallying the number of lives saved by any given crew. To keepers and surfmen, preventing the loss of life and property was an everyday reality, not a means by which to keep score. Nevertheless, Pea Island had a remarkable record. By a conservative estimate, the Pea Island surfmen saved over two hundred shipwrecked mariners and lost only thirteen lives.

Of the 131 medals awarded surfmen during the first three decades of the LSS's existence, 33 went to North Carolinians. Patrick Etheridge is remembered as the consummate coastal hero, stories of his deeds the stuff of folklore. So, too, with other Tar Heel lifesavers: Dunbar Davis, L. B. and

Erasmus Midgett, Malachi Corbell, all of whom won medals for valor. The *Newman* rescue, and the man behind it, faded into obscurity.

By that time, the Sand Banks were changing. The shad were gone, or at least nothing of what they had been. Telephone lines stretched the length of the Banks. The Nags Head Hotel, refurbished and under new ownership, braced itself for twentieth-century entertainment: Victrolas, motion pictures. African-Americans still could not stay there.

In 1903, Orville and Wilbur Wright chose the Outer Banks as the site at which they would test their theories on human flight, and nearby lifesavers helped them with their experimentation. Although Orville's first jaunt spanned only one hundred feet and lasted just twelve seconds, its success heralded the dawn of a new era. This same technology that the Kitty Hawk surfmen helped the Wright brothers test would eventually contribute to the end of coastal lifesaving.

In 1915, the Life-Saving Service and the Revenue Cutter Service merged to form the Coast Guard, a semimilitary organization. Only with its formation were lifesavers granted pension and retirement benefits. Their duties, however, were reduced to little more than helping free the tires of automobiles stuck in the sand and, during the wars, watching the shores for signs of U-boats. Modern advances such as the internal combustion engine, aviation, wireless radio, improved weather-forecasting techniques, navigational aids and instruments made the surfmen obsolete. Ships became larger, more powerful, and safer than ever before. Rescues did occur, but with hardly the frequency as during the Age of Sail. By the 1930s, the black lifesavers described their equipment—the Lyle gun and shot, the breeches buoy—as "museum pieces."

Two years after World War II, Pea Island, like most of its sister stations, was decommissioned. The station was sold and relocated, leaving the long stretch of beach empty and awash with broken surf.

But the end of the Pea Island story is triumphant. On February 29, 1992, the Coast Guard honored the memory of the African-American lifesavers by christening a 110-foot cutter, the U.S.C.G.C. *Pea Island.* The event brought renewed energy to recovering their history. The authors, in collaboration with Captain Steve Rochon, petitioned the service to recognize Etheridge and his men for their heroism the night the *Newman* came ashore. The request stalled until fourteen-year-old Katie Burkhart joined the team.

Burkhart, after interviewing the authors, protested to her senator: ultra-conservative Jesse Helms. Helms was preparing for what the *Raleigh News and Observer* was billing as a "tough, expensive political rumble" for his U.S. Senate seat against black challenger Harvey Gantt, the popular former mayor of Charlotte. Helms seized the opportunity, endorsing Burkhart's letter and passing it on to the commandant of the Coast Guard. Although just two years before, the Coast Guard's Medals and Awards Panel had refused a proposal to pay tribute to the 1896 crew, the commandant, in a surprising turn, overruled the decision.

On March 5, 1996, almost one hundred years after the daring feat, Richard Etheridge and his men were posthumously awarded a Gold Life-Saving Medal, the service's highest peacetime honor, by the Coast Guard's Commandant Admiral Robert E. Kramek at a ceremony at the Naval Memorial in Washington, D.C. A right was wronged, forgotten history recovered.

ACKNOWLEDGMENTS

The authors are indebted to more people than we can name here. Thanks to Wynne Dough, a veritable repository of facts, information, and stories, whose knowledge filled in gaps and opened up avenues of inquiry; Brian Edwards, Sarah S. Downing, and the crew at the Outer Banks History Center, our HQ during much of our research; Maurice Duke, who guided us in our earliest meandering and stuck with us; Patricia Click of the University of Virginia; Joe Mobley of the North Carolina Department of Cultural Resources; Geneva Perry of the University of Wyoming; Keith Harrison of the Cape Hatteras National Seashore; Mike Halminski, Richard Darcey, Bob Huggett, and the helpful volunteers of the Chicamacomico Life-Saving Museum; Alyson Hagy; John Edgar Wideman; Jay Neugeboren; Dr. Robert Browning, the Coast Guard Historian; Joanna Ord, of the Interlibrary Loans Department of the University of Wyoming; Anne Giffey and Irene Ponce, of the Knox College library; and the anonymous "Reviewer B" of Naval Institute Press, whose excoriating, vituperative feedback made us better historians.

Mimi and Vincent Zoby housed and fed us, loaned us cars, came to our lectures, and even took photographs. Lucette Mayer put us up and put up with us. Thank you. Special thanks to our patient readers Ray Harvey, Harpo Power, Elisa Carbone, Jill Petty, and especially Audrey Petty, who, as my (Wright's) wife, was subjected to countless drafts. And thanks to Lisa Drew and her assistant Jake Klisivitch, who prove in so many ways that writers need—and always will—good editors, and John McGregor, our agent, who knows a good story when he hears it.

Heartfelt thanks to William C. Bowser, Nicholas Meekins (deceased), Miss Pinky Berry (deceased), Agatha Gray, Izetta Bowser Redmon, Chelsley Midgett (deceased), and all the people of Roanoke Island, whose memories helped us imagine a world.

We also wish to thank for generous financial assistance: the Afro-American Studies and Research Program of the University of Illinois, where Wright spent a year as a postdoctoral fellow; the Dean's Office and the John and Elaine Fellowes Fund of Knox College, for sustained support; the Munson Institute of American Maritime Studies, Mystic, Connecticut, for a Paul Cuffe Memorial Fellowship, which helped us know we were on the right track; the Wyoming Council for the Humanities; the Illinois Arts Council; and the English Department of Virginia Commonwealth University and the North Carolina Humanities Council, whose early support made everything possible.

AUTHORS' NOTES
AND SOURCES

Tracing Richard Etheridge's passage through life, given his bondage, was tremendously difficult. Records in the Outer Banks are inconsistent to begin with, but are especially so for African-Americans, particularly former slaves. A slave was property, like cattle or a plow, and as a result appeared in the federal census in a separate "Schedule of Slave Inhabitants," recorded only by age and gender under his owner's name. The few other records that exist are equally vague. The records for the U.S. Colored Troops, though more plentiful, rarely addressed the cases of specific troopers and also left holes in Etheridge's story.

Consequently, the authors attempted to uncover Etheridge's past by reconstructing the history of the time and place in which he lived. By constructing the histories of the people near Etheridge and, with the details that exist about his life, situating him in those stories, a vivid picture of the man begins to emerge. For instance, we could not know for certain that Etheridge saw specifically the details we describe him seeing during various actions of the Civil War; however, those details and actions occurred as described, and he was near them.

In reconstructing Etheridge's early life for the chapters "Youth: The Outer Banks," "War," and "Home," his wife Frances's application for pension benefits (Record Group 94, National Archives, Washington), though limited, offered important information. Several other sources proved invaluable, most notably the Currituck and Dare County Records

303

(Accounts of Sales, Bonds, Census, Court, Estate, Inventories of Estates, Marriage/Divorce/Vital Statistics, Miscellaneous, Records of Accounts, and Wills). The *North Carolina Business Directory,* for the years 1867–68, 1869, 1872, and 1878 (the only ones extant), were also useful in imagining the Outer Banks of that era. Sheer luck led us to Etheridge's letter of protest about the mistreatment of freedpeople on Roanoke Island when, while flipping through Ira Berlin, et al.'s *The Black Military Experience,* we came across Etheridge's name in the index. This proved to be an invaluable piece that gave us Richard's voice as well as an important example of his leadership. Patricia C. Click's forthcoming study, *A Time Full of Trial: The Freedmen's Colony on Roanoke Island, 1862–1867,* is the keystone work on the colony. Dr. Click also very generously provided us with important documents from the Records of the Bureau of Refugees, Freedmen and Abandoned Lands (Record Group 105, National Archives). These sources, bolstered by Fred M. Mallison's *The Civil War on the Outer Banks: A History of the Late Rebellion along the Coast of North Carolina from Carteret to Currituck,* Gary S. Dunbar's *Historical Geography of the North Carolina Outer Banks,* and David Stick's important works, *The Outer Banks of North Carolina, 1584–1950, Dare County: A History,* and *An Outer Banks Reader,* helped fill in the narrative.

The primary sources for the chapters describing the Thirty-sixth and Etheridge's life in the unit—"War," "Wild's December Raid," "Point Lookout: The Bottom Rail on Top," "Before Richmond: In the Trenches," and "Armistice: Texas"—were contained in the Records of the United States Colored Troops (Record Group 94, National Archives), which included regimental descriptive books, military service records, and, importantly, applications for pensions; and *A Compilation of the War of the Rebellion: Compiled and Arranged from Official Records of the Federal and Confederate Armies' Reports of the Adjutant Generals of the Several States, the Army Regulations and Other Reliable Documents and Sources.* It was also useful to read the chronicles of the times in *Harper's Weekly* and *Frank Leslie's Illustrated Newspaper,* as well as Thomas Morris Chester's dispatches for the *Philadelphia Press,* collected in *Thomas Morris Chester, Black Civil War Corespondent: His Dispatches from the Virginia Front.*

These records, though more plentiful, still left holes in Etheridge's biography. Finding a sketch of Alonzo Draper's story helped immensely which, fortunately, Thomas Waln-Morgan Draper recorded in the family history: *The Drapers in America, Being a History and Genealogy of Those of That Name and Connection.* Likewise, Richard Reid's "Raising the African Brigade: Early Black Recruitment in Civil War North Carolina," Jerry V. Witt's *Wild in North Carolina: General Edward A. Wild's December 1863 Raid into Camden, Pasquotank and Currituck Counties,* Edwin Beitzell's *Point Lookout Prison Camp for Confederates,* Mallison's *The Civil War on the Outer Banks,* and Kenneth J. Bryant II's " 'A Model Regiment': The 36th U.S. Colored Infantry in the Civil War" were each great resources and complements to the primary sources. Joseph T. Glatthaar's *Forged in Battle: The Civil War Alliance of Black Soldiers and White Officers* is the best source on the USCT experience in Texas.

The history of the Life-Saving Service (for Part Two, "National Calamity or National Crime?") was more easily reconstructed as a wealth of sources still exists. The jumping-off point was the *Annual Report of the Operations of the United States Life-Saving Service,* for the years 1876–1914. Likewise, many of the reports and much of the official correspondence between Sumner Kimball and his chief officers can be found in the Records of the Life-Saving Service (Record Group 26) in the National Archives (at East Point, Georgia; Philadelphia, Pennsylvania; and Washington, D.C.). We stumbled upon two gems when we found the assistant inspector's "Letter Book" and the one for his sloop, the *Saville,* in the Southern Historical Collection at the University of North Carolina. Also of great use were the following secondary sources: Stick's *Graveyard of the Atlantic,* Joe Mobley's *Ship Ashore! The U.S. Lifesavers of Coastal North Carolina,* Dennis Noble's *That Others Might Live: The U.S. Life-Saving Service, 1878–1915* and Irving H. King's *The Coast Guard Expands, 1865–1915: New Roles, New Frontiers.*

The events at the sites of shipwrecks were culled primarily from official Wreck Reports, log entries from stations concerned in the rescues, and print media coverage. The principle sources for the *Lancaster* disaster ("Prologue") were: the LSS's *Annual Report,* 1881; the Pea Island, Chicamacomico, and Gull Shoal logbooks; the Record of American and Foreign Shipping, 1880, of the American Shipmaster's Association; and news stories in the *Elizabeth City Economist* and the *Norfolk Virginian.* The account of the *Nuova Ottavia* disaster ("North Carolina's Lifesaving Woes") comes from: the LSS's *Annual Report,* 1876; Signal Service reports from Kitty Hawk station; and secondary sources, Mobley, Stick, and Noble. Much has been written about the wrecks of the *Huron* and *Metropolis.* The LSS's *Annual Report* for 1878 and the *Congressional Record* for the Forty-fifth Congress served as principle sources in describing the wrecks, as did *Frank Leslie's Illustrated Newspaper* and the *Norfolk Virginian,* which also reported extensively on the disasters. Likewise, Joe D. Friday's unpublished manuscript, "A History of the Wreck of the USS Huron," proved indispensable in dramatizing the warship's demise. Stick's *Graveyard of the Atlantic* and his collection of interviews, letters, and reports located among his papers at the Outer Banks History Center also added. Primarily, we used print reports form the *Virginia Landmark,* the *Norfolk Virginian,* and the *Elizabeth City Economist* to document the wreck of the *Metropolis.* Of particular importance was Revenue Marine Captain John H. Merryman's report to the secretary of the treasury, dated February 9, 1878 (copy in the David Stick Papers, Outer Banks History Center).

The political fallout that resulted from the disasters and the reform measures that followed ("The Reformation of the Sixth District") were reconstructed from the official correspondence between LSS officials in RG 26 (East Point and Washington) and from the *Congressional Record.* Reports in the *Elizabeth City Economist* and *North Carolinian* and Dare County records were also invaluable in understanding and re-creating the tumultuous times. Inspector Charles Shoemaker's letter to Superintendent Kimball of January 6, 1880 (RG 26, Washington) details the investigation of the *M&E Henderson* debacle. Other correspondence between him, Inspector Newcomb, and Superintendent Kimball (RG 26, Washington and East Point) helped us put together the facts surrounding the botched rescue, the ensuing cover-up, and the recommendation of Etheridge for the keepership at Pea Island. Information on conditions of the North Carolina stations at that time and on the service of African-Americans in the LSS likewise came primarily from East Point and Washington, as well as from the LSS "Letter Book" in the Southern Historical Collection.

Much of the information about the staffing of the first black crew ("Segregation for the Good of Progress") and on the subsequent fire ("Fire on the Beach") was culled from documents found in the National Archives, Washington, notably the official correspondence and registers of letters received. Newcomb and Joseph W. Etheridge's reports to Kimball about their ongoing investigation (letters dated June 24, August 5, and

September 11, 1880, RG 26, Washington) provided bountiful facts and insight. The *Saville*'s "Letter Book" also had important information. To understand the historical context of that era, Eric Foner's *Reconstruction: America's Unfinished Revolution, 1863–1877* is the definitive source on Reconstruction and its close. George Fredrickson's *The Black Image in the White Mind: The Debate on Afro-American Character and Destiny, 1817–1914* and Eric Anderson's *Race and Politics in North Carolina, 1872–1901: The Black Second* also proved invaluable.

For Part Three, "The Life of a Surfman," several varied sources helped us reconstruct the nature of life at Pea Island over the course of Richard Etheridge's tenure as keeper. Of primary importance were the station logbooks, from 1880 through the turn of the century. We also read those of other North Carolina stations, from Big Kinnakeet to Creeds Hill, as well as some from Virginia's Fifth District. The logs accurately inform contemporary historians of day-to-day routine at the station, of the conditions of the wind and surf on any given day over a hundred years ago, and, in the instances of disasters or extraordinary circumstances, of the details of those events. Unfortunately, as the logs were written in strict military fashion, they offer little insight into the personalities of these early lifesavers.

To help flesh out the characters of the principal players, we relied on correspondence, reports, and other archival material from a variety of sources, most notably RG 26, the Outer Banks History Center, the holdings of the Cape Hatteras National Seashore, and the Southern Historical Collection. We also combed the extant local, regional, and state newspapers—most importantly, Elizabeth City's *Economist*, *North Carolinian*, and *Fisherman and Farmer*, and Norfolk's *Pilot* and *Virginian*—for any articles and columns about the lifesavers, stations, or other relevant information.

For a better understanding of the coastal environment, we went to Dunbar's *Historical Geography of the North Carolina Outer Banks*, Dirk Frankenberg's *The Nature of the Outer Banks*, and the articles and essays in Stick's *An Outer Banks Reader*, all of which provided many insightful observations about the Banks, its history, climate, and geography. Information on the conditions of life for the African-American surfmen ("Pressures Particular to Pea Island Surfmen") come from the logs, registers, and correspondence found in RG 26 (East Point, Washington, and

Philadelphia), the Pea Island Papers at the Cape Hatteras National Seashore, the Records of the Civil Service Commission (RG 146), and the records of the Surfmen's Mutual Benefit Association. Likewise, several secondary sources were of particular use in understanding evolving race relations during the era of Southern "Redemption," most notably: Edward Ayers's *The Promise of the New South: Life after Reconstruction*, Raymond Gavins's "The Meaning of Freedom: Black North Carolina in the Nadir, 1880–1900," Howard N. Rabinowitz's "From Exclusion to Segregation: Southern Race Relations, 1865–1890," and Joseph F. Steelman's dissertation "The Progressive Era in North Carolina, 1884–1917." Also, many Roanoke Islanders gave generously of their time and graciously of their patience as we conducted several interviews with the descendants and family members of Pea Island surfmen. In most things, William C. Bowser was our guide.

In Part Three, for narrative drive, we occasionally took small liberties with the available records, although, as a practice, we avoided it. Throughout the book, when conversation or dialogue is rendered, it was taken directly from primary source material. However, the *Newman* rescue, the subsections entitled "Life of a Surfman," and G. R. Midgett's patrol (the end of "Patrolling the Beach") were places where we allowed our imaginations to help drive the scenes forward, not in any of the facts of those events, but with the specific workings of the individuals involved.

In the case of the *Newman* rescue, we cannot know specifically what happened on the beach that night. Only broad brushstrokes are available: the conditions of wind and surf, the equipment hauled to the site, the seeming impossibility of rendering any assistance, Meekins's daring. We do not know, for example, that the Pea Islanders chanted or sang while towing the cart to the site of the *Newman* wreck. Work songs were an important part of African-American cultural tradition; in the Outer Banks, "shanty songs," originated by slaves at Beaufort and in the Core Banks area, have survived to this day. It made sense to us that the Pea Islanders—some of whom had been slaves, the rest, the children of former slaves—might sing as a way to keep beat and better drive the cart forward. It is possible that other crews also did so to facilitate this arduous task. In no instance in the book did we allow ourselves to imagine without firm foundation in historical fact and record.

The events of the *Newman* rescue were taken from the official Wreck

Report, from the Pea Island log, from the LSS's *Annual Report,* 1896, and from the oral testimonies of surviving relatives of Pea Island surfmen. Signal Service observers from Kitty Hawk recorded the weather patterns for September and October 1896. To gauge the magnitude of the hurricane, we looked at log entries up and down the coast, including those of Cape Hatteras, Chicamacomico, Oregon Inlet, and Wash Woods stations. The hurricane and its wake of destruction were well documented in the *Economist,* the *Virginian,* and the *Norfolk Pilot.* When we needed to dramatize events aboard the *Newman,* we relied upon the knowledge of sailor and historian Dr. Maurice Duke (USN Ret.).

A note on spelling and grammar in quoted passages: In the days before word processors with spell checkers, errors in type often went unnoticed and uncorrected. Likewise, many Outer Bankers of that era were barely literate or altogether unlettered. As a result, most original documents that we cite contain numerous grammatical and orthographic errors. To preserve the flavor of the voice, as a rule we left the language intact. However, in order to avoid having to overburden the quotes with redundant [sic]'s, we have not used them at all, except when necessary for clarity or comprehension.

A note on names: In the insular and relatively isolated communities of the Outer Banks, it was not uncommon for families, black as well as white, to share the same name. In some cases, this indicated a familial tie, albeit perhaps a distant one; in others, the connection was too many generations removed to be significant. When familial relation seemed of consequence to the narrative, we made a point to signal it.

Finally, concerning Richard Etheridge's paternity: With no extant record of slave unions or births and, in the Outer Banks, few of slave sales, it is impossible to determine for sure who his father was. The scenario presented in the text was the one that seemed most likely to us. Here follow other possibilities.

According to county records, Richard's mother, Rachel Dough, along with the slave "Lewis," were regularly hired out by Warren Dough, most often to the elderly Abiah Dough. When Warren died in 1843, Rachel and Lewis were kept together as a pair whereas the other four Dough slaves were sold. Rachel and Lewis were of compatible ages. They may have been conjugal partners. If they were a couple, Lewis may have fathered Richard.

However, if he did, it does not explain how Richard came to be born in the Etheridge household, as Rachel Dough was not John B.'s property. It's possible that, during the time that she gave birth to Richard, Rachel was hired out to John B. This seems unlikely, however, as a pregnant slave would seem to have little value as rental property. Also, there are no extant records of this transaction, nor are there any of the sale of a slave infant between John and either Warren or Abiah Dough. Further, if Lewis was Richard's father, it does not explain why Richard, in later life, took the name Etheridge as opposed to Dough. Slaves, both during slavery and immediately after, often used naming as a way to connect themselves to family from whom they were separated by their bondage. Though an Etheridge slave, Richard could well have chosen to be known as Dough, after Lewis and Rachel, particularly with his freedom when war came. He did not. Lewis, in fact, never comes up in Richard's records. Interestingly, although his mother is buried beside him on his family plot, no father is. Richard's paternity is never accounted for, a silence that may be due to its socially proscribed origins.

Another even more remote possibility is that Richard Etheridge was fathered by the slave "Dick" (possibly short for Richard), who was owned by William Etheridge (a cousin of John B.'s). When William died in 1837, Thomas Dough bought Dick. Thomas Dough ran in the same circles as John B. Etheridge and Warren Dough, Rachel Dough's owner (Thomas and Warren may even have been related). So it is possible that the slave Dick and Rachel Dough conceived Richard (who would also later be called Dick), that the young Richard was born while Rachel was hired out to John B., and that the baby was sold to him. Richard would then have been carrying his father's surname, which only coincidentally was the same as that of the family to whom he belonged. This seems even more speculative and unlikely.

BIBLIOGRAPHY

ARCHIVAL MATERIALS

Atlantic Mutual Insurance Company. *M&E Henderson* and *E. S. Newman* Wreck Files, Administrative Center, Madison, N.J.

Coast Guard Materials. North Carolina Division of Archives and History, Raleigh.

Colyer, Vincent, Superintendent of the Poor, under Major General Burnside. *Brief Report of the Services Rendered by the Freed People to the United States Army in North Carolina, in the Spring of 1862, after the Battle of Newbern.* New York: Vincent Colyer, 1864. Copy at Outer Banks History Center, Manteo, N.C.

Congressional Record: Containing the Proceedings and Debates of the Forty-fifth Congress, Second Session. Washington, D.C.: Government Printing Office, 1878.

Currituck County Census, 1840, 1850, with Slave Schedule; 1870. Microfilm. North Carolina Division of Archives and History, Raleigh.

Currituck County Records (Accounts of Sales, Bonds, Court, Estate, Inventories of Estates, Miscellaneous, and Wills). North Carolina Division of Archives and History, Raleigh.

Dare County Census, 1870, 1880, 1890, 1900, and 1910. Microfilm. North Carolina Division of Archives and History, Raleigh.

Dare County Records (Court, Estate, Marriage/Divorce/Vital Statistics, Miscellaneous, Records of Accounts, and Wills). North Carolina Department of Archives and History, Raleigh.

Keeper Application Files. Outer Banks History Center, Manteo, N.C.

Letter Book, U.S. Life-Saving Service, 1878–81. William F. Martin Papers. The Southern Historical Collection, Louis Wilson Library, University of North Carolina, Chapel Hill.

Letter Book, U.S. Revenue Sloop *Saville*, 1872–75. William F. Martin Papers. The Southern Historical Collection, Louis Wilson Library, University of North Carolina, Chapel Hill.

North Carolina Business Directory, 1867–68, 1869, 1872, and 1878. The Reverend L. Branson, ed. The North Carolina Collection, Louis Wilson Library, University of North Carolina, Chapel Hill.

North Carolina Year Book (News and Observer, Raleigh), 1901–10. Outer Banks History Center, Manteo, N.C.

Pea Island Station Papers, 1883–1909. Holdings in the Collection of the Cape Hatteras Group, Cape National Seashore, Fort Raleigh, N.C.

Record of American and Foreign Shipping, 1880. American Shipmaster's Association, New York, 1880. Mariners' Museum, Newport News, Va.

Records of the Assistant Commissioner for the State of North Carolina (in Records of the Bureau of Refugees, Freedmen and Abandoned Lands). Record Group 105, copies, North Carolina Division of Archives and History, Raleigh.

Records of the Civil Service Commission. Record Group 146, National Archives, College Park, Md.:
—General Letters Sent, 1897–1904;
—Minutes of Proceedings, 1886–1929.

Records of the Coast Guard. Record Group 26, National Archives, Washington, D.C.:
—Public Information Office, Miscellaneous Reference Materials, 1910–41 ("Negroes in the Coast Guard");
—Records of the Mutual Aid Association, 1891-1933.

Records of the Life-Saving Service. Record Group 26, National Archives, East Point, Ga.:
—Letter Books, Letter from General Superintendent, 1900–1904;
—Letter Books, Sixth and Seventh Districts, 1899–1900;
—Letter Books, Sixth District, 1881–83, 1892, 1893–95;
—Logbooks, Big Kinnakeet Life-Saving Station, 1880–90;
—Logbooks, Bodie Island Life-Saving Station, 1874–77, 1879–90;
—Logbooks, Cape Fear Life-Saving Station, 1880–1900;
—Logbooks, Cape Hatteras Life-Saving Station, 1887–1910;
—Logbooks, Chicamacomico Life-Saving Station, 1878–90;
—Logbooks, Creeds Hill Life-Saving Station, 1880–90;
—Logbooks, Gull Shoal Life-Saving Station, 1881;
—Logbooks, Hatteras Life-Saving Station, 1896;
—Logbooks, Kitty Hawk Life-Saving Station, 1875–91;
—Logbooks, Little Kinnakeet Life-Saving Station, 1874–85;
—Logbooks, Nags Head Life-Saving Station, 1874–92;
—Logbooks, New Inlet Life-Saving Station, 1883–1915;
—Logbooks, Oregon Inlet Life-Saving Station, 1880–93;
—Logbooks, Pea Island Life-Saving Station, 1880–1915;
—Logbooks, Wash Woods Life-Saving Station, 1896.

Records of the Life-Saving Service. Record Group 26, National Archives, Philadelphia, Pa.:
—Logbooks, Cape Henry Life-Saving Station, 1875–80.

Records of the Life-Saving Service. Record Group 26, National Archives, Washington, D.C.:

—Applications for Superintendent of the Life-Saving Service Districts, 1874–1900;

—Articles of Engagement, Fifth and Sixth Districts, 1876–78, 1880–84, 1901–6;

—Correspondence (Letters Sent; Letters Sent "Unrecorded"; Letters Received; Miscellaneous Letters; Correspondence of Life-Saving Keepers; Correspondence of the General Superintendent), Fifth and Sixth Districts, 1847–1915;

—Inventory of Letters of Stations, Sixth District;

—Life-Saving Scrapbook;

—Nominations of Keepers;

—Register of Letters Received, 1879–80;

—Register of Officers and Employees, 1866–1913;

—Report of Examination of Keepers and Surfmen, 1876–80;

—Wreck Reports of Stations.

Records of the United States Colored Troops (in Records of the Adjutant General's Office). Record Group 94, National Archives, Washington, D.C.:

—Applications for Pensions, various names;

—Military Service Records, various names;

—Regimental Descriptive Book, Thirty-seventh USCT;

—Regimental Descriptive Book, Thirty-sixth USCT.

Registration Papers, *Thomas J. Lancaster.* Mariner's Museum, Newport News, Va.

Shoemaker, Charles F., Lieutenant, United States Revenue Marine. "The Evolution of the Life-Saving System of the United States from 1837 to June 30, 1892: An Outline of the Part Taken in Its Development by the U.S. Revenue Marine." Unpublished MS, U.S. Coast Guard Academy, London, Conn.

Statutes of the United States of America, Passed at the Second Session of the Forty-fifth Congress, 1877. Washington, D.C.: Government Printing Office, 1878.

Stick, David, Papers. Boxes of notes, Outer Banks History Center, Manteo, N.C.

Surfmen's Mutual Benefit Association. *Official Manual and Convention Book.* Boonisar Collection, available from R. M. Boonisar, U.S. Life-Saving Service Heritage Association, P.O. Box 75, Caledonia, MI 49316-0075.

U.S. Life-Saving Service. *Annual Report of the Operations of the United States Life-Saving Service,* 1876–1914. Washington, D.C.: Government Printing Office, 1876–1915.

U.S. Life-Saving Service. *List of Persons Who Have Died by Reason of Injury Received or Disease Contracted in the Line of Duty in the Life-Saving Service Since the Origin to the Present System, as Shown by the Records of the Treasury Department.* Washington, D.C.: Government Printing Office, 1914.

U.S. Signal Service. Monthly Observations, Kitty Hawk, October 1881, September 1896, October 1896, Outer Banks History Center, Manteo, N.C.

U.S. War Department. *The War of the Rebellion: A Compilation of the Official Records of the Union and Confederate Armies.* Published under the direction of Russel A. Alger, Secretary of War. Washington, D.C.: Government Printing Office, 1891.

NEWSPAPERS AND MAGAZINES

Along the Coast (later, *Along the Coast: The Official Organ of the Surfmen's Mutual Benefit Association,* Boston, Mass.), 1909–10.
Coast Guard Magazine (U.S. Coast Guard Academy, New London, Conn.), 1927–54.
Dare County Times (Manteo, N.C.), 1935–49.
Edenton American Banner, 1856.
Elizabeth City Economist, 1872–1907.
Elizabeth City Fisherman and Farmer, 1889–1900.
Elizabeth City North Carolinian, 1876–88.
Frank Leslie's Illustrated Newspaper, 1861–65, 1877–78.
Harper's New Monthly, "The American Life-Saving Service," February 1882.
Harper's Weekly, 1861–65, 1877–78.
Newbernian, 1874–76, 1880.
New York Times, 1877–78.
New York World, 1877–78.
Norfolk Pilot, 1876–78, 1896.
Norfolk Virginian, 1876–79, 1881, 1896.
Raleigh News and Observer, 1906–7 (copies in Coast Guard Materials, North Carolina Department of Cultural Resources, Raleigh).
Scribner's Monthly, "The United States Life-Saving Service," January 1880.

ORAL HISTORIES

Berry, Arounia, and Agatha Gray. Tape recording with authors, Manteo, N.C., June 8, 1993.
Bowser, William C. Tape recording with authors, Norfolk, Va., May 8, 1993, and Manteo, N.C., June 24, 1994; no recordings are available for July 4–5, 1993 (personal), and January 5 and June 12, 1997, and May 23, 1998 (telephone).
Gray, Agatha. Telephone interview with authors, June 9, 1997, and personal interview with authors, October 10, 1997.
Meekins, Nicholas. Tape recording with authors, Manteo, N.C., July 8, 1993.
Redmond, Izetta. Personal interview with authors, Manteo, N.C., July 5, 1993.
Reenactment of Beach Drill. Chicamacomico Station, August 12, 1999.

SECONDARY SOURCES

Alexander, Roberta Sue. *North Carolina Faces the Freedmen: Race Relations during Presidential Reconstruction, 1865–1867.* Durham, N.C.: Duke University Press, 1985.
Anderson, Eric. *Race and Politics in North Carolina, 1872–1901: The Black Second.* Baton Rouge: Louisiana State University Press, 1981.

Aron, Cindy Sondik. *Ladies and Gentlemen of the Civil Service: Middle-Class Workers in Victorian America*. New York: Oxford University Press, 1987.

Ashley, Clifford. *The Ashley Book of Knots*. New York: Doubleday, 1944.

Ayers, Edward. *The Promise of the New South: Life after Reconstruction*. New York: Oxford University Press, 1992.

Barfield, Rodney. *Seasoned by Salt: A Historical Album of the Outer Banks*. Chapel Hill: University of North Carolina Press, 1995.

Barnes, Jay. *North Carolina's Hurricane History*. Chapel Hill: University of North Carolina Press, 1995.

Barnett, Thomas. "Hatteras Surf Reminiscences." *U.S. Coast Guard Magazine* 5, no. 5 (November 1932).

Barrett, John G. *The Civil War in North Carolina*. Chapel Hill: University of North Carolina Press, 1963.

Beitzell, Edwin W. *Point Lookout Prison Camp for Confederates*. Leonardtown, Md.: St. Mary's County Historical Society, 1983.

Bennett, Robert F. "The Life-Savers: 'For Those in Peril on the Sea.'" *United Naval Institute Proceedings* 102, no. 3 (March 1976).

———. *Surfboats, Rockets, and Carronades*. Washington, D.C.: Government Printing Office, 1976.

Benson, Rodney J. "Romance and the Story of Pea Island." *U.S. Coast Guard Magazine* 6, no. 1 (November 1932).

Berlin, Ira, Joseph P. Reidy, and Leslie S. Rowland, eds. *The Black Military Experience*. Series II of *Freedom: A Documentary History of Emancipation, 1861–1867*. Cambridge, Mass.: Cambridge University Press, 1982.

———. *The Wartime Genesis of Free Labor: The Upper South*. Series I, vol. 2, of *Freedom: A Documentary History of Emancipation, 1861–1867*. Cambridge, Mass.: Cambridge University Press, 1993.

Blackett, R. J. M., ed. *Thomas Morris Chester, Black Civil War Correspondent: His Dispatches from the Virginia Front*. Baton Rouge: Louisiana State University Press, 1989.

Boatner, Mark Mayo, III. *The Civil War Dictionary*. New York: David McKay Company, 1959.

Bowditch, Nathaniel. *The American Practical Navigator: An Epitome of Navigation*. Washington, D.C.: U.S. Navy Hydrographic Office, 1966.

Brimley, H. H. *A North Carolina Naturalist, H. H. Brimley: Selections from His Writings*. Ed. by Eugene P. Odum. Chapel Hill: University of North Carolina Press, 1949.

Bryant, Kenneth J., II. "'A Model Regiment': The 36th U.S. Colored Infantry in the Civil War." Master's thesis, University of Vermont, May 1996.

Butler, Benjamin F. *Butler's Book: Autobiography and Personal Reminiscences of Major-General Benj. F. Butler: A Review of His Legal, Political, and Military Career*. Boston: A. M. Thayer and Co., 1892.

Canfield, Edward J., and Thomas A. Allan. *Life on a Lonely Shore: A History of the Vermilion Life-Saving Station*. Sault Ste. Marie, Mich.: Lake Superior State University Press, 1991.

Carter, Kathleen S. Untitled article on Life-Saving Service practices in North Carolina. Available from the author, c/o High Point University, Department of History, Political Science and Geography, University Station, Montlieu Avenue, High Point, NC 27262-3598.

Click, Patricia C. *A Time Full of Trial: The Freedmen's Colony on Roanoke Island, 1862–1867.* Chapel Hill: University of North Carolina Press, forthcoming.

Cohn, Michael, and Michael K. H. Platzer. *Black Men of the Sea.* New York: Dodd, Mead, 1978.

Crawford, William. *Mariner's Weather.* New York: Norton, 1992.

Creecy, Richard B. *Grandfather's Tales of North Carolina History.* Raleigh: Edwards and Broughton Printers, 1901.

Crow, Jeffrey. *The Black Experience in Revolutionary North Carolina.* Raleigh: North Carolina Division of Archives and History, 1996.

Crow, Jeffrey, Paul Escott, and Flora Hatley. *A History of African Americans in North Carolina.* Raleigh: North Carolina Division of Archives and History, 1992.

Crow, Jeffrey, and Larry Tise, eds. *Writing North Carolina History.* Chapel Hill: University of North Carolina Press, 1979.

Crow, Jeffrey, and Robert E. Winters Jr., eds. *The Black Presence in North Carolina.* Raleigh: North Carolina Museum of History, 1978.

Davis, Major George B., U.S. Army, Leslie J. Perry, and Joseph W. Kirkley. *The Official Military Atlas of the Civil War.* Comp. by Capt. Calvin D. Cowles. New York: Gramercy Books, 1983.

Draper, Thomas Waln-Morgan. *The Drapers in America, Being a History and Genealogy of Those of That Name and Connection.* New York: John Polhemus Printing Company, 1892.

Druett, Joan. *Hen Frigates: Passion and Peril, Nineteen-Century Women at Sea.* New York: Simon & Schuster, 1998.

Dunbar, Gary S. *Historical Geography of the North Carolina Outer Banks.* Coastal Studies Series, no. 3. Ed. by James P. Morgan. Baton Rouge: Louisiana State University Press, 1958.

Dyer, Frederick H. *A Compilation of the War of the Rebellion: Compiled and Arranged from Official Records of the Federal and Confederate Armies' Reports of the Adjutant Generals of the Several States, the Army Regulations and Other Reliable Documents and Sources.* Dayton, Ohio: The Press of Morningside, 1908.

Evans, W. McKee. *Ballots and Fence Rails: Reconstruction on the Lower Cape Fear.* Chapel Hill: University of North Carolina Press, 1966.

Falconer, William. *Falconer's Marine Dictionary.* New York: A. M. Kelley, 1780.

Foner, Eric. *Reconstruction: America's Unfinished Revolution, 1863–1877.* New York: Harper and Row, 1988.

Foote, Shelby. *The Civil War: A Narrative.* 3 vols. New York: Random House, 1958.

Frank Leslie's Illustrated History of the Civil War: The Most Important Events of the Conflict between the States Graphically Pictured. New York: Fairfax Publications, 1977.

Frankenberg, Dirk. *The Nature of the Outer Banks: A Guide to the Dynamic Barrier*

Island Ecosystem from Corolla to Ocracoke. Chapel Hill: University of North Carolina Press, 1995.

Franklin, John Hope. *The Free Negro in North Carolina, 1790–1860.* Chapel Hill: University Press of North Carolina, 1995.

Franklin, John Hope, and Alfred A. Moss Jr. *From Slavery to Freedom: A History of Negro Americans.* New York: McGraw-Hill, 1947.

Fredrickson, George. *The Black Image in the White Mind: The Debate on Afro-American Character and Destiny, 1817–1914.* New York: Harper and Row, 1971.

Friday, Joe D., Jr. "A History of the Wreck of the USS *Huron.*" Unpublished MS, Outer Banks History Center.

Gavins, Raymond. "The Meaning of Freedom: Black North Carolina in the Nadir, 1880–1900." In *Race, Class, and Politics in Southern History: Essays in Honour of Robert F. Durden.* Ed by Jeffrey J. Crow, Paul D. Escott, and Charles L. Flynn Jr. Baton Rouge: Louisiana State University Press, 1989.

————. "A 'Sin of Omission': Black Historiography in North Carolina." In *Black Americans in North Carolina and the South.* Ed. by Jeffrey Crow and Flora J. Hatley. Chapel Hill: University of North Carolina Press, 1984.

Gladstone, William A. *United States Colored Troops, 1863–67.* Gettysburg, Pa.: Thomas Publications, 1990.

Glassner, Greg. "Coast Guard Heritage in Mackey Family Nearly a Century Old." *The Chesapeake Post,* November 29, 1984.

Glatthaar, Joseph T. *Forged in Battle: The Civil War Alliance of Black Soldiers and White Officers.* New York: The Free Press, 1990.

Gutman, Herbert G. *The Black Family in Slavery and Freedom, 1750–1925.* New York: Pantheon Books, 1976.

Hagar, George J. "The United States Life-Saving Service: Its Origin, Progress, and Present Condition." *Frank Leslie's Popular Monthly* 5, no. 2 (February 1878).

Harris, Carl V. "Right Fork or Left Fork? The Section-Party Alignments of Southern Democrats in Congress, 1873–1897." *Journal of Southern History* 42, no. 4 (November 1976).

Heinegg, Paul. *Free African Americans of North Carolina and Virginia.* Baltimore: Genealogical Publications, 1993.

Johnson, Charles. *The Long Roll.* East Aurora, N.Y.: The Roycrofters, 1911; reprint, Shepherdstown, W.Va.: Carabelle Books, 1986.

Johnson, Guion Griffis. *Ante-Bellum North Carolina: A Social History.* Chapel Hill: University of North Carolina Press, 1937.

Kay, Marvin L., Michael Cary, and Lorin Lee Cary. "A Demographic Analysis of Colonial North Carolina with Special Emphasis upon the Slave and Black Populations." In *Black Americans in North Carolina and the South.* Ed. by Jeffrey J. Crow and Flora J. Hatley. Chapel Hill: University of North Carolina Press, 1984.

King, Irving H. *The Coast Guard Expands, 1865–1915: New Roles, New Frontiers.* Annapolis, Md.: Naval Institute Press, 1996.

Levine, Lawrence. *Black Culture and Black Consciousness: Afro-American Folk Thought from Slavery to Freedom.* New York: Oxford University Press, 1977.

Lossing, Benson J. *Mathew Brady's Illustrated History of the Civil War, 1861–65, and the Causes That Led Up to the Great Conflict.* Reprint, New York: Gramercy Books, 1994.

Mallison, Fred M. *The Civil War on the Outer Banks: A History of the Late Rebellion along the Coast of North Carolina from Carteret to Currituck.* Jefferson, N.C.: McFarland and Co., 1998.

Manarin, Louis H., ed. *North Carolina Troops, 1861–1865: A Roster.* 13 vols. Raleigh, N.C.: State Department of Archives and History, 1966.

Means, Dennis R. "A Heavy Sea Running: The Formation of the U.S. Life-Saving Service, 1846–1878." *Prologue: Journal of the National Archives* 19, no. 4 (winter 1987).

Merryman, J. H. "The United States Life-Saving Service—1880." *Scribner's Monthly;* reprint, Golden, Colo.: Outback Books, 1981.

Mobley, Joe. *James City: A Black Community in North Carolina, 1863–1900.* Raleigh, N.C.: Department of Cultural Resources, 1981.

———. *Ship Ashore! The U.S. Lifesavers of Coastal North Carolina.* Raleigh: North Carolina Division of Archives and History, 1994.

Montgomery, Horace. "A Union Officer's Recollections of the Negro as a Soldier." *Pennsylvania History* 28 (April 1961): 156–86.

Moore, Frank, ed. *The Rebellion Record: A Diary of American Events, with Documents, Narratives, Illustrative Incidents, Poetry, Etc.* Vol. 8. New York: D. Van Nostrand, 1865.

Nalty, Bernard C. *Strength for the Fight: A History of Black Americans in the Military.* New York: The Free Press, 1986.

Nalty, Bernard C., Dennis L. Noble, and Truman R. Strobridge. *Wrecks, Rescues and Investigations: Selected Documents of the U.S. Coast Guard and Its Predecessors.* Wilmington, Del.: Scholarly Resources Inc., 1978.

Nathans, Sydney. *Quest for Progress: The Way We Lived in North Carolina.* Chapel Hill: North Carolina Department of Cultural Resources, by University of North Carolina Press, 1983.

Noble, Dennis. *That Others Might Live: The U.S. Life-Saving Service, 1878–1915.* Annapolis, Md.: Naval Institute Press, 1994.

Noble, Dennis, and T. Michael O'Brien. *Sentinels of the Rocks: From "Graveyard Coast" to National Lakeshore.* Marquette: Northern Michigan University Press, 1979.

O'Brien, T. Michael. "Black Heroes of Pea Island." *Commandant's Bulletin* (U.S. Coast Guard), pts. 1–3, June–August 1980.

Prather, H. Leon. *We Have Taken a City!: The Wilmington Racial Massacre and Coup of 1898.* Rutherford, N.J.: Associated University Press, 1984.

Rabinowitz, Howard N. "From Exclusion to Segregation: Southern Race Relations, 1865–1890." *Journal of American History* 63, no. 2 (September 1976).

Redkey, Edwin S., ed. *A Grand Army of Black Men: Letters from African-American Soldiers in the Union Army, 1861–1865.* New York: Cambridge University Press, 1992.

Reid, Richard. "Raising the African Brigade: Early Black Recruitment in Civil War North Carolina." *North Carolina Historical Review* 70 (1993); reprint, on-line: www.ccharity.com.

Seaworthy, Gregory (George H. Throop). *Nag's Head: or, Two Months Among "The Bankers." A Story of Sea-Shore Life and Manners.* Philadelphia: A. Hart, late, Carey and Hart, 1850.

Shanks, Ralph, and Wick York. *The U.S. Life-Saving Service: Heroes, Rescues, and Architecture of the Early Coast Guard.* Ed. by Lisa Woo Shanks. Petaluma, Calif.: Costano Books, 1996.

Sommers, Richard J. *Richmond Redeemed: The Siege at Petersburg.* Garden City, N.Y.: Doubleday, 1981.

Steelman, Joseph F. "The Progressive Era in North Carolina, 1884–1917." Ph.D. diss., University of North Carolina.

Stevenson, Brenda E. *Life in Black and White: Family and Community in the Slave South.* New York: Oxford University Press, 1996.

Stick, David. *Dare County: A History.* Raleigh: State Department of Archives and History, 1970.

———. *Graveyard of the Atlantic.* Chapel Hill: University of North Carolina Press, 1952.

———. *The Outer Banks of North Carolina, 1584-1950.* Chapel Hill: University of North Carolina Press, 1958.

———, ed. *An Outer Banks Reader.* Chapel Hill: University of North Carolina Press, 1998.

Stobridge, Truman. *The History of Blacks in the Coast Guard from 1790.* U.S. Dept. of Transportation, n.d.

Toppin, Edgar. Tape recording of public lecture, Manteo, N.C. June 17, 1994.

Trelease, Allen W. "Republican Reconstruction in North Carolina: A Roll-Call Analysis of the State House of Representatives, 1868–1870." *Journal of Southern History* 42, no. 3 (August 1976).

Trudeau, Noah A. *The Last Citadel: Petersburg, Virginia, June 1864–April 1865.* Boston: Little, Brown and Company, 1991.

———. *Like Men of War: Black Troops in the Civil War, 1862–1865.* Boston: Little, Brown and Company, 1998.

———. *Out of the Storm: The End of the Civil War, April–June 1865.* Boston: Little, Brown and Company, 1994.

U.S. Coast Guard. *African Americans in the U.S.C.G.: Historic Role Models, 1790–1993.* Silver Spring, Md.: Patriot Publications, 1993.

Watson, Richard L., Jr. "Furnifold M. Simmons and the Politics of White Supremacy." In *Race, Class, and Politics in Southern History: Essays in Honour of Robert F. Durden.* Ed. by Jeffrey J. Crow, Paul D. Escott, and Charles L. Flynn Jr. Baton Rouge: Louisiana State University Press, 1989.

Wechter, Nell Wise. *The Mighty Midgetts of Chicamacomico.* Manteo, N.C.: Times Printing Co., 1974.

Whedbee, Charles H. *Legends of the Outer Banks and Tarheel Tidewater.* Winston-Salem, N.C.: John F. Blair, 1966.

———. *Outer Banks Tales to Remember.* Winston-Salem, N.C.: John F. Blair, 1985.

White, Gwen A. "Richard Etheridge: An American Coastal Hero." *Current: The Journal of Marine Education* 1, no. 4 (Summer 1980).

320 DAVID WRIGHT AND DAVID ZOBY

Williams, George W. *A History of the Negro Troops in the War of the Rebellion, 1861–1865.* New York: Harper and Brothers, 1888.

Williamson, Joel. *The Crucible of Race: Black-White Relations in the American South since Emancipation.* New York: Oxford University Press, 1984.

Witt, Jerry V. *Wild in North Carolina: General Edward A. Wild's December 1863 Raid into Camden, Pasquotank and Currituck Counties.* Arlington, Va.: J. V. Witt Publications, 1993.

Wolfram, Walt. *Hoi Tide on the Outer Banks: The Story of the Ocracoke Brogue.* Chapel Hill: University of North Carolina Press, 1997.

Woodward, C. Vann. *Origins of the New South, 1877–1913.* Baton Rouge: Louisiana State University Press, 1951.

INDEX